Guiding Clinical Experiences in Teacher Education

GOLDEN GARLAND

TEMPLE UNIVERSITY

Longman
New York & London

GUIDING CLINICAL EXPERIENCES IN TEACHER EDUCATION

GUIDING CLINICAL EXPERIENCES IN TEACHER EDUCATION

Longman Inc., 19 West 44th Street, New York, N.Y. 10036
Associated companies, branches, and representatives
throughout the world.

Copyright © 1982 by Longman Inc.

Developmental Editor: Nicole Benevento
Editorial and Design Supervisor: Diane Perlmuth
Interior and Cover Design: Diana Hrisinko
Manufacturing and Production Supervisor: Anne Musso
Composition: A & S Graphics
Printing and Binding: Quinn-Woodbine Incorporated

Library of Congress Cataloging in Publication Data

Garland, Colden.
    Guiding clinical experiences in teacher education.
    Includes index.
    1. Teachers, Training of—United States.
2. Individualized instruction. I. Title.
LB1715.G28   370′.7′10973   81-1831
ISBN 0-582-28162-8   AACR2

Manufactured in the United States of America

9 8 7 6 5 4 3 2 1

FOR A NUMBER of years I have participated in clinical experiences in a wide range of public school settings and in a variety of teacher education programs. As diverse as these experiences have been, they have had one aspect in common. In each experience, I have encountered teacher education students, cooperating teachers, and college supervisors who

- worked conscientiously and enthusiastically to make the clinical experience in which they were participating productive and satisfying
- offered ideas and suggestions for ways of increasing the effectiveness of clinical experiences
- provided feedback that I found useful in refining my participation in clinical experiences

acknowledgments

I am pleased to have this opportunity to thank these colleagues for providing the context that encouraged the writing of this book.

I am particularly grateful to the following individuals for their contributions to the overall development of the book: Teresa Richardson, for providing the careful research assistance, thoughtful suggestions, and constant encouragement that enabled me to complete the manuscript; Dr. Sandra Jorgensen, for listening to ideas and providing helpful feedback; and Susan Adair, for her competence in carrying out the many tasks involved in the final stages of manuscript preparation.

CONTENTS

chapter **7** providing guidance
through observation
and conferencing   127

chapter **8** the evaluation process   154

part **4** looking ahead   171

chapter **9** perspectives on the future   173

appendixes   182

appendix A

appendix b

List of figures

list of Analysis Guides

A significant trend in teacher education is that of providing more clinical experiences for prospective teachers than was formerly the case, and offering them earlier in teacher preparation programs. This has created a need to offer instructional programs for the growing numbers of cooperating teachers, college supervisors, and other teacher educators who now participate in these experiences. A major problem in designing such programs is the shortage of relevant and current instructional materials. *Guiding Clinical Experiences in Teacher Education* represents an effort to address this problem.

The intent in this book is to help teacher educators acquire an understanding of the dimensions of clinical experiences and develop the ability to implement them in their unique situations. To facilitate this objective, the material included here combines significant research findings with current thinking regarding effective practice. It is hoped that this combination will provide a base from which partici-

INTRODUCTION

pants in clinical experiences can approach this important effort with competence and confidence.

The organization of the book and its use by specific groups of teacher educators are described in the initial section of this introduction. Following this discussion are sections that contain suggestions for the program or course instructor and for the reader. The final introductory section presents definitions of the major terms used throughout the book.

The book is organized in four parts. Part One, which includes Chapters 1 through 3, provides perspectives from which to view emerging concepts in clinical experiences. This is accomplished through a discussion of research and practice in the areas of teacher effectiveness, teacher education, and supervision. These discussions are essential in establishing the current context of clinical experiences in teacher education.

Part Two, which consists of Chapter 4, deals with the concept of *role* and its application in clinical experiences. While the role concept appears frequently in material written about clinical experiences, it is rarely defined clearly or used in a way that demonstrates consistency. In this chapter, the role concept is defined in terms of its components and is systematically applied to the interacting relationships among participants in clinical experiences. The chapter then identifies the first of the strategies for working through the phases of clinical experiences presented in the book. Included in the description of this strategy are activities that enable participants to experience the process of analyzing role expectations.

Part Three, which covers Chapters 5 through 8, delineates the dimensions of clinical experiences: preparing for and initiating the experience, providing guidance in planning and assuming teaching responsibility, providing guidance through observation and conferencing, and implementing the evaluation process. A strategy for implementing each dimension is presented as that area is addressed. The description of each strategy includes activities that enable participants to develop the skills needed to apply the strategy in their own situations.

Part Four, the single Chapter 9, presents thinking about the future of clinical experiences in teacher education. Included in this chapter are discussions of pressures toward change, problems in the use of research, and roles and priorities that seem to be emerging.

The book is addressed primarily to the cooperating teachers in whose classrooms preservice students participate in clinical experiences. This focus was selected because of the close working relationship that exists between cooperating teachers and students, and because of the importance of cooperating teachers in determining the quality of students' clinical experiences. Much of the material written for the occupants of this role has consisted only of general guidelines. In this book, cooperating teachers are given opportunities, particularly in Chapters 4 through 8, to develop the specific skills they need to provide productive and satisfying clinical experiences for students, for themselves, and for the pupils they teach. Cooperating teachers also will find Chapters 1, 2, 3, and 9 useful. Cooperating teachers frequently feel that they lack up-to-date knowledge of the overall field of teacher education. These four chapters provide background information designed to help cooperating teachers feel confident of their ability to participate in clinical experiences as knowledgeable teacher educators.

College supervisors will also be aided by the book. In fulfilling their role, college supervisors are expected to demonstrate many of the competencies needed by cooperating teachers. The material and activities presented here provide college supervisors with opportunities to increase the effectiveness of their interaction with students. In addition to their work with students, college supervisors are often asked to provide orientation sessions and inservice programs for cooperating teachers. The strategies and activities included here can serve as a framework for designing such programs.

While cooperating teachers and college supervisors interact most closely with preservice students, additional teacher educators participate in clinical experiences: school administrators, directors of clinical experiences, school district coordinators of teacher education, and college faculty who teach courses that include a field component. This book can benefit these teacher educators by increasing their awareness of current thinking regarding the development and implementation of clinical experiences.

SUGGESTIONS FOR THE INSTRUCTOR

Instructional programs for cooperating teachers, college supervisors, and other teacher educators are offered in a variety of contexts: college and university graduate courses, workshops, inservice staff development programs. This book is designed for flexible use. Ways in which the material can be used in various instructional settings are suggested.

The most extensive treatment of the material probably will take place in graduate courses because they typically are of longer duration than workshops and inservice programs. In this setting, participants can explore in depth the implications for clinical experiences of the issues, concepts, and strategies presented. Furthermore, class members can participate fully in the activities, included in Chapters 4 through 8, that are a major focus of the book. The suggested procedure for carrying out each activity encourages participants (1) to complete the analysis guide that accompanies the activity and (2) to share their work in order to provide feedback for one another. In several activities role playing is suggested, both as a way of experiencing the process being considered and as a means of viewing that process from the perspective of other role occupants. Full participation in these procedures will enable group members to become actively involved in developing the understandings and skills presented in the text.

If the book is to be used in settings where time is limited, such as workshops or inservice programs, the instructor can consider several options. One approach is to focus on selected dimensions of the clinical experience rather than deal superficially with every topic presented in the material. Topic selection can be made by the instructor or the participants on the basis of their interests and needs. A second option is to ask participants to complete the analysis guides outside of the instructional setting. They can then share their work and complete the activities when they come together as a group. A third alternative is to ask the participants to form subgroups according to shared interests or needs. These groups can select the activities they wish to pursue and share the results of their work with others at the completion of the activities.

Although the procedures for completing the activities included here are directed toward participants in group settings, this does not preclude the use of the material on an independent study basis. Contracts can be developed by the instructor with individuals who want to pursue selected aspects of the material. A procedure for completing the activities on an independent basis is included in Activity 1, which appears in Chapter 4.

The instructor should not feel restricted by the suggestions given here for using the book. Undoubtedly, many instructors will want to adapt the material in other ways in order to meet the needs of their particular instructional settings.

A final point regarding the activities included in the book. With two exceptions, the activities are self-contained and can be completed without additional material or equipment. (Activities 13 and 14 involve the use of a tape recorder.) Instructors and participants may want to supplement the illustrative material provided here with materials of their own. They are encouraged to do so. Such materials might include the following:

- handbooks developed by cooperating teachers or college supervisors
- daily and weekly schedules
- plans developed by students or cooperating teachers
- evaluation forms developed by colleges or school districts
- audiotapes or videotapes of lessons or conferences

SUGGESTIONS FOR THE READER

The trend toward including clinical experiences early in programs of teacher education has created a growing demand for teacher educators who have the skills to work with preservice students in these experiences. As a result, increasing numbers of cooperating teachers, college supervisors, and other teacher educators are searching for resources that will help them fulfill their roles successfully. The development of *Guiding Clinical Experiences in Teacher Education* represents an effort to respond to that search.

The book is addressed primarily to cooperating teachers in whose classrooms preservice students participate in clinical experiences. Nevertheless, college supervisors and other teacher educators can also increase the effectiveness of their participation in clinical experiences through reading the material presented and participating in the activities included in the book.

The book is organized in four parts. The material included in each part is described in the initial section of this introduction. A brief summary of each part is included here for your convenience.

Part One establishes the current context of clinical experiences in teacher education. This is accomplished through a discussion of research and practice in the areas of teacher effectiveness, teacher education, and supervision. Part Four offers an analysis of the current scene that provides the basis for projecting the future of teacher education.

Part Two examines the roles that interact in clinical experiences. Part Three addresses the specific dimensions of clinical experiences (e.g., planning, observing, evaluation) through which this interaction takes place. A strategy for implementing each dimension is presented as that area is considered.

The description of each strategy includes activities that enable you to develop the skills needed to apply the strategy in your own situation. The procedure for carrying out each activity encourages you to complete the analysis guide that accompanies the activity and then share your work with others in order to give and receive feedback.

While the procedures for completing the activities included here are directed toward participants in group settings, this does not mean that you cannot complete the activities on your own. Following your independent completion of the analysis guide for each activity, you can invite one or more colleagues to participate with you in the steps of the feedback process. A suggested procedure for completing the activities on an independent basis is included in Activity 1, which appears in Chapter 4.

TERMINOLOGY

Changing patterns in teacher education have resulted in an expanded vocabulary to describe the components and roles involved in preservice programs. In addition, there is some variation in the meanings of many terms currently being used. In order to avoid confusion and misunderstanding, the following terms are presented here with the definitions that they are given throughout the book.

Preservice teacher education: A college or university program consisting of course work and supervised direct experiences in teaching. Successful completion of the program is required for teacher certification.

Teacher education student: A college or university student who is participating in a program of preservice teacher education. The terms *preservice college student* and *student* are used synonymously with *teacher education student.*

Teacher educator: An educator in a school or college setting who participates in planning, implementing, or evaluating programs of preservice teacher education.

Clinical experiences: Supervised, direct experiences in teaching provided for teacher education students in nursery, elementary, middle, and secondary schools. The term *clinical experience,* as used here, includes participation in pre-student teaching, student teaching, or internship experiences. In the context of this book, *clinical experience* is used synonymously with the following terms: *professional laboratory experience, field experience,* and *practicum.*

Cooperating teacher: A classroom teacher whose role in teacher education is to work directly with preservice students who are participating in clinical experiences. The term *supervising teacher* is also used to designate this role.

College supervisor: A college or university representative whose role in teacher education is to work directly with preservice students and cooperating teachers in clinical experiences.

PART 1

THE CONTEXT OF clinical experiences

What is teaching? How can we define, assess, and develop teacher effectiveness? Vast amounts of time, money, and effort have been expended in the search for answers to these questions. The results of this expenditure, though not yet as clear-cut and definitive as we would like, need to be examined by those who participate in providing clinical experiences for teacher education students.[1] Cooperating

[1]Throughout this book, the designation *teacher education student,* or *student,* is used to identify a preservice teacher engaged in direct teaching experience in an elementary, middle, or secondary school. The traditional, more limited, designation *student teacher* has not been used because of the current trend toward providing a wide variety of preservice teaching experiences (pre-student teaching, student teaching, and internship experiences).

CHAPTER TEACHING AND TEACHER EFFECTIVENESS

teachers, college supervisors, and others who play a part in this important effort must make the clinical experience an opportunity for systematically studying teaching. In order to fulfill this responsibility, every teacher educator needs to be aware both of his own conception of *teaching* and *teacher effectiveness* and of alternative conceptions that are useful in the study of teaching. As those who share in the responsibility for providing clinical experiences examine ways of analyzing teaching and teacher effectiveness, and clarify or modify their own conceptions, they will develop a sound basis for their efforts in guiding students in the complex process of studying teaching.

DEFINING *TEACHING*

The attempt to define teaching has a history as long as that of education itself and has resulted in definitions as varied as the settings in which education has taken place. When teaching was viewed as a simple process, defining it merely as "telling" or "imparting knowledge" seemed adequate. Teaching is not a simple process, however; it involves an interactive situation in which teachers create conditions under which pupils will come to learn and to act upon their knowledge (Sprinthall and Sprinthall 1974, p. 253). Once educators began to identify the complexities involved in teaching, defining the process simply as "telling" was recognized as inadequate.

Models for the Analysis of Teaching

Recognition of the complexities involved in the teaching process has led to the development of ways of describing and analyzing teaching that attempt not only to include the major dimensions of the process but also to identify the relationships among these dimensions. A number of conceptions, or models, of the teaching process have been proposed, and it is probable that additional models will be forthcoming as educators, psychologists, sociologists, and others continue to search for useful ways of analyzing teaching. It is beyond the scope of this chapter to attempt to describe all the models that currently exist, but it is important to present several views of the teaching process. After these models have been described, it will be possible to examine their usefulness in designing experiences for teacher education students.

Broad Models of Teaching.   Sprinthall and Sprinthall (1974, pp. 253–57) present three teaching models, representing three different views of the teacher's role. In the first model, teaching is viewed as the transmission of knowledge. What is emphasized here is giving children facts and information. The teacher's role is one of assigning work and making the majority of decisions, rather than one of helping children develop initiative.

The second model, with which Jerome Bruner's name is often linked, views teaching as the process of helping children discover the structure of a discipline through a process of inquiry. In this approach the teacher's role is one of asking questions that help children discover answers for themselves, rather than one of giving answers to them. One question raised with regard to this teaching model is whether pupils have the cognitive sophistication necessary for dealing with the abstract concepts and processes involved in understanding the structure of a discipline taught in this way. The authors suggest that this is a problem at both elementary and secondary school levels.

The third model views teaching as a process of developing positive interpersonal relationships between teachers and pupils. The major focus is on creating an environment in which children feel free to learn, rather than on how to present the actual content involved. Carl Rogers (1969), a proponent of this approach, suggests that in order to free children to learn, teachers need to provide three conditions: empathy, unconditional positive regard, and genuineness. Teachers must communicate to students that they understand their feelings, accept them as they are, and are being "real" in their relationships with them. According to Rogers, these conditions provide a better climate for learning than the impersonality and aloofness that characterize the traditional learning environment.

Applied Psychological Models.   Several theories of human behavior have been used as sources for the development of approaches to teaching. Frostig and Maslow (1973, pp. 43–48) discuss the implications for teaching of four psychological theories: humanistic psychology, behavior modification, cognitive-developmental psychology, and psychoanalysis. Table 1.1 compares the application of these theories to twelve dimensions of the teaching process.

Table 1.1   Comparison of Implications of Behavior Modification, Humanistic Psychology, Psychoanalysis, and Cognitive-Developmental Psychology for Education

	Individualization	Motivation
Behavior Modification	Individualization of task assignment taking the child's level of functioning into account. Individualization of rewards and of discipline.	The child's interests and needs are not accepted as a "given"; they are to be changed and manipulated whenever this seems of advantage. A reward system motivates the child. Motivation is extrinsic. Rewards may be material, social, or fulfill other needs. In contrast to psychoanalysis and humanism, satisfaction of needs is the consequence and not the precondition of learning.
Humanistic Psychology	Individualization of total approach according to needs and individuality of child, on	Satisfaction of needs is necessary for optimum learning ability. The child's need for

Table 1.1 Comparison of Implications of Behavior Modification, Humanistic Psychology, Psychoanalysis, and Cognitive-Developmental Psychology for Education *(continued)*.

	Individualization	*Motivation*
	an intuitive basis as a consequence of shared experience.	experience, his wish to be helpful and to communicate with others—in short, social motives and need for experience—are emphasized. Motivation is mainly intrinsic.
Psychoanalysis	Individualization in relation to differences of needs and maturational level, task assignments, personal relationships, and total approach.	Satisfaction of needs regarded as the prime source of motivation ("the pleasure principle"). Needs for love, security, and mastery and emotional and social needs must be satisfied before energy and interests are available for learning. Motivation is both extrinsic and intrinsic.
Cognitive-Developmental Psychology	Adaptation of tasks to child's developmental stage and previous experiences.	Interests are the expression of a "drive" toward equilibrium. Knowing is a motive in itself. Motivation is intrinsic. The need for equilibrium is as compelling as physiological needs.

	Degree of Systematization	*Methodology*
Behavior Modification	Very specific methods of classroom management and teaching are prescribed. Systematization is emphasized. Programmed material is suggested.	Extensive and detailed methods and sequences to develop skills and specific knowledge are advocated. Use of computer and other machine technology to assist teacher.
Humanistic Psychology	A balanced curriculum and balance between freedom and discipline is advocated. Recognition of developmental progression is only one of the factors to be taken into account in adjusting to the child's needs. The	Emphasis on integrated project approach, with particular stress on social studies.

teacher must be attuned to the child's intellectual, emotional, and social needs.

Psychoanalysis	Systematization is not especially stressed; the classroom environment must be stable but flexible. Teaching takes developmental level of child into account. Curriculum usually shows progressive steps, except in the type of school like Summerhill.	No special developments or innovations, except in the type of school like Summerhill where total freedom prevails.
Cognitive-Developmental Psychology	Progress in teaching is systematic, but classroom environment free enough for exploration and discovery. Theory of cognitive development results in definite teaching approaches suitable for the child's developmental level.	Materials and curricula to develop basic cognitive skills, such as classification, seriation, conservation, imagery, and problem-solving have been developed, as well as specific curricula in science, math, and social studies.

	Curricular Objectives	*Form of Classroom Management*
Behavior Modification	Focus on academic knowledge and skills and on socially defined personal and social behavior characteristics.	Teacher-centered. The teacher prescribes curriculum and classroom procedures. Social relationships are not emphasized as goals but utilized as means.
Humanistic Psychology	Focus on social development, communication skills, and sensitivity to beauty and other humanistic values. The child's sensitivity to group needs as well as to individual needs is to be enhanced. Social influences are more emphasized than biological ones. The goal is optimum interrelationship with the environment, not adjustment.	Child-centered. The teacher assists child but does not direct him in his learning. The classroom structure permits freedom of choice for the child and fosters creativity and exploration. The importance of human relationships is recognized. The classroom situation permits and should foster social learning.
Psychoanalysis	Focus on emotional development, communication skills, and social institutions. Social interaction is used as a tool to	Opinions among this group vary. In certain schools it is partly child-centered, with the roles of teacher and child

	Curricular Objectives	*Form of Classroom Management*
	further emotional growth. Academic knowledge and skills are tools to achieve the main objectives of later mature adjustment.	specified in relation to each other. The teacher's role includes her influence on character formation and adjustment of the child. In others, a Summerhill-like atmosphere prevails, and the school is totally child-centered. The value of peer relationships is emphasized.
Cognitive-Developmental Psychology	Focus on total development: sensory-motor, language, and cognitive. Social interaction serves as a tool to develop decentration, intelligence, and logical thought.	Child-centered. The teacher assists the child and guides him in his learning, explorations, and discovery. The classroom structure permits and fosters self-direction.

	Making Teaching Meaningful	*Active Participation*
Behavior Modification	Emphasis is usually not on integration of topics but rather on a linear progression in teaching content and skills. Behaviorists are not concerned with "meaning" except as meaning is derived from understanding previous steps. Mastery is emphasized in behavioristic terms of specific mastery of subject matter or adjustment to classroom demands. Mastery or attainment of extraneous rewards make learning meaningful.	Behaviorists are little concerned with activity, except if the activity is the behavior to be elicited. The child may be a rather passive recipient of knowledge, and should follow directions. The behavior is shaped, not guided.
Humanistic Psychology	As in psychoanalytically influenced teaching, meaning derives from integration of topics and relating the content to child's personal needs. Additional emphasis is put on human needs in gen-	Experience requires action. The child needs to relate himself actively to the environment and to share with others in common activities. Also, the child's need for play and activity has to be satisfied.

eral, on creativity and involvement, and on developing the child's feeling of "being in the world" and awareness of the world around him.

| Psychoanalysis | Meaningfulness of material taught is achieved through integration of topics, and by relating topics to satisfaction of the child's past experiences, present needs, and future goals. In certain schools, the child chooses the topic he wants to study and even whether or not he wants to learn. | Activity is deemed necessary, first, because it is the mode in which younger children can best express thoughts and feelings. Activity, including play, also helps the child to understand and to adjust to the environment. Finally, the physiologic need for movement has to be satisfied. |
| Cognitive-Developmental Psychology | Integration of knowledge is emphasized. Integration is not merely achieved by associations between thoughts or between contents of curricula or by addition of new knowledge. The hierarchical order of concepts and skills must be grasped to make meaningful what has been learned. Concepts are related to other coordinated, supraordinated, and subordinated concepts. | Activity is regarded as the basis of all mental development. The child learns by exploring and experimenting. In new learning, he proceeds from activity (enactive learning) to perceptual learning (iconic) and then to symbolic learning. To make symbolic learning possible, he must learn to read, write, make graphs, use mathematical language, etc. |

	Use of Early Symbolic Abilities *(not including language)*	*Language Instruction*
Behavior Modification	The topic of symbolic play and imagery has not been discussed by behaviorists, as these are activities which are not at all or only partly overt. Repetition, modified repetition, and imitating a model are methods used extensively in teaching.	The approach to language teaching is structured. Syntax, vocabulary, and articulation are taught specifically. Imitation is used in the teaching of language, as well as modified imitation and the learning of rules. Correct use of language is the goal of language instruction, and includes oral and written language.

Table 1.1 **Comparison of Implications of Behavior Modification, Humanistic Psychology, Psychoanalysis, and Cognitive-Developmental Psychology for Education** (continued).

	Use of Early Symbolic Abilities (not including language)	Language Instruction
Humanistic Psychology	Experience involves imagery. Empathy requires imagery and is developed by imagining playing another person's role. Imagery is basic to all understanding and must be developed; one method is symbolic (dramatic) play.	Language is developed through use of creative language, poems, story-writing, and dramatic play. Expressions of feelings and ideas are furthered. Language includes body language, gestures, and creative expression.
Psychoanalysis	Imagery and role-taking are forms of learning. Imaginative and symbolic play assist the child in adjusting to reality and in his emotional growth. Imitation helps the child to learn behavior patterns.	Language is enhanced through social contacts and small group learning. Little formal teaching of language. Reading and writing are introduced late. The child is taught to substitute language for "acting out" in achieving need satisfaction.
Cognitive-Developmental Psychology	Imitation, symbolic play, and imagery are basic to symbolic behavior. Imitation and symbolic play are therefore utilized in instruction. Development of images (kinetic and anticipatory) must occur prior to logical thought and can be developed through planning and self-direction.	Language and thought cannot be separated in instruction. Language is the most important form of symbolic expression. Language needs to be used to describe and explain action. Written language is taught very early, together with beginning reading.

	Rote versus Insight Learning	Goals
Behavior Modification	Rote learning and associational learning in small steps are emphasized. Skills are greatly emphasized.	A person able to fill a job well or to continue with his education because he has mastered skills and knowledge taught on a lower level. Competence is the goal of education.
Humanistic Psychology	Emphasis is on insight learning and understanding, in contrast to mere acquisition of knowledge.	A loving, creative human being with a strong social conscience, aware of the needs of others, feeling fulfilled, and helping others to feel fulfilled. Self-fulfillment and

		understanding are the goals of education.
Psychoanalysis	Emphasis is on insight learning and understanding. The importance of understanding current behavior in light of the child's previous experiences is also stressed.	A person free of neuroticism and not suppressed by cultural demands who is socially aware and responsive, cherishes human values, is self-assured, and feels enriched by his culture, to which he adjusts and attempts to contribute. Adjustment and interaction with society are both goals of education.
Cognitive-Developmental Psychology	Emphasis is on insight learning and understanding.	A person who has optimally developed his cognitive functions and who is innovative and flexible in his thought processes. Most important, he is a person who can de-centrate, especially by taking into account the points of view of others as well as all possible outcomes in making decisions and carrying out actions. Intelligence used equally well in decisions pertaining both to oneself and to others is the goal of education.

SOURCE: From Marianne Frostig and Phyllis Maslow, *Learning Problems in the Classroom* (New York: Grune & Stratton, 1973), pp. 97–103. Reprinted with permission.

Frostig and Maslow point out that the differences among these theories derive in part from differences in focus or emphasis. Humanists emphasize the goals of education, while the focus of behaviorism is methodology. The psychoanalytic and cognitive-developmental viewpoints give equal emphasis to the curriculum, the methodology, and the goals of education. All four approaches agree, however, on the results to be achieved: "the development of friendly, happy children, who will find life meaningful" (p. 44). The authors conclude their discussion of the four theories by pointing out that the application of one theory to certain dimensions of teaching does not preclude the application of the other theories to different dimensions of the teaching process. They encourage teachers to combine these approaches and use them in different situations. For example, a teacher might select one approach as a basis for developing objectives and another as a basis for the development of classroom management strategies.

A Pedagogical Model. B. Othanel Smith (1960) presents a model of teaching that differs considerably from those described here. He begins his discussion of teaching by identifying three ways in which it has been defined:

> *Teaching:* arrangement and manipulation of a situation in which there are gaps or obstructions which an individual will seek to overcome and from which he will learn in the course of doing so.

> *Teaching:* intimate contact between a more mature personality and a less mature [one] which is designed to further the education of the latter.

> *Teaching:* impartation of knowledge to an individual by another in school. (p. 230)

According to Smith, each of these definitions has the same defect. Each one "smuggles in its own particular view of how teaching is to be carried on" (p. 230). Smith contends that these definitions confuse teaching with the ways in which it can be performed, and therefore represent normative rather than descriptive concepts of teaching.

Smith's conception of teaching, he argues, avoids the problems he has pointed out in other definitions. He defines teaching as "a system of actions intended to induce learning" (p. 230). To explain this concept of teaching Smith proposes a pedogogical model that identifies the variables involved in and related to the actions that make up teaching. Smith's model is presented in Figure 1.1.

Figure 1.1   A Pedagogical Model

I *Independent Variables* *(Teacher)*	*II* *Intervening Variables* *(Pupils)*	*III* *Dependent Variables* *(Pupils)*
(1) Linguistic behavior	These variables consist of postulated explanatory entities and processes such as memories, be- liefs, needs, inferences, and associative mechanisms.	(1) Linguistic behavior
(2) Performative behavior		(2) Performative behavior
(3) Expressive behavior		(3) Expressive behavior

SOURCE: From B. Othanel Smith, *Teachers College Record* (February 1960, *61* (5)), p. 234. Reprinted with permission.

Smith contends that all these variables can be classified into three categories: (1) independent variables, (2) dependent variables, and (3) intervening variables. In the model, the arrows indicate the direction of causal influences. The independent variables, actions of the teacher, are followed by states, events, or processes in the pupil, represented by the intervening variables. The pupil, then, as a result of these variables, exhibits one or more of the behaviors indicated in the dependent variables column.

The teacher's actions, the independent variables, consist of linguistic, performative, and expressive behaviors. In the linguistic category, according to Smith, the teacher performs three kinds of actions. The first consists of the performance of logically relevant tasks—those tasks that involve logical operations. For example, the teacher defines terms, explains events, and compares and contrasts objects, factors, and processes. In taking each action, the teacher is performing a logical operation. The second kind of action that teachers perform with language is called directive action. Here the teacher gives instructions; for example, he may tell the pupil how to perform a skill, what to do to correct a mistake, or how to set up a piece of equipment. The pupil is not expected to learn what the teacher has said, in the sense of being able to repeat the words the teacher used, but rather to follow the instructions as a means of improving his performance. Finally, in the linquistic category, the teacher performs admonitory acts. He praises and criticizes. He advises the pupil to follow one course of action rather than another. The significance of these admonitory acts lies in their social or emotional impact rather than in their cognitive content.

In addition to their verbal actions, teachers perform two kinds of nonverbal actions. The first of these Smith calls performative action. The teacher *shows* the pupil how to operate the filmstrip projector by performing the act himself. Verbal behavior may accompany performative actions, but the actions themselves are motor performances. The second kind of nonverbal action is called expressive behavior. Posture, facial expression, and tone of voice are examples of this behavior. Smith points out that these behaviors typically are neither purposeful nor addressed to anyone. They have a function in teaching, however, because pupils take them as signs of the psychological state of the teacher.

Actions performed by teachers, the independent variables, are paralleled by actions performed by pupils, the dependent variables in Smith's model. Pupils perform linguistic actions, just as teachers do. They define terms, explain events, and compare and contrast objects and factors. By performing these actions they indicate that they are taking part in the instructional process. Smith states that pupils perform directive and admonitory verbal actions infrequently. With regard to this statement, it can be suggested that pupils probably engage in these behaviors more frequently today than they did at the time Smith developed his model. In the more open settings found in many of today's schools, for example, children instruct one other in the operation of classroom equipment; and they praise, blame, and advise one another regarding work they have completed or are in the process of completing.

Pupils, as well as teachers, exhibit nonverbal performative and expressive behavior. When a pupil shows another pupil how to operate the tape recorder by performing the action himself, he is exhibiting performative behavior. Pupils exhibit expressive behaviors as they smile, frown, and sit in a variety of postures. In doing this, they communicate to the teacher, though not necessarily with the intent to do so, their feelings, thoughts, and motivations.

Smith admits that teaching is more complex than his pedagogical model. He suggests, however, that one advantage in having a model is that it presents a simplified picture of the phenomenon it depicts. This particular model is useful, according to Smith, because it enables researchers to examine the *concept* of teaching without becoming involved in controversy about *how* teaching should be performed.

Using Models of Teaching

Everyone who works with teacher education students in clinical experiences can contribute to the effectiveness of those experiences through an awareness of the variety of ways in which teaching is described. This section addresses the question of how cooperating teachers, in particular, can use their knowledge of models of teaching to help students study teaching in the context of the classroom.

A consideration of the diverse ways in which teaching is viewed suggests, first, that it is essential that the cooperating teacher communicate to preservice students his[2] own current conception of teaching. In doing this, the cooperating teacher provides students with the basis they need for understanding and interpreting the instructional process as they observe it in his classroom.

Cooperating teachers also can help students explore alternative models of teaching and consider their use in planning for instruction. For example, a cooperating teacher and student may decide to employ concepts from humanistic psychology as they plan a sequence of lessons in language instruction or design a series of activities for self-concept development. At another time, they may consider the use of behavior modification techniques in individualizing instruction in particular areas of the curriculum.

An understanding of a variety of models of teaching can be useful in yet another way: Cooperating teachers can stay alert to the need to be concerned with a broad range of educational outcomes—the need to include affective as well as cognitive objectives in their planning, for example. Cooperating teachers who focus on a broad range of outcomes in their own teaching will recognize, as a result, the importance of providing teacher education students with opportunities to guide children's development toward a comprehensive, rather than a limited, range of objectives.

The usefulness of models of teaching is not limited to the few suggestions made here nor to the models described in the previous section. Both the models and the suggestions for their use, however, can serve as a starting point in guiding students in their study of teaching.

STUDIES OF TEACHER EFFECTIVENESS

The efforts of everyone participating in the process of educating teachers are directed toward one objective: the preparation of teachers who can demonstrate effectiveness in facilitating pupils' learning. Clearly there is agreement with regard to this objective, but it is equally clear that a considerable lack of agreement emerges when questions of how to define, assess, and develop *teacher effectiveness* are raised.

[2]Authors try to avoid overusing the generic pronoun *he* when *she* is equally appropriate. The roles of teacher education student, cooperating teacher, and college supervisor are occupied by members of both sexes. In order to avoid ambiguity and stereotyping, pronouns will be used to designate the occupants of these roles in the following manner throughout this book: teacher education student: *she*; cooperating teacher: *he*; college supervisor: *she*.

Recognition of the critical nature of these questions has resulted in research efforts that have produced literally thousands of studies. These studies, often derived from models of teaching such as those discussed here, have investigated a wide range of dimensions viewed as central to the teaching process. And yet, as Medley (1979) notes, their impact on the education of teachers has been slight. Medley suggests that one reason teacher effectiveness research has failed to have more impact on teacher education is that many of the findings have been irrelevant or inconsistent. He goes on to contend, however, that reliable information about the nature of effective teaching is available today. It is important that cooperating teachers develop an understanding of this current information, both as a basis for their own instructional decision making and as a basis for guiding teacher education students in the process of learning to make sound instructional decisions.

Since past research efforts have influenced current efforts in studying teacher effectiveness, it seems useful to place the information to which Medley refers in perspective by tracing the development of research on teacher effectiveness. This will enable us to examine current findings with an understanding of how teacher effectiveness research has come to the stage at which it is now.

The Development of Teacher Effectiveness Research

Rosenshine (1979) suggests that research on teacher effectiveness can be viewed as moving through three cycles. In the first cycle, the focus was identifying the characteristics of effective teachers. Investigators examined a wide range of variables such as mental abilities, attitudes, and personality traits in efforts to determine whether any of these characteristics were consistently related to teacher effectiveness. A major problem in these studies was the measurement of the variables. None of them can be observed directly, and considerable controversy arose regarding the "best" way to measure the characteristics being examined (Biddle 1964, p. 10). Overall attempts to measure and relate teacher characteristics to effectiveness failed to produce useful results. As Gage (1963) has stated: ". . . these studies have yielded disappointing results: correlations that are nonsignificant from one study to the next, and usually lacking in psychological and educational meaning" (p. 118).

In the second cycle of teacher effectiveness research, which began in the 1950s, investigators focused on relationships between teacher behavior and pupil learning. The method in this research involves (1) the systematic counting of teacher and pupil behaviors and (2) relating the frequency of these behaviors to measures of pupil gains in achievement. Because this research focuses both on measures of behavior (process) and gains in pupil learning (product), it has come to be known as "process-product research." In process-product studies, teacher behaviors (and in some cases pupil behaviors) are recorded using observational category systems or rating systems. The behaviors are then related to measures of pupil performance using the statistical procedure of correlation. In their review of process-product research, Rosenshine and Furst (1971) pointed out that the results of these studies, which are correlational and not experimental, should be viewed with caution. They suggested that "the results of such studies can be deceptive in that they suggest causation although the teacher behaviors which are related to student achievement may be only minor indicators of a complex of behaviors that we have not yet identified" (p. 42).

Rosenshine and Furst identified additional limitations before presenting the results of the process-product studies they reviewed. The first was that all the studies were conducted with normal children. The second was that in most studies, only the class mean was used in the analyses; few attempts were made to assess the relationships between teacher behavior and pupil achievement for subgroups of pupils differing in personality, aptitude, or achievement. The third limitation was that their review included only the relationships between teacher behaviors and pupil achievement. It did not include a discussion of other important outcomes, such as pupil attitudes toward self and school.

Rosenshine and Furst then described the eleven strongest variables produced by process-product studies at the time of their review. The best results had been obtained on the first five variables: clarity of the teacher's presentation, use of varied activities during the lesson, teacher's enthusiasm, task-oriented and businesslike behaviors, and student opportunity to learn the material. Less conclusive results were obtained on the last six variables: teacher use of student ideas during discussion, criticism (negatively related to achievement), use of structuring statements at the start and at the end of lessons, use of varied types of questions, teacher's probing of students' responses, and perceived difficulty of the course.

In a recent review of process-product research, Rosenshine (1979) discusses what has been learned about several of these variables from studies conducted since the time of his first review. Clarity of presentation, enthusiasm, and use of student ideas are no longer the significant predictors of student achievement, in kindergarten through fifth grade, that they were in earlier studies. Rosenshine suggests that this change in the significance of these verbal variables in predicting achievement may have occurred because of a decrease in the frequency of verbal interaction in elementary classrooms in recent years. He states that since today's students spend from 50 to 70 percent of their time working alone, the verbal behaviors of teachers are now less important than they once were. The variable "use of varied activities" has correlated negatively, rather than positively, with student achievement in recent studies. These findings may indicate that when too many activities occur simultaneously, students are less attentive because the teacher is unable to monitor all the activities. Both amount of content covered in the classroom (student opportunity to learn the material) and task-oriented behaviors have continued to yield excellent results in recent research, according to Rosenshine. Finally, criticism of students by teachers continues to be negatively correlated with achievement.

In another recent review of process-product research, Medley (1977) reports 613 relationships between teacher behaviors and pupil learning resulting from 14 studies. One limitation in these studies, as Medley notes, is that most of them were conducted with one segment of the school population—with classes of Grade III or below in which most of the pupils came from homes of low socioeconomic status. Medley summarizes the findings of these studies and presents his interpretation of them in a verbal picture of the effective teacher of low SES (socioeconomic status) pupils whose classes show high mean gains on achievement tests of arithmetic, reading, or both:

The Effective Teacher of Low SES Pupils in the Primary Grades

Teacher Use of Time
Compared with the less effective teacher, the effective teacher
- devotes more class time to task-related or "academic" activities
- spends less class time discussing matters unrelated to lesson content

Organizing for Instruction
Compared with the less effective teacher, the effective teacher
- spends more time with large groups and less with small ones
- individualizes assignments more

Quality of Instruction
Compared with the less effective teacher, the effective teacher
- asks more questions classifiable in the lower levels of the Bloom taxonomy[3]
- is less likely to amplify, discuss, or use pupil answers

Environmental Maintenance
Compared with the less effective teacher, the effective teacher
- has a classroom characterized by less deviant or disruptive pupil behavior
- controls the classroom with less criticism and uses a more varied repertory of techniques in doing so
- uses more praise or positive motivation

Individual Attention
Compared with the less effective teacher, the effective teacher
- spends more time checking pupils' work during seatwork periods
- tends to talk longer and to pay closer attention when talking to an individual pupil

Medley also examines the data from these studies in terms of affective outcomes and makes two generalizations: (1) The effective teacher of subject matter is likely to be developing positive pupil attitudes toward school as well; and (2) those teachers who produce significant achievement gains are also likely to improve pupils' self-concept the most.

While process-product research is, in the words of Rosenshine (1979), "alive, well, and continuing" (p. 31), he identifies a third cycle that is now in progress. The emphasis in this cycle is on the student, particularly the student's mastery of content and the number of minutes the student is attending to academically relevant tasks. Before reporting studies investigating these variables, Rosenshine notes an overall caution: The studies were limited to instruction in reading and mathematics of students in grades 1 through 5.

[3]Benjamin S. Bloom (Ed.). *Taxonomy of educational objectives.* New York: Longman Inc., 1977.

According to Rosenshine, the results of the studies reveal a fairly clear and consistent pattern. Teachers who are effective in bringing about student gains in achievement place students in contact with curriculum materials and find ways of keeping them academically engaged for many minutes each day. In addition, when they place children in groups, these teachers actively supervise the groups, rather than let the children work on their own. Their classrooms are structured, and they select the activities. Finally, these teachers tend to ask questions that have specific answers in a controlled-practice format.

These findings should not leave the reader with an image of a formal classroom that is cold and regimented. Rosenshine cites additional studies that indicate that "in general, classrooms that show high gains in achievement and a high number of academically engaged minutes are usually moderate to high with respect to having a warm classroom atmosphere" (p. 40). This statement is further supported by the findings of studies dealing with teacher criticism, ridicule, and sarcasm; these behaviors are consistently related negatively to gain in achievement.

The Current Status of Teacher Effectiveness Research

In looking at Rosenshine's three cycles, what major changes in teacher effectiveness research can be identified? Earlier efforts attempted to define effective teaching in terms of personality traits or attitudes, and to determine the presence or absence of these characteristics through paper-and-pencil tests or the rating of "experts." This represented an attempt to determine what an effective teacher *is*. A major step forward was taken when the focus shifted to investigations of what an effective teacher *does*. This resulted in the search for relationships between specific teacher behaviors and student gains in achievement. The value in this shift lies in the fact that teachers can change their behaviors, whereas it is doubtful that they can change their personality characteristics. Progress has also been made in defining teacher behavior more precisely. For example, knowing what effective teachers do while their pupils are engaged in seatwork is more useful than knowing that effective teachers are "enthusiastic."

A major criticism of teacher effectiveness research over the years has been that it is of little value because the findings have been so inconsistent. This criticism is becoming less valid. Both Rosenshine and Medley were able to identify consistent findings in the studies they examined. In addition, when the results reported in these two reviews are compared, consistencies emerge.

Advances in teacher effectiveness research are being made. This in no way implies that the information we have is either sufficient or conclusive. Much additional research is needed, both to produce new knowledge and to confirm current findings. The value in understanding the information currently available is that it broadens the base from which we approach the teaching process. As McNeil and Popham (1973) point out: "The practical utility of research should be seen as allowing all students of teaching—teachers, administrators, and researchers—to be more flexible in planning, executing, analyzing and evaluating the teaching act" (p. 241).

REFERENCES

Biddle, Bruce J. The integration of teacher effectiveness research. In Bruce J. Biddle and William J. Ellena (Eds.), *Contemporary research on teacher effectiveness.* New York: Holt, Rinehart and Winston, 1964.

Frostig, Marianne, and Maslow, Phyllis. *Learning problems in the classroom.* New York: Grune & Stratton, 1973.

Gage, Nathaniel L. Paradigms for research on teaching. In Nathaniel L. Gage (Ed.), *Handbook of research on teaching.* Chicago: Rand McNally, 1963.

McNeil, John D., and Popham, W. James. Chap. 7, The assessment of teacher competence. In Robert M. W. Travers (Ed.), *Second handbook of research on teaching.* A Project of the American Educational Research Association. Chicago: Rand McNally, 1973.

Medley, Donald M. *Teacher competence and teacher effectiveness: A review of process-product research.* Washington, D.C.: American Association of Colleges for Teacher Education, 1977.

Medley, Donald M. The effectiveness of teachers. In Penelope L. Peterson and Herbert J. Walberg (Eds.), *Research on teaching: Concepts, findings, and implications.* Berkeley, CA: McCutchan, 1979.

Rogers, Carl R. *Freedom to learn.* Columbus, OH: Merrill, 1969.

Rosenshine, Barak V. Content, time, and direct instruction. In Penelope L. Peterson and Herbert J. Walberg (Eds.), *Research on teaching: Concepts, findings, and implications.* Berkeley, CA: McCutchan, 1979.

Rosenshine, Barak, and Furst, Norma. Research on teacher performance criteria. In B. Othanel Smith (Ed.), *Research in teacher education: A symposium.* Englewood Cliffs, NJ: Prentice-Hall, 1971.

Smith, B. Othanel. A concept of teaching. *Teachers College Record,* February 1960, *61* (5), 229–41.

Sprinthall, Richard C., and Sprinthall, Norman A. *Educational psychology: A developmental approach.* Reading, MA: Addison-Wesley Publishing, 1974.

The word *diversity* probably best describes the field of teacher education today. Current programs for the preparation of teachers differ widely along many dimensions: objectives, content, structure, field experiences, and assessment of student performance. Programs differ, moreover, not only from institution to institution, but also within institutions. It is not uncommon for students at the same college or university, seeking the same certification, to be able to select from among alternative programs the one they wish to pursue.

Cooperating teachers cannot be expected to know in detail the varied approaches to program development being described and debated in the literature of teacher

CHAPTER **2** TRENDS AND PATTERNS IN TEACHER EDUCATION

education today. It is important, however, that they develop an awareness of the major trends that are influencing program development as a basis for understanding the experiences their students have had prior to their field experience or are having in conjunction with the field experience. To provide the maximum benefit, field experiences must be integrated with other components of students' programs. Cooperating teachers who are knowledgeable about current trends and patterns in teacher education can contribute significantly to the achievement of this integration.

A TIME OF CHANGE IN TEACHER EDUCATION

The 1960s and 1970s were exciting and challenging times in teacher education. They were exciting because teacher educators across the country were given the opportunity, through extensive federal funding during the earlier part of the period, to develop a wide range of innovative programs and techniques for preparing teachers. They were challenging because everyone involved in teacher education sought ways of responding to the criticisms and pressures for change that characterized this period.

Criticism from Many Sources

The views of one group of critics that emerged during the 1960s are described by Woodring (1975):

> During the late 1960s the schools and teacher education came under fresh attack from a group of critics whose views were almost directly opposite to those of the critics of the early 1950s. These new critics, Paul Goodman, John Holt, and Edgar Friedenberg, among others—who were variously described as "liberal," "radical" and "romantic"—held a view of individual freedom and of the corrupting influence of society that was reminiscent of Rousseau and some of the early progressive educators of the 1920s. Some of them contended that, because schools often do more harm than good, attendance should not be compulsory. All of them were highly critical of the way teachers were educated and contended that conventionally educated teachers were prone to force children into conventional molds. They supported the development of "free schools" with teachers selected on the basis of their personal traits and social attitudes rather than their professional or academic education. (p. 23)

Pressures for change in teacher education came also from the increasing demand that teachers be held accountable for the achievement of their pupils. Teachers responded to this demand for accountability by claiming that their preservice training had not provided them with the skills necessary for ensuring student achievement at the level being called for (Gage and Winne 1975).

Finally, a clear call for change came from the authors of two critiques of teacher education: James B. Conant in *The Education of American Teachers* (1963) and James D. Koerner in *The Miseducation of American Teachers*

(1963). Both books generated considerable discussion and debate among teacher educators concerning the direction in which the profession should move.

Elementary Teacher Education Models

In 1967 the U.S. Office of Education responded to the pervasive criticisms of the status quo in teacher education. Consultants were asked to meet with Office of Education personnel to discuss the need for improvement in teacher education and the possibility of funding elementary teacher education models. As a result of this conference, a request for proposals for teacher education models was issued. Among the components to be included in a program proposal were program goals expressed in terms of expected and measurable teacher behaviors, professional learning experiences and content to be provided trainees, evaluation and feedback techniques, and a multipurpose management and evaluation system (Clarke 1969).

Eighty proposals were received in response to the request, and nine were subsequently funded. As Clarke points out, at the time the proposals were developed, an extensive literature existed detailing teacher education goals, programs, techniques, and related ideas. What, then, was new in the nine models? Clarke suggests several features that were unique. First, they were developed by teams of scholars, and in many cases these teams were interdisciplinary. Second, they were complete models; that is, they included goals, teacher behaviors, the treatment and materials needed to produce the behaviors, and evaluation techniques to determine whether the criteria had been met. Third, they attempted to specify the support systems and other conditions needed to implement them. Finally, the models provided a "gold mine" of new ideas in teacher education. Since their development, many of these ideas have had a significant and lasting impact on teacher education. In 1969 Clarke concluded that "teacher education will never be the same after this tour de force . . ." (p. 285). A dozen years later, it is apparent that his prediction was accurate. Several ways in which Office of Education models have affected teacher education are examined in subsequent sections of this chapter.

New Techniques for the Analysis of Teaching

In the early 1960s, descriptions of innovative techniques for the analysis of teaching began to appear in the literature of teacher education. Many of the techniques were designed as components of the Office of Education models, but their use quickly spread to other programs. Three of them, in particular, have been used extensively in connection with clinical experiences: microteaching, simulation, and interaction analysis.

Microteaching. The term *microteaching* appeared in 1963. The procedure was developed as part of the teacher education program at Stanford University. James Cooper and Dwight Allen (1971), both of whom participated in the development of the techniques at Stanford, define microteaching as ''a teaching situation that is scaled down in terms of time and numbers of students'' (p. 1). In this procedure, the teaching act is analyzed into specific skills, each of which can then become the focus of a microteaching episode. Each episode usually takes from four to twenty minutes and involves from three to ten pupils. Scaling the lesson down in this way helps reduce the complexities involved and allows the teacher to focus on selected aspects of teaching.

Cooper and Allen describe the usual format for using microteaching at the preservice level. The trainees first receive instruction in the skill they are going to practice. This instruction may be presented orally, in writing, or through the use of film or videotape. Following the explanation of the skill, the trainees may see a film of a teacher demonstrating that skill. Cooper and Allen indicate that Ward, in a national survey conducted in 1969, found that the following skills were the most often used: Asking Questions, Using Reinforcement Techniques, Establishing Set, Using Examples, and Varying the Stimulus.

Each trainee then teaches a short lesson, dealing with the skill that has been presented, to a small number of students. If possible, the lesson is recorded on videotape or audiotape. Typically a supervisor helps the trainee analyze the lesson he has taught and discusses with him ways in which the lesson can be improved. In addition, trainees often observe one another's teaching and provide feedback.

After the critique session, the trainee replans the lesson on the basis of the comments and suggestions he has received. He then teaches the lesson again, but to a different group of students. Following the reteach lesson, feedback is again provided in a critique session. This teach-critique/reteach-critique cycle can be repeated as often as is needed in order to master the skill being learned.

Cooper and Allen summarize several of the advantages in using the microteaching procedure:

1. Microteaching provides a way of reducing the complexities of classroom teaching.
2. The immediate feedback from videotape recorders, supervisors, and peers helps the trainee modify his behavior.
3. Microteaching provides a low-threat situation, in comparison with an actual classroom, in which to learn teaching skills.
4. Through repetitive practice in the microteaching setting, the trainee can master specific skills that he will subsequently need in actual teaching.

Microteaching can be used for varied purposes and can occur at different points in teacher education programs. When it is used as part of the pre-student teaching phase of a program, it provides students with opportunities to learn teaching skills in controlled, but at the same time *real*, teaching situations. This helps prepare students for more extensive classroom involvement. When it is used during the student teaching or internship phase of the clinical experience, microteaching can help students focus on problem areas that may develop. By isolating a particular area and dealing with it in the controlled microteaching setting, the student is better able to analyze the difficulty and develop the skills he lacks.

Simulation. According to Cruickshank (1971), simulation was first used in teacher education at the Teaching Research Laboratory of the Oregon State System of Higher Education. The central objective in this technique is to provide students with opportunities to respond to selected aspects of teaching and receive feedback concerning their responses.

The simulations developed for use in teacher education programs vary widely with regard to materials, procedures, and specific areas of focus. Since it is not possible to describe simulations in general, the essential features of one project are discussed here as an example of the work done with this technique.

The efforts of Cruickshank, Broadbent, and Bubb (1967) at the State University of New York at Brockport resulted in the development of a simulation called the *Teaching Problems Laboratory*. Cruickshank (1971) explains that participants in this simulation assume the role of newly appointed fifth-grade teachers and are first oriented to the town and school system in which they will teach. As new staff members, each "teacher" receives a handbook, an audiovisual manual, sociograms, samples of children's work, and various school district forms. The "teachers" are then presented with thirty-one teaching problems through films, in role plays, or as written incidents. Each participant is asked to respond independently to each problem by (1) defining the problem, (2) identifying the factors that seem to be contributing to it, (3) locating related information, (4) projecting alternative courses of action, (5) selecting a more desirable course of action, and (6) preparing to communicate or implement a decision. After the period of independent problem solving using the materials provided, including selected reading, the participants are asked to share their solutions in small groups. During this time they are encouraged to role-play and to exchange roles. Finally, each problem is discussed by the total group. Through the use of the *Teaching Problems Laboratory*, participants are helped to increase their skill in identifying problems, using related data, and employing a greater variety of response strategies.

Cruickshank lists many advantages in the use of simulation in teacher education. He suggests that several advantages can be identified specifically in the use of simulation in conjunction with clinical experiences. First, simulation can give students exposure to severe or frequent problems that they may not encounter during student teaching or other clinical experiences. Second, this technique affords students opportunities to become actively involved in solving problems. Third, if cooperating teachers and students participate in simulations together, their interaction creates the potential for eliminating barriers to communication. Finally, the use of simulations in clinical experiences can provide the basis for diagnosing students' needs and for individualizing their experiences in the school and community.

Interaction Analysis. Numerous category systems have been developed for use as tools in collecting information on specific aspects of the interaction taking place in classrooms. Many of these systems have been used not only in teacher effectiveness research but in teacher education programs as well.

One of the most widely used systems is that of Flanders (1970). This system consists of ten categories for recording teacher talk and student talk (see Figure

Figure 2.1   Summary of Categories for Interaction Analysis

Teacher Talk	Indirect Influence	1.* *ACCEPTS FEELING:* accepts and clarifies the feeling tone of the students in a nonthreatening manner. Feelings may be positive or negative. Predicting or recalling feelings is included.
		2.* *PRAISES OR ENCOURAGES:* praises or encourages student action or behavior. Jokes that release tension, but not at the expense of another individual; nodding head, or saying "um hm?" or "go on" are included.
		3.* *ACCEPTS OR USES IDEAS OF STUDENTS:* clarifying, building, or developing ideas suggested by a student. As teacher brings more of his own ideas into play, shift to Category 5.
		4.* *ASKS QUESTIONS:* asking a question about content or procedure with the intent that a student answer.
	Direct Influence	5.* *LECTURING:* giving facts or opinions about content or procedures; expressing his own ideas, asking rhetorical questions.
		6.* *GIVING DIRECTIONS:* directions, commands, or orders with which a student is expected to comply.
		7.* *CRITICIZING OR JUSTIFYING AUTHORITY:* statements intended to change student behavior from nonacceptable to acceptable pattern; bawling someone out; stating why the teacher is doing what he is doing; extreme self-reference.
Student Talk		8.* *STUDENT TALK—RESPONSE:* talk by students in response to teacher. Teacher initiates the contact or solicits student statement.
		9.* *STUDENT TALK—INITIATION:* talk by students, which they initiate. If "calling on" student is only to indicate who may talk next, observer must decide whether student wanted to talk. If he did, use this category.
		10.* *SILENCE OR CONFUSION:* pauses, short periods of silence, and periods of confusion in which communication cannot be understood by the observer.

SOURCE: From Edmund J. Amidon and Ned A. Flanders, *The Role of the Teacher in the Classroom* (Rev. Ed.) (Minneapolis, MN: Association for Productive Teaching, 1971), p. 14. Reprinted with permission.

*There is NO scale implied by these numbers. Each number is classificatory; it designates a particular kind of communication event. To write these numbers down during observation is to enumerate—not to judge a position on a scale.

2.1). The procedure for using the system originally proposed by Amidon and Flanders (1971) involved recording the category numbers corresponding to the interactions being observed at three-second intervals throughout the observation period. The resulting sequence of numbers was then entered in a matrix.

In their discussion of the Flanders system, Acheson and Gall (1980) suggest that a more recently developed procedure, known as timeline coding, is simpler to use and interpret than the one identified by Amidon and Flanders.

Two examples of timelines used in conjunction with the Flanders system are shown in Figure 2.2.

In describing these timelines, Acheson and Gall point out that each has thirty columns. Since a tally is recorded every three seconds, each timeline accounts for one and one half minutes of classroom interaction.

The rows in the timelines represent the categories of interaction. Categories reflecting indirect teaching (1, 2, and 3) and the category reflecting student-initiated responses (9) are above the middle row. The middle row is for teacher questions (category 4). Categories indicating direct teaching (5, 6, and 7) and the category for structured student responses (8) are below the middle row. Category 10 (silence or confusion) is not represented by a row. Tallies for this category are recorded below the timeline. In two rows categories are paired (1 and 2, 6 and 7) to conserve space.

The first timeline in Figure 2.2 shows alternating 4s and 8s. This pattern reflects a series of teacher questions and student responses, with the questions directed toward the recall of factual information.

The interaction in the second timeline is more indirect. After the teacher gives some information on a topic, the students are encouraged to offer their own ideas on the subject. The teacher responds to students' ideas with acceptance and praise.

A considerable amount of research has been conducted using the Flanders system. Included in this research are studies in which student teachers have been trained in the use of this system of interaction analysis. Furst (1971) summarized studies of this kind completed in the 1960s and concluded that a common feature among them was that there were significant changes in either the attitudes or the behaviors of students trained in the use of the Flanders system when compared with students who did not receive the training. These changes were reflected in students' use of indirect teaching patterns: They exhibited more acceptance of pupil ideas, used more praise and encouragement, and used less criticism.

The results of the most recent teacher effectiveness research, summarized in Chapter 1, give the overall impression that direct teaching behaviors are more effective in the classroom than are indirect behaviors. If we were to look at the results that lead to this impression and go no further, we might conclude that we ought not to expose teacher education students to the indirect behaviors in the Flanders system. It is important, therefore, that we keep in mind some additional findings. Rosenshine indicated that classrooms that show high gains in achievement are usually moderate to high with respect to having a warm classroom atmosphere (indirect influence in the Flanders system). He also stated that teacher ridicule, sarcasm, and criticism are consistently related negatively to gain in achievement. When these findings are considered along with the findings concerning direct teaching behaviors reported by Medley and Rosenshine, it is apparent that teachers need to be able to exhibit both direct and indirect teaching behaviors. This suggests, in turn, that teacher education students be provided with opportunities to use an interaction analysis system such as Flanders to analyze their patterns of indirect and direct behaviors and then, on the basis of their analyses, to modify these patterns if the need for this is indicated.

Figure 2.2 Timelines

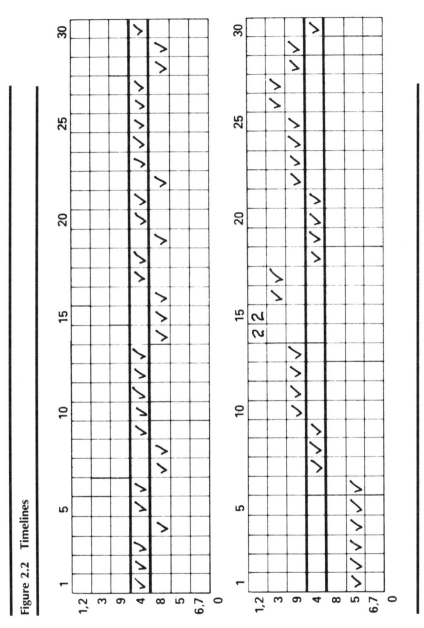

SOURCE: Copyright 1974 Far West Laboratory for Educational Research and Development, San Francisco, California. Published by Paul S. Amidon & Associates, Inc., 1966 Benson Avenue, St. Paul, Mn, 55116.

THE COMPETENCY-BASED APPROACH TO TEACHER EDUCATION

The competency-based movement has unquestionably been the most widely discussed and debated innovation in teacher education in the last decade. Writing in 1972, Houston and Howsam described the potential impact of this movement:

> Rarely, if ever, has any movement swept through teacher education so rapidly or caught the attention of so many in so short a time as has the competency-based movement. Already well underway, the approach holds promise of renovating and regenerating teacher education. Equally significantly, it appears probable that it will do so in record-setting time. (p. viii)

Has the competency-based movement had the impact predicted by Houston and Howsam? Before attempting to answer this question, let us examine the origins, essential features, and major criticisms of competency-based teacher education, or CBTE, as it is frequently abbreviated.

Origins of CBTE

The competency-based movement emerged in the context of teacher and teacher education criticisms discussed earlier in this chapter. These criticisms, and the increased demand for accountability, provided the impetus at all levels of education for the development of more precise definitions of objectives and more effective ways of assessing their achievement.

In its application specifically to teacher education, the competency-based movement seems to have originated with the development of the Office of Education teacher education models. According to Houston and Howsam (1972), each model arrived relatively independently at an emphasis on competencies. Another feature common to the models was the inclusion of performance modules (Clarke 1971). A third dimension emphasized in all models was individualization of instruction. These elements rapidly began to be associated with the development of competency-based teacher education programs.

Essential Features of CBTE Programs

The emergence of competency-based teacher education was accompanied by a vast amount of literature in which writers defined the concept, enumerated characteristics, and gave detailed descriptions of implementation plans. Unfortunately, this literature reflected such confusion and lack of consensus, particularly with regard to terminology, that it often obscured, rather than clarified, the essential features of the movement. Rather than attempt to present a variety of viewpoints here, it seems more useful to present only one, while noting that other writers might not be in total agreement with the approach selected. Because of their prominent association with CBTE from its inception, the writing of Robert B. Howsam and W. Robert Houston (1972) is used as the source for the discussion that follows.

Howsam and Houston suggest that the meaning of *competency based* is best derived from a consideration of its characteristics, rather than from an attempt to define it in a simple phrase. They identify two characteristics that are essential to the concept of competency-based instruction. The first is that objectives, defined in behavioral terms, must be made known both to teacher and learner. These objectives are accompanied by an identification of the means that will be used to determine whether they have been met. A variety of alternative learning activities that can be pursued in reaching the objectives is provided. The second characteristic is accountability. The learner knows that he is expected to demonstrate the competencies specified. He accepts this responsibility and expects to be held accountable.

The authors identify a third characteristic that is widely associated with competency-based instruction, but that does not necessarily distinguish it from other programs. This is individualization. Competency-based programs are self-paced and also offer the learner some choice in the selection of objectives and learning experiences.

According to Howsam and Houston, the confusion that surrounds further characteristics is the result of the failure to differentiate the essential characteristics of competency-based instruction—those just identified here—from related concepts or ways of implementing the approach. One example of this problem is the widespread idea that competency-based instruction is synonymous with the use of *modules*. Modules are instructional units that include statements of objectives (or competencies), alternative learning activities, and procedures for assessment. They are clearly useful in individualizing instruction. For this reason, modules are widely used in competency-based instruction; but, as Howsam and Houston point out, they are not synonymous with the concept.

What advantages result when competency-based instruction is applied to teacher education? First, students know, from the beginning of their program, the specific skills they will be expected to demonstrate in order to complete the program successfully. Second, because CBTE programs are individualized, students can proceed at their own rates in mastering competencies. Third, the results of the evaluation process are much more meaningful than is the case in traditional programs. A list of the competencies that a student has mastered communicates far better about her potential for teaching than does a record of how many grades of *A* she has received.

Critics of CBTE

Not all the literature dealing with competency-based teacher education has been written by its proponents. Critics, particularly those concerned with humanistic education, have identified what they consider to be significant weaknesses in the CBTE approach. Cohen and Hersh (1972) summarize the major criticisms:

1. Behaviorists specify only the most easily observable objectives, with the result that many of the objectives are trivial. Objectives dealing with the affective areas of values and attitudes are largely neglected.
2. Behaviorists advocate a lock-step approach that ignores individual differences.
3. Assessment of instruction, as carried out by behaviorists, is restricted to the measurement of observable behavior.

Responses to these and other criticisms have come from a variety of sources. Many have criticized the humanistic approach to teacher education; these criticisms are identified in the section of this chapter examining that approach. Then, since it is the view of this writer, and of others, that competency-based and humanistic approaches to teacher education need not be considered dichotomous, this position will be explored.

What, then, of the question raised by the statement of Howsam and Houston at the beginning of this section: Has the competency-based movement had the impact they predicted? Current evidence suggests that it has not renovated teacher education to the extent that they thought it would. That the impact has been less than expected seems to have been caused by the feasibility problems encountered in attempting to implement such a comprehensive concept. The impact has still been significant. While it is often difficult to implement complete CBTE programs, many programs have been designed to include one or more of the elements associated with CBTE. Finally, the competency-based movement has heightened the awareness of teacher educators of the need for more precision both in defining program objectives and in evaluating students' progress in meeting the stated objectives.

THE HUMANISTIC APPROACH TO TEACHER EDUCATION

Educators agree that concern for the individual has always been reflected in statements of humanistic goals for education in this country. In recent years, however, many educators have felt that humanistically oriented goals were receiving far less attention in actual practice than their importance warranted. As a result, there has been a renewed effort, on the part of individuals and groups, to focus attention on those goals of education concerned with the rights, dignity, and self-fulfillment of the individual.

In the sections that follow, we examine the origins, characteristics, and criticisms of the humanist movement as it has been applied in teacher education.

Origins of the Current Focus on Humanistic Education

The demand for accountability that served as a force in the development of the competency-based movement has also been a major factor contributing to the resurgence of concern for humanistic education. Elizabeth S. Randolph (1978), a past president of the Association for Supervision and Curriculum Development (ASCD), summarizes the response of many educators to the accountability movement:

> Most educators are aware of the social, political, and economic phenomena that have created the demand for accountability in public education. The public has been especially insistent on the development of measurement instruments for competence in the basic skills. Many educators committed to the goal of humanizing education have been fearful that the accountability and "back to basics" movements could turn back the advances in humanistic education that have been made in the past decade. (p. v)

The authors of a recent ASCD monograph (1978) on humanistic education see the emergence of the humanist movement as a response to the change in human problems brought about by the social, political, and economic forces to which Randolph refers. In their view, the problems we face today—ecology, starvation, overpopulation, nuclear power, and others—require for their solution responsible, caring persons. This group of educators, who comprise the ASCD Working Group on Humanistic Education, considers the humanist movement an expression of people throughout the world seeking to defend human dignity and individual freedom. The results of this expression can be seen, they contend, in civil rights legislation, mental health research, and the women's liberation movement, to name just a few areas.

The authors of this monograph conclude their discussion of the forces giving rise to the humanist movement by speaking directly to the task of education today. In doing this, they issue a clear call for an educational system that is humanistically oriented: "The greatest problems facing all of us are essentially human ones. If education is to assume its responsibility to prepare young people to meet the challenges of the future, it must number humanistic objectives high among its priorities" (p. 2).

Characteristics of Humanistic Teacher Education Programs

The professional literature concerned with the humanist movement and its application to teacher education is similar, in some respects, to the literature dealing with the competency-based movement. While there is no doubt less confusion and more agreement with regard to basic definitions and assumptions than is the case with CBTE, descriptions of humanistic teacher education programs reflect considerable variety with regard to program components and their implementation. For this reason, the writing of one widely read proponent of humanism, Arthur W. Combs, is used here as the basis for examining the characteristics of the humanistic approach to teacher education.

Combs (1978) first cites research that supports his contention that good teaching is a product of teacher perceptions in five areas: (1) Good teachers are aware of the perceptions of others and use this understanding in guiding their own behavior; (2) good teachers see themselves in positive ways; (3) good teachers see others in positive ways; (4) the purposes of good teachers are facilitating and process oriented; (5) good teachers are genuine and self-revealing. Combs then suggests that these findings point to the need for change in four areas of teacher education.

Combs argues, first, that the importance of the teacher perceptions he has identified calls for a "self-as-instrument" concept of teaching that makes teacher education a problem in personal becoming; that is, of helping students discover how best to use themselves as educators. In a program directed toward this objective, according to Combs, learning must be experiential and personal. Merely giving students objective information "about teaching" is insufficient. In a program for becoming, students must be provided with opportunities for continuous exploration of beliefs about self, others, ideas, and purposes, and of ways of implementing these beliefs in action.

Combs suggests, next, that a self-as-instrument approach to teacher education implies that learning must begin with students' needs. This is not characteristic of the logically sequenced traditional course organization. Combs calls for programs in which traditional courses are replaced by learning experiences that will enable students to explore professional problems and discover appropriate personal solutions. This approach will require individualized processes that involve students in decision making and assuming responsibility for their own learning.

Combs' third area of concern is the relationship between field experiences and university-based study. In the kind of program he proposes, field experience would be provided for students continuously, not merely for a semester at the conclusion of the professional sequence. In these supervised field experiences, students would discover their strengths and weaknesses, assess their growth, and decide what steps to take next.

Lastly, Combs describes the faculty that will be needed to implement the personal approach to teacher education. These faculty will not be the traditional specialists in discrete content areas. Instead, they will be process facilitators skilled in helping students explore problems, themselves, and others. Experiential learning, according to Combs, calls for persons who are not so much teachers with answers as persons capable of helping students arrive at appropriate personal solutions.

Critics of Humanistic Education

As noted in the section of this chapter that dealt with competency-based teacher education, proponents of this approach have responded to the criticisms of humanists by identifying the weaknesses they find in the humanistic approach. Cohen and Hersh (1972) summarize the major areas of criticism:

1. Humanists state goals that sound nice, but present little or no evidence that the goals can be attained.
2. Humanists are not concerned with, or are incapable of, examining their instructional procedures systematically.
3. Humanists either assess instruction in terms of whether they feel good about it, or fail to assess at all.

Following their summary of the criticisms of humanistic education, and of competency-based education (presented in the previous section of this chapter), Cohen and Hersh propose that a synthesis of humanism and behaviorism is not only possible but necessary. They point out, first, that since teaching is an intentional activity, it is imperative that we state objectives and provide evidence that their attainment can be measured. It is in this area that the behaviorists have been strong and the humanists weak. Second, they suggest that through their concern for children and society, humanists have refocused our attention on the importance of examining our rationale for the objectives we select. In this area, while the humanists have been strong, the behaviorists have been weak. Cohen and Hersh contend that a synthesis of humanism and behaviorism would combine the strengths, and eliminate the weaknesses, of both approaches. Indeed, it is their position that the questions that must be addressed by every educator can be answered only through the combined efforts of humanists and behaviorists:

> Once we have agreed upon objectives and a rationale to support them, a behavioral humanism requires that evidence be gathered such that one can infer that the goals have been achieved and that the teaching techniques are efficacious. Humanists and behaviorists together need to answer these questions. Each is necessary, but neither alone is sufficient. (p. 176)

CLINICAL EXPERIENCES IN TEACHER EDUCATION

Preservice experience in teaching has been considered an essential component of teacher education from the days of the early normal schools, but the nature of the experience has changed in several ways over the years. The major impetus for change has been the periodic effort to redefine the objectives of preservice teaching experiences. The redefinition of objectives, in turn, has often called for a reexamination of the roles of the participants. As changes in objectives and role relationships occurred, they became reflected in changes in the terminology used to designate both the experience and the roles of the participants. In this section, then, we examine the development of clinical experiences from earlier patterns to those that have emerged recently.

The Development of Clinical Experiences

The earliest teacher training institutions in the United States were the normal schools that began to appear in the early nineteenth century. The first of these schools opened in 1839 in Lexington, Massachusetts. The name "normal school," from the French *écoles normales primaires*, was selected because it was the term used at the time to designate similar institutions in France (Lang, Quick, and Johnson 1975). In the practice schools that adjoined the normal schools, students were provided with direct experiences in teaching. The concept underlying the experiences was one of apprenticeship: learning a trade from one who has already acquired the skills of that trade. As Bennie (1972) indicates: "The approach was largely that of 'practicing' the teaching act until one was pronounced a qualified teacher" (p. 4). The vocabulary that developed as part of the normal school movement clearly reflected the way in which teaching was viewed at the time: *Apprentices*, in *training* schools, learned to teach by *practicing*. The objective was to produce teachers who performed in exactly the same way as those who trained them.

As a result of new developments in education, state teachers colleges began replacing the normal schools at the beginning of the twentieth century. A major factor contributing to this transition, according to Haberman and Stinnett (1973), was the rapid expansion of public high schools, which created a trend toward requiring high school teachers to be college graduates. Faced with this trend, some normal schools made the transition to teachers colleges, while others simply stopped preparing teachers.

The emergence of teachers colleges was accompanied by the laboratory school movement. Teachers colleges, and many universities, developed campus laboratory schools to provide a controlled setting in which their students could have direct experiences in teaching. Highly qualified teachers were sought to staff these lab schools, as they became known. These teachers provided the supervision for preservice teachers, and in some cases also participated in the teaching of methods courses. The concept underlying laboratory schools was that of providing a series of graduated experiences for teacher education students. While variations existed, a typical sequence began with observation, moved to participation at the next level, and culminated with the assumption of full teaching responsibility.

The development of laboratory schools was viewed as a significant advance in teacher education. By 1950, however, problems surrounding the schools began to emerge. Teachers colleges expanded rapidly after World War II, and the typical laboratory school became increasingly unable to accommodate the growing numbers of students. At the same time, it was becoming more and more difficult to justify the expense of maintaining laboratory schools when public school facilities were available. Finally, many teacher educators were encouraging the increased use of public schools for direct experience in teaching, arguing that these schools provided a more "real" setting than did the laboratory schools. As these factors combined, there was a marked increase in the numbers of teacher education students who were receiving their classroom teaching experience in off-campus settings.

The focus, as well as the setting, of direct experience in teaching changed during this period. The objective of the direct experience now became that of *studying* the teaching act instead of merely *practicing* it. Students now were "students of teaching," or student teachers, and their classroom experience was designated as student teaching, rather than practice teaching. The student teaching experience was viewed as a time for integrating theory and practice; a time for testing ideas in real situations and studying the results. The person most involved in helping a student achieve this integration was, of course, the teacher in whose classroom the student teacher was placed, and a new role designation for this person was emerging. Gradually, a teacher who worked with student teachers became known as a "supervising teacher," and the earlier labels, "master teacher" or "critic teacher," began to disappear.

Typically, student teaching was the final experience in programs of teacher education. In the majority of programs it was the *only* direct experience provided for students. Increasingly, teacher educators became concerned with the need for providing direct experience in addition to student teaching. Writing in 1956, Sharpe documented this trend:

> Most members of the teaching profession are evincing increased interest in laboratory experiences. If there is any one point that is common to most of the two hundred twenty-five evaluation reports made by the two hundred twenty-five different teams who participated in the intervisitation program of the American Association of Colleges for Teacher Education it is the almost universal suggestion that more opportunities for professional laboratory experiences prior to student teaching be provided. (p. 185)

The rationale for providing direct experiences in teaching, or "professional laboratory experiences" as they are called, in addition to student teaching is that there must be an interaction between thinking and doing if real learning is to occur. This suggests that students need a variety of direct experiences throughout their program, not just at the conclusion. The nature of these experiences is described by Sharpe (1956): "The laboratory experiences for the teacher-to-be must be those which will contribute to his ability to make judgments in a problem situation—to apply principles to new situations or to develop skills in new surroundings" (p. 184).

Recent Trends in Clinical Experiences

The movement toward providing a wider variety of preservice teaching experiences clearly gained momentum in the 1960s and '70s. Influenced by the Office of Education models and the concept of competency-based education, teacher educators began to design programs that included a range of graduated experiences leading to a period of full-time, supervised teaching. At the same time, concern for the preparation of teachers for urban schools led to the development of programs, such as the federally funded National Teacher Corps, that placed a heavy emphasis on direct involvement in school and community activities. This interest in increasing students' supervised teaching experiences resulted not only in the provision for pre-student teaching experiences but also in the extension of student teaching in the form of an internship. While the internship concept has been defined in diverse ways, in some programs it has meant an experience beyond student teaching in which the intern assumes responsibility for a classroom, is paid, and is supervised jointly by college and school personnel.

A second emphasis in the 1960s and '70s was that of helping students acquire skill in recording and analyzing specific components of the teaching act. The new techniques of microteaching, simulation, and interaction analysis began to be widely used in conjunction with pre-student teaching, student teaching, and internship experiences to help students learn to analyze, modify, and refine their teaching behaviors. As Bennie (1972) observed, "the entire supervisory process is rapidly becoming more analytical and more clinical in its approach" (p. 6).

It is interesting to note that as the supervisory process has become more clinical, the term "clinical" has begun to appear in other contexts. For example, direct experiences in teaching are now frequently referred to as "clinical experiences," although the terms "professional laboratory experiences" and "field experiences" are still being used. In the early 1960s the term "clinical" also appeared in the suggestion that a new position in teacher education be created, that of "clinical professor" (Davies and Amershak 1969, p. 1378). This term was defined to mean either (1) a skilled classroom teacher who works with preservice college students on a continuing basis or (2) a college faculty member who works closely with preservice students and cooperating teachers. While the concept of the clinical professor was apparently well-received, it has not been widely implemented, according to Kazlov (1976).

A third focus emerged during the 1960s as colleges placed increased numbers of students in schools for a wider range of teaching experiences, and as a result, the need for closer school-college cooperation became apparent. The recognition of this need for joint responsibility in planning and implementing clinical experiences led to the development of the concept of teacher centers. While various approaches to the organization of teacher centers exist, the following statement by McGeoch and Quinn (1975) gives a clear picture of the overall structure:

> A Teacher Education Center is created when a school or schools agree to work cooperatively with a university for a specific period of time. The university supervisor becomes a clinical professor spending the greater part of his/her time in the schools working with the school staff and students assigned to him/her from the university. School administrators, university students, classroom teachers, and university staff together discuss the functioning of the program. These four groups constitute a team for planning experiences, reporting progress, and evaluating results. In order to facilitate communication, a committee is formed with members selected from the four constituent groups. This committee is referred to as the Teacher Education Council. (p. 176)

The emphasis in the teacher center concept on cooperation between school and university is reflected in the term "cooperating teacher" that began to be used to designate classroom teachers who work with students in clinical experiences. The designation "cooperating teacher" certainly seems preferable to the earlier terms used to identify this significant role for at least two reasons: (1) It underscores the importance of joint responsibility and (2) it does not have the negative connotations implicit in "critic teacher" and "supervising teacher." Although these advantages appear to make the use of "cooperating teacher" more appropriate, "supervising teacher" continues to be widely used.

The development of cooperative structures in teacher education has received a great deal of attention in the professional literature (James and Brown 1975; Kerber and Protheroe 1973; Smith, Olsen, Johnson and Barbour 1968). It seems likely that the new patterns that emerge from these structures will continue to be of major interest to teacher educators. In concluding his summary of the teacher center movement, Bennie (1978) predicts that "while the future of this movement is still to be decided, enough activities are currently centered around this approach to teacher education that it bodes well to be a significant force in the future" (p. 7).

Writing in 1956, Sharpe projected the role of direct experience in teaching: "Direct experience will continue to play an expanding role in the education of teachers" (p. 229). Current data confirm Sharpe's prediction. In their survey of over 500 programs in more than 140 teacher education institutions, Howey, Yarger, and Joyce (1978) found that in a variety of programs, clinical experiences are available at every level from freshman year through fifth-year programs. The three most prevalent clinical experiences, according to their findings, are sophomore-year observation and participation, junior-year observation and participation, and senior-year student teaching.

Many forces, operating at different times over the past twenty years, have been responsible for directing increased attention to clinical experiences. What forces are operating currently? Elliott (1978) suggests four reasons for the increased emphasis on field experiences in teacher education:

1. The field setting is an integral part of a great many of the competency-based teacher education programs which have been widely initiated in schools of education in recent years.
2. There is a growing demand from practitioners that they become more involved in the process of teacher preparation; it is their position that the translation of theory into practice is best accomplished in the setting in which they operate.
3. When some dissatisfaction exists with the performance of students in educational institutions, as at present, alternative forms of functioning in all areas related to the institution are usually sought out as a means of redress for the grievances, whether founded or unfounded.
4. In this time of lower enrollments, many schools of education are seizing this period of lessened teaching demands on faculty to experiment with and implement more time-consuming programs and interfacing activities with other agencies in the field of education. (p. 2)

Elliott's analysis suggests that clinical experiences will continue to play a major role in this effort in the years ahead.

REFERENCES

Acheson, Keith, A., and Gall, Meredith Damien. *Techniques in the clinical supervision of teachers.* New York: Longman Inc., 1980.

Amidon, Edmund J., and Flanders, Ned A. *The role of the teacher in the classroom* (Rev. ed.). Minneapolis, MN: Association for Productive Teaching, 1971.

The ASCD Working Group on Humanistic Education. *Humanistic education: Objectives and assessment.* Washington, DC: Association for Supervision and Curriculum Development, 1978.

Bennie, William A. *Supervising clinical experiences in the classroom.* New York: Harper & Row, 1972.

Bennie, William A. The prologue of the past. *Action in Teacher Education,* Summer 1978, *1* (1), 3–7.

Clarke, S. C. T. The story of elementary teacher education models. *Journal of Teacher Education,* Fall 1969, *10* (3), 283–93.

Clarke, S. C. T. Designs for programs of teacher education. In B. Othaniel Smith (Ed.), *Research in teacher education: A symposium.* Englewood Cliffs, NJ: Prentice-Hall, 1971.

Cohen, Stuart, and Hersh, Richard. Behaviorism and humanism: A synthesis for teacher education. *Journal of Teacher Education,* Summer 1972, *23* (2), 172–76.

Combs, Arthur W. Teacher education: The person in the process. *Educational Leadership,* April 1978, 35 (7), 558–61.

Conant, James G. *The education of American teachers.* New York: McGraw-Hill, 1963.

Cooper, James M., and Allen, Dwight W. Microteaching: History and present status. In *Microteaching: Selected papers* (ATE Research Bulletin 9). Washington, DC: Association of Teacher Educators and ERIC Clearinghouse on Teacher Education, 1971.

Cruikshank, Donald R. *Simulation as an instructional alternative in teacher preparation.* (ATE Research Bulletin 8). Washington, DC: Association of Teacher Educators and ERIC Clearinghouse on Teacher Education, 1971.

Cruickshank, Donald R.; Broadbent, Frank W.; and Bubb, Roy L. *Teaching problems laboratory.* Chicago: Science Research Associates, 1967.

Davies, Don, and Amershak, Kathleen, Student teaching. In Robert L. Ebel (Ed.), *Encyclopedia of educational research* (4th ed.). New York: Macmillan, 1969.

Elliott, Peggy G. *Field experiences in preservice teacher education* (Bibliographies on Educational Topics No. 9). Washington, DC: ERIC Clearinghouse on Teacher Education, 1978.

Flanders, Ned A. *Analyzing teaching behavior.* Reading, MA: Addison-Wesley, 1970.

Furst, Norma. Interaction analysis in teacher education: A review of studies. In *Interaction analysis: Selected papers* (ATE Research Bulletin 10). Washington, DC: Association of Teacher Educators and ERIC Clearinghouse on Teacher Education, 1971.

Gage, Nathaniel L., and Winne, Philip H. Chap. 6, Performance-based teacher education. In Kevin Ryan (Ed.), *Teacher education.* The Seventy-fourth Yearbook of the National Society for the Study of Education (Part II). Chicago: The National Society for the Study of Education, 1975.

Haberman, Martin, and Stinnett, T. M. *Teacher education and the new profession of teaching.* Berkeley, CA: McCutchan, 1973.

Houston, W. Robert, and Howsam, Robert B. Foreword in W. Robert Houston and Robert B. Howsam (Eds.), *Competency-based teacher education: Progress, problems, and prospects.* Chicago: Science Research Associates, 1972.

Howey, Kenneth R.; Yarger, Sam J.; and Joyce, Bruce R. *Improving teacher education.* Palo Alto, CA: Association of Teacher Educators, 1978.

Howsam, Robert B., and Houston, W. Robert. Chap. 1, Change and challenge. In W.

Robert Houston and Robert B. Howsam (Eds.), *Competency-based teacher education: Progress, problems, and prospects.* Chicago: Science Research Associates, 1972.

James, Richard, and Brown, Ray (Eds.), *Emerging concepts for collaboration: Selected papers* (ATE Bulletin 40). Washington, DC: Association of Teacher Educators, 1975.

Kazlov, Gertrude. Whatever happened to the clinical professor? *Journal of Teacher Education,* Winter 1976, 27 (4), 340–41.

Kerber, James E., and Protheroe, Donald W. *Guiding student teaching experiences in a cooperative structure* (ATE Bulletin 33). Washington, DC: Association of Teacher Educators, 1973.

Koerner, James D. *The miseducation of American teachers.* Baltimore, MD: Penguin Books, 1963.

Lang, Duaine C.; Quick, Alan F.; and Johnson, James A. *A partnership for the supervision of student teachers.* Mt. Pleasant, MI: Great Lakes Publishing, 1975.

McGeoch, Dorothy, and Quinn, Peter J. Clinical experiences in a teacher education center. *Journal of Teacher Education,* Summer 1975, 26 (2), 176–79.

Randolph, Elizabeth S. Foreword. In *Humanistic education: Objectives and assessment,* a report of the ASCD working group on humanistic education. Washington, DC: Association for Supervision and Curriculum Development, 1978.

Sharpe, Donald M. Chap. 6, Professional laboratory experiences. In Donald P. Cottrell (Ed.), *Teacher education for a free people.* Oneonta, NY: The American Association of Colleges for Teacher Education, 1956.

Smith, E. Brooks; Olsen, Hans C.; Johnson, Patrick J.; and Barbour, Chandler (Eds.), *Partnership in teacher education.* Washington, DC: The American Association of Colleges for Teacher Education and The Association for Student Teaching, 1968.

Woodring, Paul. Chap. 1, The development of teacher education. In Kevin Ryan (Ed.), *Teacher education.* The Seventy-fourth Yearbook of the National Society for the Study of Education (Part II). Chicago: The National Society for the Study of Education, 1975.

Most, if not all, classroom teachers have experienced supervision in some form. These experiences no doubt have been highly varied, ranging from those that were satisfying and productive to those that were threatening and dehumanizing. Many teachers, perhaps, would place their experiences in being supervised at some midpoint on the continuum and would find themselves in agreement with Blumberg (1980): "... much of what occurs in the name of supervision in the schools (the transactions that take place between supervisor and teacher) constitutes a waste of time, *as teachers see it.* In many instances, the best evaluation that teachers give of their supervision is that it is not harmful" (p. 5).

CHAPTER **3** EMERGING CONCEPTS IN SUPERVISION

Achieving the goal of providing experiences that are positive and productive is highly desirable in the supervision of inservice teachers and *essential* in the supervision of preservice teachers. Competent inservice teachers will continue to be effective; they may also be able to withstand the effects of negative supervisory practices. Preservice teachers, however, because they are "students of teaching," must have productive and positive clinical experiences if they are to make progress in becoming competent and self-directed teachers. Classroom teachers who accept the role of cooperating teacher assume the responsibility of helping teacher education students develop both professionally and personally. The guidance cooperating teachers provide must be at a level that is beyond just "not harmful"!

The intent in this chapter is to provide an overview of recent developments in the field of supervision. This overview will serve as a basis for examining, in subsequent chapters, specific ways in which cooperating teachers can provide meaningful, productive guidance for prospective teachers.

FACTORS CONTRIBUTING TO CHANGE IN THE FIELD OF SUPERVISION

Writing in 1973, Frymier contended that "until recently, supervision had changed very little from the theory and practice of half a century or more ago" (p. v). What factors have emerged to stimulate this current movement toward change in the field of supervision?

It is clear that one factor is the "accountability movement." As taxpayers demand that teachers be held accountable for the achievement of their students, teachers respond by voicing their dissatisfaction with the ways in which their teaching effectiveness is evaluated by supervisory personnel. According to data reported by McNeil (1971), teachers have good reason to be dissatisfied. Two national surveys revealed that "only about half the school systems in the United States follow any formal procedures in evaluating their teachers, and the procedures used are most inadequate" (p. 4). This situation clearly makes necessary a reexamination of the process of supervising and evaluating teachers.

Berman and Usery (1966) have suggested that the movement toward increased precision in studying the nature of teaching is another factor that has contributed to bringing about change in the field of supervision. Techniques such as the Flanders system of interaction analysis, developed for use in studying teaching, have now been applied to the process of supervision.

Finally, Frymier (1973) cites the creation of the Regional Educational Laboratories as a significant factor in changing the supervisory process. These labs have developed materials, often incorporating the use of audiotaping and videotaping, that can be used by teachers in assessing and increasing their instructional competence. When these materials are used, the supervisor's role becomes more that of "facilitator" and less that of "observer-critiquer."

THE FUNCTIONS OF SUPERVISION

Two major functions of supervision can be identified: the teaching function and the evaluating function. This section looks at the teaching function through a consideration of those elements common to teaching and supervision. The evaluating function of supervision is dealt with only briefly here, since it is considered in greater detail in Chapter 8.

The Teaching Function

The relationship between teaching and supervision has been examined by a number of educators (Anderson 1967, Berman and Usery 1966, Olsen 1968). A highly detailed analysis of this relationship is presented by Anderson in his contribution, "Supervision as Teaching: An Analogue," to a publication of the Association for Supervision and Curriculum Development. Anderson views supervision as teaching teachers about teaching. When the supervisory process is defined in this way, the role of the supervisor is virtually the same as the role of the classroom teacher. Just as the classroom teacher facilitates the efforts of his pupils to learn, the supervisor, as teacher, facilitates the efforts of teachers to increase their competence. In fulfilling his role as teacher, the supervisor diagnoses the needs of the teachers with whom he works. Moreover, the supervisor establishes a relationship with teachers that will enable him to work with them effectively. In carrying out these responsibilities, the supervisor performs the same functions as those performed by the classroom teacher.

Anderson applies his analogy between supervision and teaching to the relationship between supervisors and inservice teachers. Can the analogy be applied, also, to the "supervisory" relationship between cooperating teachers and teacher education students? It seems that it can, for at least two reasons: (1) Prospective teachers are already functioning in the role of student and come to the clinical experience expecting to learn from their cooperating teachers; and (2) cooperating teachers, because of their experience, have the skills and the perspective needed in helping students study teaching in classroom settings. For these reasons, applying the concept of *supervision as teaching* to clinical experiences seems to provide a useful framework for looking at the relationship between cooperating teachers and teacher education students. Certainly, one effect of using this framework is immediately evident: The cooperating teacher who views teaching as a major function of supervision will perform his role differently from the way in which the same role was performed by the "critic" or "master" teacher of the past.

The Evaluating Function

Traditionally, evaluation has been the major function of supervision. Evaluation of the beginning teacher determines whether tenure is awarded at the conclusion of the probationary period. Evaluation of the experienced teacher can determine whether a promotion is received or a salary increase gained.

Unfortunately, as important as this function is in teachers' careers, there has been little effort on the part of supervisors and administrators, until recently, to develop objective programs for the evaluation of teachers. In fact, as was pointed out by McNeil, only about half the school systems in the United States attempt to use any formal evaluation procedures. It is not surprising, then, to find that McNeil also reports that while three out of four principals and superintendents express confidence in their evaluation procedures, one half of their teachers do not.

The problems surrounding the evaluation of preservice teachers, particularly student teachers and interns, are no less serious than those occurring in the evaluation of inservice teachers. Student teachers and interns feel that they are being treated unfairly when evaluation procedures are not made clear to them. They feel equally disturbed when cooperating teachers and college supervisors fail to use objective criteria in judging their performance.

A supervisory pattern known as *clinical supervision* has, in recent years, shown promise in providing a framework for the solution of a major problem in evaluation: the lack of a precise, objective procedure for collecting and analyzing evaluative data. This pattern is described in the following section.

THE DIMENSIONS OF SUPERVISION

Approaches to the problem of making the supervisory process more analytical are receiving considerable attention in the professional literature. At the same time, the literature reflects a continuous search for techniques that will be effective in establishing mutually satisfying relationships between supervisors and those they supervise. This section examines recent developments that have significance for both dimensions of supervision: the analytical and the interpersonal. This will provide a basis for proposing that an adequate conception of supervision requires the integration of the analytical and the interpersonal dimensions of this process.

The Analytical Dimension

Recent efforts to improve supervision by making it more analytical are reflected in the emergence of a supervisory cycle referred to as *clinical supervision*. Morris Cogan (1964), who was associated with the development of the concept, has defined clinical supervision as "supervision focused upon the improvement of the classroom performance of the teacher by way of observation, analysis, and treatment of that performance" (p. 118). While some variation exists in the specific steps identified for this process, Reavis (1978) suggests that the dominant pattern is the five-step sequence proposed by Goldhammer (1969). Reavis summarizes these five steps:

1. *Preobservation conference.* In this conference, the supervisor is oriented to the class, objectives, and lesson by the teacher. Then the

teacher and supervisor decide on a contract (purposes of the observation).

2. *Observation*. The supervisor observes the lesson, taking verbatim notes as much as possible or recording the lesson by mechanical means.

3. *Analysis and strategy*. The supervisor considers his or her notes with respect to the contract emphasis and also to discover any patterns, either favorable or unfavorable, that might characterize this teacher's behavior. After the lesson has been analyzed, the supervisor considers this teacher, his or her level of self-confidence, maturity, experience, and so on, [and] decides on a strategy for the conference.

4. *Postobservation conference*. The supervisor implements his or her strategy. He or she deals with the contract terms first and, with the consent of the teacher, may introduce comments on patterns not a part of the original contract that he or she has identified. Planning with the teacher for a future lesson that incorporates mutually-agreed-upon changes may also occur.

5. *Postconference analysis*. The supervisor analyzes his or her own performance and makes plans for working with this teacher in a more . . . productive manner in the future. (p. 580)

The process of clinical supervision has been used with both inservice and preservice teachers. We examine the specific ways in which cooperating teachers can use this five-step sequence in their work with teacher education students in Chapter 7.

The Interpersonal Dimension

The process of clinical supervision described in the preceding section involves face-to-face interaction between supervisors and those they supervise. This interaction plays a critical part in determining the effectiveness of the supervisory process. It is important, therefore, to examine current knowledge that contributes to an understanding of the interpersonal dimension of supervision.

Blumberg (1980) reports the findings of studies in which he examined teachers' perceptions of their interaction with supervisors. Note that the studies dealt with *perceptions* of behavior, not behavior itself. As Blumberg points out, however, a person's perceptions of another's behavior are significant in determining his reaction to that person, regardless of whether the perceptions are congruent with the actual behavior.

The first question Blumberg investigated was whether teachers perceive supervisors as having different behavioral styles. He found that they do. On the basis of the data he obtained, Blumberg was able to develop the following set of four supervisory styles:

STYLE A. *High Direct, High Indirect*
The teacher sees the supervisor emphasizing both direct and indirect behavior: he tells and criticizes, but he also asks and listens.

STYLE B. *High Direct, Low Indirect*

    The teacher perceives the supervisor as doing a great deal of telling and criticizing but very little asking or listening.

STYLE C. *Low Direct, High Indirect*

    The supervisor's behavior is rarely direct (telling, criticizing, and so forth); instead he puts a lot of emphasis on asking questions, listening, and reflecting back the teacher's ideas and feelings.

STYLE D. *Low Direct, Low Indirect*

    The teacher sees the supervisor as passive, not doing much of anything. Our hunch is that some supervisors may appear passive as they try to engage in a rather misguided democratic role. (p. 66)

Having found that teachers do discriminate behavioral patterns of supervisors, Blumberg questioned whether their discrimination makes a difference. One area he investigated was the relationship between teachers' descriptions of their supervisors' styles and their descriptions of the communicative freedom of their interaction with their supervisors. Blumberg reports that the following patterns resulted from this investigation: Teachers who described their supervisor's style as predominantly high direct, low indirect (Style B) felt that the communicative climate focused on control, superiority, strategy, and evaluation. Supervisory behavior described as low direct, high indirect (Style C), on the other hand, led to the development of empathic relationships. Behavior perceived as high direct, high indirect (Style A) was associated, as was Style B, with feelings of defensiveness on the part of teachers. Lastly, behavior described as low direct, low indirect (Style D) was associated, along with Style C, with feelings of supportiveness.

A second area of interest to Blumberg was the relationship between the four supervisory styles and teachers' ratings of the productivity of supervision. The results indicated that the four styles were perceived differently with regard to productivity. The order of productivity, from highest to lowest, corresponded to supervisory styles C, A, D, and B. Blumberg notes that the ratings for C and A were very close, while there was a sharp break between A and D and between D and B. He interprets these results to mean that teachers find their interaction with supervisors productive when the supervisors are either primarily indirect or both indirect and direct. When supervisors are predominantly direct or do very little, their interaction with teachers is viewed as unproductive.

Following these initial investigations, Blumberg tested the hypothesis that different descriptions of the behavioral styles of their supervisors by teachers would produce different evaluations of the overall quality of their interpersonal relationships. The results of the study he conducted supported this hypothesis. Blumberg makes two major points in discussing his findings:

1. Generally *positive* evaluations by teachers of the quality of their supervisory interpersonal relations appear to develop when a teacher perceives his supervisor's behavior as consisting of a heavy emphasis on both telling, suggesting, and criticizing, and on reflecting, asking for information, opinions, etc. (high direct, high indirect); or when a

teacher perceives his supervisor as putting little emphasis on telling and much on reflecting and asking (low direct, high [in]direct).

2. Generally *less positive* or even *negative* evaluation by teachers of the quality of their supervisory interpersonal relationships appear to develop when a teacher perceives his supervisor as predominantly telling and not doing much reflecting or asking (high direct, low indirect); or when a teacher sees his supervisor's behavior as relatively passive (low direct, low indirect). (p. 80)

Blumberg's research findings can help us understand the perceptions teachers have of different supervisory styles. They are potentially useful, also, in considering the development of interpersonal relationships in clinical experiences. We return to these findings, and their implications for the interaction between cooperating teachers and teacher education students, in Chapter 7.

Integrating the Dimensions of Supervision

Clearly, the supervisory process cannot be effective unless sufficient attention is given to both the analytical and interpersonal dimensions of supervision. As Blumberg points out, interpersonal work can be productive only when there is a balance between the energy devoted to the work itself and the energy devoted to the development of positive relationships among those engaged in the work. We are currently at a point at which the objective of achieving this balance is not only desirable but also attainable by those in supervisory roles. The concept of clinical supervision provides us with a framework for making the supervisory process objective and analytical. Research such as Blumberg's provides us with useful information regarding the effects of different supervisory styles on interpersonal relationships. When we integrate the knowledge currently available to us concerning the analytical and interpersonal dimensions of supervision, we have the necessary tools to ensure that the outcomes of the supervisory process are both productive and satisfying.

REFERENCES

Anderson, Robert H. Supervision as teaching: An analogue. In William H. Lucio (Ed.), *Supervision: Perspectives and propositions.* Washington, DC: Association for Supervision and Curriculum Development, 1967.

Berman, Louise M., and Usery, Mary Lou. *Personalized supervision: Sources and insights.* Washington, DC: Association for Supervision and Curriculum Development, 1966.

Blumberg, Arthur. *Supervisors and teachers: A private cold war* (2nd ed.). Berkeley, CA: McCutchan, 1980.

Cogan, Morris L. Clinical supervision by groups. In *The college supervisor: Conflict and challenge.* The Forty-third Yearbook of the Association for Student Teaching. Dubuque, IA: Wm. C. Brown, 1964.

Frymier, Jack R. Foreword. In Fred T. Wilhelms, *Supervision in a new key*. Washington, DC: Association for Supervision and Curriculum Development, 1973.

Goldhammer, Robert. *Clinical supervision: Special methods for the supervision of teachers*. New York: Holt, Rinehart and Winston, 1969.

McNeil, John D. *Toward accountable teachers: Their appraisal and improvement*. New York: Holt, Rinehart and Winston, 1971.

Olsen, Hans C. Innovation in supervision today. In E. Brooks Smith, Hans C. Olsen, Patrick J. Johnson, and Chandler Barbour (Eds.), *Partnership in teacher education*. Washington, DC: The American Association of Colleges for Teacher Education and the Association for Student Teaching, 1968.

Reavis, Charles A. Clinical supervision: A review of the research. *Educational Leadership*, April 1978, *35* (7), 580–84.

PART 2
THE INTERACTION SYSTEM

Much of the diversity in current approaches to teacher education is reflected in the patterns of clinical experiences that have emerged. On the basis of their survey of over 550 programs, Howey, Yarger, and Joyce (1978) report that the range of clinical experiences available to preservice college students includes unsupervised contact, structured observation, observation with participation, student teaching, and various kinds of internships. This recent emphasis on providing a variety of preservice teaching experiences for students has made it necessary for college and school personnel to develop new roles or redefinitions of existing roles in order to implement changing patterns of clinical experiences.

CHAPTER 4 **defining roles in clinical experiences**

The new or redefined roles make it essential that participants in clinical experiences examine carefully the role definitions applied in their particular setting. When this process of role examination does not take place, consensus regarding role definitions often can be *assumed* to exist when in reality it does not. If this misperception persists, it can prevent the development of effective role relationships (Sarbin 1954, Twyman and Biddle 1963). What is needed, if the process of role definition is going to result in viable relationships, is a systematic approach that can be used to analyze both existing roles and those that are emerging. In this chapter we examine a framework for role analysis that can be used in defining role relationships and then consider its application in specific contexts.

APPLICATION OF THE ROLE CONCEPT IN CLINICAL EXPERIENCES

A survey of the literature dealing with the clinical experience component of teacher education reveals frequent use of the role concept with regard to the activities of the participants in these experiences. In books, journal articles, and research reports, the various dimensions of student teaching and other clinical experiences are often discussed in terms of "the role of the cooperating teacher," or the "role of the college supervisor."

A major difficulty that becomes apparent when this use of the role concept is considered closely involves a general lack of clarity and consistency regarding the way in which "role" is employed. For example, one writer may use "role" to refer to *expectations for behavior,* while a second writer may use the term to refer to *actual behavior.* Furthermore, it is not uncommon to find that neither author explains the reasons for his particular use. Even more confusing to the reader is material in which the author has made no attempt to define his use of "role" or has defined the concept obscurely. The assumption that seems to underlie the use of the role concept is that there is a single definition of "role" and that this definition is well understood by everyone.

An examination of the use of the role concept in the literature dealing with clinical experiences leads to the conclusion that at least two needs must be met if the concept is to be applied effectively to this component of teacher education. First, it is necessary to identify a set of specific, consistent definitions of the elements that comprise the concept of role. Second, a need exists for a framework within which the roles to be examined can be related. The role concept implies complementarity in the sense that the content of a specific role can be defined only with reference to counter positions or roles. This means that one cannot consider the "role of the student teacher" or the "role of the cooperating teacher" in isolation from the roles with which each interacts.

A Framework for Role Analysis in Clinical Experiences[1]

The framework for role analysis developed by Gross, Mason, and McEachern (1958) meets both the need for specific definitions of role elements and the need for a way of viewing sets of complementary roles as interaction systems.

[1]Parts of the following discussion are taken from Dean Corrigan and Colden Garland, *Studying role relationships* (AST Research Bulletin 6). Cedar Falls, IA: Association for Student Teaching, 1966.

Recognizing the problems surrounding the language of role analysis, Gross, Mason, and McEachern developed a set of consistent definitions that can be employed in examining role conflict and role consensus in any setting. This set of concepts also provides a framework for relating complementary roles.

Elements of the role concept that can provide the basis for analyzing relationships in clinical experiences are defined here. With the exception of the term "role consensus," these definitions are adapted from the definitions developed by Gross, Mason, and McEachern.

Position: the location of an individual, or class of individuals, in a system of social relationships.

Role expectation: an evaluative standard applied to an occupant of a position (i.e., what an individual is expected to do in a given situation, both by himself and by others).

Role: a set of expectations applied to an occupant of a particular position.

Role consensus: a state that exists when similar expectations are held for an occupant of a position.

Role conflict: a state that exists when contradictory expectations are held for an occupant of a position.

In order to examine expectations for roles in clinical experiences, it is necessary to view the roles as an interaction system. Figure 4.1 represents a way of viewing the relationships among the positions of cooperating teacher, college supervisor, and teacher education student as an interaction system. The way in which the positions are related is indicated by the double arrows, which signify two-way relationships. Each position is separated into positional sectors that illustrate the relationship of one position to the other two positions. For each of the three positions, two positional sectors have been left blank to indicate that only a limited set of positions is shown in the diagram. Cooperating teachers, preservice students, and college supervisors, for example, also interact with pupils, principals, and a variety of other school personnel. In separating each position into sectors, recognition is given to the existence of these additional relationships.

Within this framework, each role can be viewed in terms of its relationship to the other roles. For example, attention can be focused on consensus between cooperating teachers and college supervisors on the expectations they hold for student teachers. Another possibility would be to examine the expectations held for cooperating teachers by college supervisors, interns, and cooperating teachers themselves. Additional positions, such as clinical professor or coordinator of clinical experiences, can be added to the framework or substituted for one or more of the positions identified here. As the framework is used to analyze the expectations held for various roles, the amount of consensus that exists on role definitions can be assessed. The identification of potential conflict and ambiguity, through this analysis, can serve as the starting point for planning and implementing ways of bringing about increased clarity and consensus with regard to role definitions.

Figure 4.1   System Diagram Indicating Relationships Among the Positions of Teacher Education Student, Cooperating Teacher, and College Supervisor

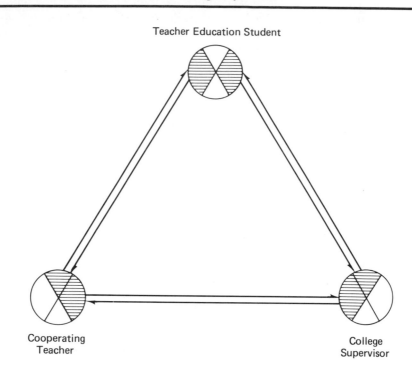

Studies of Role Conflict and Consensus

Three studies of role expectations in clinical experiences have been conducted using a modification of Gross, Mason, and McEachern's framework for role analysis. The first study (Garland 1964) assessed conflict and consensus on expectations held for the role of student teacher by cooperating teachers, college supervisors, and prospective student teachers. A role expectation instrument was constructed that consisted of 76 items most frequently identified in the literature on student teaching as functions that student teachers do perform, should be expected to perform, or should not be expected to perform (see Appendix A). Cooperating teachers, college supervisors, and prospective student teachers were asked to indicate their opinions regarding what should or should not be expected of student teachers by choosing one of the following responses for each item: *absolutely must, preferably should, preferably should not,* or *absolutely must not* be expected to perform.

The responses of the three groups showed that there were significant differences between cooperating teachers and prospective student teachers on 4 items, between college supervisors and prospective student teachers on 3 items, and between cooperating teachers and college supervisors on 3 items. These were interpreted to reflect disagreement on expectations, which could result in conflict for those involved. The expectations that reflected disagreement are shown in Table A in Appendix D.

The responses to items that did not reflect disagreement were analyzed to determine the amount of consensus that existed on those items. When the items were classified into levels of consensus, it was found that there was high consensus among the three groups on 24 items. The expectations that reflected high consensus are shown in Table D in Appendix D.

An interview schedule was developed on the basis of the analysis of responses to the role expectation instrument. The questions on the interview schedule were designed to obtain information regarding perceived reasons for disagreement or lack of agreement among the three groups.

Interviews were conducted with one-third of the respondents in each of the three groups. The major factors the interviewees perceived as contributing to disagreement or lack of agreement were different points of view in focusing on the student teaching experience, the frequent lack of awareness of position occupants of the expectations held by those occupying other positions, and a lack of communication both among and within the groups.

In the second study, Kaplan (1967) investigated the role expectations for college supervisors held by student teachers, supervising (cooperating) teachers, and college supervisors. Members of each of the three groups were asked to indicate their opinions regarding what should or should not be expected of college supervisors by responding to a role expectation instrument that included 40 items (see Appendix B).

The responses of the three groups revealed disagreement between cooperating teachers and student teachers on 11 items, between college supervisors and student teachers on 8 items, and between college supervisors and cooperating teachers on 5 items. The expectations that reflected disagreement are shown in Table B in Appendix D.

When the items that did not reflect disagreement were classified into levels of consensus, high consensus among the three groups was found on 7 items. The expectations that reflected high consensus are shown in Table D in Appendix D.

After the response data were analyzed, Kaplan conducted interviews with one-third of the respondents in each of the three groups. The major factors the three groups viewed as contributing to lack of agreement were different perceptions of the role of the college supervisor, particularly in the areas of evaluation and in acting as a resource consultant. The lack of awareness of the expectations held by others for the role of the college supervisor and a lack of communication among and within the three groups were seen as possible sources of conflict.

The focus of the third study in this series (Castillo 1971) was the role of the cooperating teacher. Student teachers, college supervisors, and cooperating teachers were asked to indicate their opinions regarding what should or should not be expected of cooperating teachers by responding to a role expectation instrument that included 50 items (see Appendix C).

An analysis of the response differences among the groups showed that cooperating teachers and college supervisors disagreed on 14 items, college supervisors and student teachers disagreed on 12 items, and cooperating teachers and student teachers disagreed on 9 items. The expectations that reflected disagreement are shown in Table C in Appendix D.

Classifying the items that did not reflect disagreement into levels of consensus showed that there was high consensus among the three groups on 7 items. The expectations that reflected high consensus are shown in Table D in Appendix D.

Castillo conducted interviews with 20 percent of the respondents in each of the three groups to determine reasons for the low consensus found on 14 items. The major reasons given by the interviewees for the low consensus were that (1) cooperating teachers do not have the time to perform a number of the role expectations, (2) certain expectations are neither mandatory nor specified as "formal" expectations for the cooperating teachers, (3) many cooperating teachers may not have the ability or necessary expertise to perform some of the role expectations, (4) performance of the expectations by the cooperating teacher is dependent upon the specific situation or need of the student teachers, and (5) the responsibility in performing some of these expectations should be shared by the college supervisor or other school personnel.

The results of the studies conducted by Garland, Kaplan, and Castillo clearly demonstrate that consensus on role definitions cannot be viewed as a condition to be assumed. Rather, it must be viewed as a condition to be developed. Only as expectations are examined for areas of disagreement and consensus can a basis for effective role relationships be established.

A STRATEGY FOR ANALYZING ROLE EXPECTATIONS IN CLINICAL EXPERIENCES

In order to analyze role definitions to determine areas of consensus and conflict, it is necessary first to identify the expectations that are held for the occupants of the interacting roles. Moreover, to ensure the usefulness of this process of role analysis, the expectations should communicate clearly and include the full range of areas of responsibility of each role occupant. Once participants have identified expectations that meet these criteria, they will be able to determine areas of conflict, as well as areas in which consensus exists.

Using the Perceptions of Role Occupants in Identifying Expectations

Developing an awareness of the concerns and anxieties frequently expressed by those involved in clinical experiences can provide a useful starting point for cooperating teachers as they begin the process of identifying and clarifying role expectations. A consideration of the anxieties experienced by students prior to a clinical experience, for example, may suggest expectations on which the cooperating teacher will want to focus initially in order to increase his student's feeling of security. Similarly, knowing the concerns of college supervisors and other cooperating teachers may help the cooperating teacher identify areas in which he will want to seek clarification regarding expectations for his role and that of the college supervisor.

Anxieties of Student Teachers. That preservice teaching experiences can produce anxiety and stress in teacher education students is well documented. In their study of stress in student teaching, for example, Sorenson and Halpert (1969) found that 70 percent of the students who participated in the study experienced "considerable psychological discomfort" at the beginning of the student teaching experience. Twenty percent of the students continued to feel that discomfort throughout the assignment.

Coates and Thoresen (1976) reviewed and summarized the findings of 15 studies of the concerns of beginning teachers and student teachers. They found the similarity among the findings impressive, not only because the samples surveyed were quite different, but also because a variety of methods was used to obtain these data. After reviewing the studies, Coates and Thoresen concluded that the anxieties and concerns reported by the subjects centered on the following five areas:

1. Their ability to maintain discipline in the classroom.
2. Student's liking them.
3. Their knowledge of subject matter.
4. What to do in case they make mistakes or run out of material.
5. How to relate personally to other faculty members, the school system, and parents. (p. 164)

One study reviewed by Coates and Thoresen was Thompson's (1963) investigation of the anxieties experienced by students both prior to and during an internship assignment. One hundred twenty-five students who were nearing the end of the internship were given a checklist containing 35 questions, each defining a particular kind of anxiety. The students were asked to indicate (1) which anxieties had been experienced and (2) whether each anxiety checked had been experienced prior to or during the internship. They were also given the opportunity to write anxieties not included in the original list.

Our concern here is with the identification of role expectations at the beginning of clinical experiences. For this reason, we focus on the results of Thompson's study that report the anxieties of the students prior to their internship. The following 19 questions received the highest number of responses as being anxieties experienced prior to the internship.

Anxieties Experienced by Student Teachers

What will the critic teacher expect of me?
Will I be required to turn in my lesson plans, and who will evaluate them?
Do I really know my subject matter?
What will these pupils be like?
Will the pupils like me and respond to my guidance?
What standards does the critic teacher maintain?
Will the critic teacher allow me to use my own initiative?
Will I be able to maintain desired standards of behavior?
How will the faculty and staff accept me?
How often will my college supervisor visit and observe my teaching?

What will my supervisor be like?

How should I dress?

What will the students be likely to do "to try me out"?

What are the critic teacher's special interests, personality characteristics, and likes and dislikes?

Will the critic teacher criticize me harshly if I make a mistake?

How will I be evaluated?

Will my teaching assignment be too much for me to handle?

What are the policies concerning classroom practices, the school, the faculty, and the curriculum?

Will I be allowed to discipline students as I see fit?

Anxieties of Cooperating Teachers.   Cooperating teachers can also experience apprehension as they anticipate the arrival of teacher education students who will share their classrooms for a period of time. Already responsible for providing for the learning of their pupils, cooperating teachers also must offer the guidance necessary in helping preservice college students develop competence in teaching. Fulfilling both responsibilities simultaneously is indeed an imposing task. Furthermore, many cooperating teachers are no doubt aware that student teachers perceive their cooperating teachers as having the most significant influence on their student teaching experience (Karmos and Jacko 1977). Certainly this awareness could generate apprehension about his ability to fulfill the role in the mind of any cooperating teacher.

What specific anxieties do cooperating teachers experience as they consider the responsibilities of their role? The following are questions frequently raised by cooperating teachers and reflect concern in three major areas: (1) the cooperating teacher's feelings of personal and professional adequacy, (2) the cooperating teacher's relationship with the student, and (3) the student's relationship with the children.

Anxieties of Cooperating Teachers[2]

Will I be able to help the student become a successful teacher?

Am I sufficiently organized to be able to help a student teacher?

What will be the student teacher's reaction to my teaching?

Will I be able to be impartial, fair and free from personal bias in evaluating a student teacher?

Is my teaching of such quality that it could be an example for the student teacher?

Will I become too dependent on the student teacher so that resuming my normal load is burdensome?

Will I lose some of my program flexibility because of having a student teacher?

What if the student teacher should be more capable or more intelligent than I am?

What if things go wrong and I don't know how to take over?

[2]Dorothy E. Foster. *Some anxieties of supervising teachers.* Unpublished manuscript, n.d.

Do I have enough self-confidence to accept a student teacher?

Conferences are time-consuming. Will there be conference time available?

How do I adjust to newer methods the student teacher may suggest?

How do I know when it is helpful to interrupt a student when he is teaching?

Will there be a personality clash between me and the student teacher?

Will I be too aggressive (bossy) with the student teacher?

Will the student teacher replace me in interest and popularity with the children?

Will the student teacher be able to control the class within acceptable standards of behavior?

Will the student teacher lose control of the class?

Concerns of College Supervisors. The college supervisor may appear to students and cooperating teachers to be relatively free of apprehensions and concerns. In reality, those who occupy this role can find themselves confronted by personal and professional problems that result from the uniqueness of their position.

The college supervisor is expected to be available to provide guidance and counseling for each of the students assigned to her, even though she may be responsible for a large number of students placed in schools in widely scattered locations. She is also expected to learn, and adjust rapidly to, the policies, procedures, and personnel of the schools in which her students are placed; a task made more difficult by the fact that she may find herself in different schools each semester. Finally, if she is to advance professionally, she must find ways of maintaining contact with her colleagues at the college or university, without neglecting her students.

What specific concerns might college supervisors express as they begin a semester with student teachers or students involved in other clinical experiences? Pfeiffer (1964) identifies many of the concerns shared by college supervisors in his chapter, "Common Concerns of College Supervisors," in *The College Supervisor: Conflict and Challenge*, the Forty-third Yearbook of the Association for Student Teaching. The following questions, reflecting the concerns of college supervisors, are suggested by Pfeiffer's discussion.

Concerns of College Supervisors

For how many students will I be responsible?

How much time will I spend in travel?

Will my schedule allow me to observe each student as often as I would like to?

Will there be sufficient time to give each student the amount of help he needs?

Will the students have been adequately prepared to assume the teaching responsibilities they will be given?

Will I be able to establish effective relationships with students and with cooperating teachers?

What will the cooperating teachers expect of me? Will I be able to meet the expectations of each cooperating teacher?

If conflicts develop between a cooperating teacher and a student teacher, will I be effective in helping them resolve the conflicts?

Will I be able to schedule conferences without disrupting classroom programs?

If a cooperating teacher and I disagree in our evaluation of a student, will we be able to communicate effectively enough to resolve the disagreement?

How will the principal and other school personnel respond to me?

Will I be able to fulfill my role and still maintain my professional contacts at the college?

Identifying the Cooperating Teacher's Role Expectations

An important step for cooperating teachers in analyzing expectations for the roles involved in clinical experiences is that of identifying their expectations for the roles of student, college supervisor, and cooperating teacher. Since the student may find it overwhelming to be presented with a lengthy list of expectations at the beginning of the experience, it is probably best to focus initially on those expectations that will be most helpful as she begins the assignment. Additional expectations can be clarified as the experience progresses. The anxieties and concerns expressed by students before they begin a clinical experience, presented in the previous section, can serve as a guide in identifying the expectations that will be discussed initially.

There are other factors that the cooperating teacher will want to consider in identifying expectations for the student. These include (1) whether the student will be in the classroom on a full-time or a part-time basis, (2) the length of the assignment, (3) the point at which the student is in her professional sequence, and (4) whether the student has had previous field experiences.

Because the roles that interact in clinical experiences are complementary, the definition of expectations for one role requires the definition of expectations for the other roles. It is important, then, that the cooperating teacher identify for his role and that of the college supervisor the expectations that correspond to the expectations he is identifying for the student. This process will (1) help the cooperating teacher to clarify his thinking with regard to the definitions of all three roles and (2) serve as a basis for comparing his expectations with those of the college. The expectations regarding planning that were developed by one cooperating teacher who engaged in this process are shown in Figure 4.2.

Activity 1   In order to experience identifying and analyzing role expectations, list on Analysis Guide 1, in the column provided, the expectations you would have for a preservice college student working in your classroom on a full-time basis. Include areas you feel should be added to those already identified. As you list each expectation for the student, attempt to identify the corresponding expectations for cooperating teacher and college supervisor. Keep the information you record on Analysis Guide 1 for use with Activity 2.

After you have completed Analysis Guide 1, you will want to receive

Figure 4.2   Role Expectations and Planning

	Role Expectations		
Area	Cooperating Teacher	Student	College Supervisor
Planning	Arrange lessons with student well in advance.	Develop written lesson plans.	Guide student in writing objectives.
	Provide resources and/or assist in locating materials.	Plan a unit independently.	Suggest alternative places to find information and materials.
	Review lesson plans and discuss suitability with the student.		

feedback concerning your effectiveness in communicating expectations for the three roles. If you are participating in this activity in a group setting, exchange analysis guides with another member of the group. Analyze the expectations identified for each role and provide feedback for each other by responding to the following questions:

1. Do the expectations for each role clearly define the desired behaviors?
2. Do the expectations address the anxieties that the role occupants may have initially?
3. Do these initial expectations define the roles sufficiently, without appearing to be overwhelming?

Use the feedback you receive as a basis for rewriting, adding, or deleting expectations from your analysis guide.

While the suggestions for using this analysis guide, and those that follow throughout the text, are addressed to participants in group settings, they can be adapted for use by individuals who are completing the analysis guides independently. For example, if you have completed Analysis Guide 1 independently, ask a colleague (teacher, principal, supervisor) to analyze the expectations you have identified and provide feedback by responding to the questions listed here. On the basis of this feedback, reexamine your expectations and make whatever changes seem appropriate. The same procedure can be followed in using subsequent analysis guides.

Examining the College's Expectations for the Roles of Student, Cooperating Teacher, and College Supervisor

Once the cooperating teacher has identified expectations for his role and for the roles of student and college supervisor, he is ready to examine the college's expectations for the occupants of the three roles. Through this process he can begin to identify areas of conflict, ambiguity, and consensus.

Analysis Guide 1   Identifying the Cooperating Teacher's Expectations for the Roles of Student, College Supervisor, and Cooperating Teacher

	Role Expectations		
Area	Cooperating Teacher	Student	College Supervisor
Planning			
Observing			
Studying Children			
Evaluating Learners			
Range of Teaching Activities			
Guiding Learning Activities			
Additional Areas			

Typically, colleges and universities develop written statements of expectations for students and cooperating teachers, and these statements are given to cooperating teachers prior to, or at the beginning of, the clinical experience. When written statements are not provided, expectations are often communicated to cooperating teachers at orientation meetings held at the college. A third way in which expectations are communicated is through individual conferences between the college supervisor and each of the cooperating teachers with whom she will be working.

Colleges and universities frequently develop statements of expectations for college supervisors also. It is unlikely, however, that these expectations will be communicated to role occupants other than the supervisors themselves. This is unfortunate, because such statements can provide cooperating teachers with useful information, such as how frequently the college supervisor is expected to observe each student, when seminars are to be held if they are a part of the experience, and how often the supervisor is expected to hold conferences with the cooperating teacher. Because of the potential benefit to the cooperating teacher in knowing the college's definition of the role of the college supervisor, the cooperating teacher should not hesitate to request this information.

When the cooperating teacher has obtained the college's expectations for the roles of student, cooperating teacher, and college supervisor, he can compare them with his own expectations for the three roles. As he does this, he can identify areas of potential conflict. For example, the college's expectations for students in the area of planning may differ from those of the cooperating teacher. Next, the cooperating teacher can identify expectations, for any of the role occupants, that seem ambiguous. If the college expects the cooperating teacher to hold regularly scheduled conferences with the student, for instance, is "regularly scheduled" defined? When the cooperating teacher has completed the process of identifying areas of conflict and ambiguity, he will have a clear picture of the expectations he wants to discuss with the student and the college supervisor.

Activity 2   The statements in Figure 4.3 are selected expectations for students, cooperating teachers, and college supervisors developed at one university. Compare these expectations with the expectations you recorded on Analysis Guide 1. As you examine both sets of expectations, record on Analysis Guide 2 areas that you feel would represent potential conflict if you were working with a student from this university. Next, record any of the university's expectations that seem ambiguous.

When you have completed Analysis Guide 2, you may be interested in comparing your concerns regarding conflict and ambiguity with those identified by other group members in order (1) to determine the similarities and differences that exist in the perceptions of the participants and (2) to analyze the factors that underlie the differences when they occur.

Analyzing Role Expectations in a Three-Way Conference

To be most effective, the process of analyzing role expectations should take place in a conference in which cooperating teacher, student, and college supervisor participate. Whenever possible, the conference should be scheduled before the assignment begins. While the participants' other responsibilities will no doubt limit the amount of time that can be given to the

Figure 4.3   Role Expectations for Cooperating Teacher, Student, and College Supervisor

Cooperating Teacher	*Student*	*College Supervisor*
The cooperating teacher should insist on pre-planning of lessons. Read and comment on the lesson plans.	In general, the student teacher's responsibilities are identical with those of the cooperating teacher.	The supervisor should contact the school at least one week before the student teacher is expected.
The cooperating teacher should schedule regular conferences. Hopefully, the cooperating teacher will involve the student in planning the next week's activities and will share with the student the long range goals for the class.	The student teacher is required to prepare lesson plans as required by the cooperating teacher and/or supervisor.	If possible, the supervisor should meet with the cooperating teacher before the student teacher arrives.
The role and status of the student teacher should be clearly spelled out to the class. The cooperating teacher should introduce the student teacher as a *new* teacher, who will be working in the room for most of the semester.	With the first day, student teachers will be phased into the entire spectrum of teaching responsibilities. This phasing in period will culminate in being responsible for planning and teaching at least an entire week or more.	Supervisors are required to conduct at least one seminar a week for each group of student teachers.
The cooperating teacher should help the student teacher develop a sense of belonging by providing a place in the room to sit and work.	It is the student teacher's responsibility to become a member of the school staff in as many ways as possible, observing the regular teaching day as any staff member must do.	The supervisor should arrange a mechanism by which messages, materials, etc., can be left for the student teacher.
As soon as possible, the cooperating teacher should get the student into large group work.	Although student teachers are not evaluated on the same level as regular teachers, each is expected to change and grow in the following areas: sensitivity to children's needs, teaching techniques, knowledge of curriculum, and in management and control of groups of children.	Supervisors should set as a goal one observation cycle per week with each student teacher. Supervisors are required to observe each student an absolute minimum of three times during each placement.

Whenever possible, the
supervisor should provide
the cooperating teacher
with any information that
has been made available to
the student teacher.

SOURCE: Taken from *Steps in supervision: A resource guide for supervisors of student teachers.* College of Education, Temple University, Philadelphia, PA, 1977.

conference, it is important that there be sufficient time to explore the concerns regarding expectations that the participants bring with them. The objectives of reducing anxieties and developing consensus are so critical in establishing effective relationships that they warrant whatever expenditure of time is needed to achieve them.

In the initial three-way conference, the cooperating teacher will have the opportunity to raise questions that focus on the ambiguity and potential conflict he has previously identified. The college supervisor can then respond to the specific concerns of the cooperating teacher and can also raise questions that reflect her concerns. In this way, ambiguous expectations can be clarified. Often the increased understanding that results from this clarification process eliminates the need for further discussion. If any conflicting expectations remain, they can be explored further by considering alternative points of view, and the uniqueness of the specific setting, as a basis for cooperative effort directed toward resolving the conflict.

The student can be helped to express and clarify her expectations in a

Analysis Guide 2   Identifying Areas of Conflict and Ambiguity in Role Expectations

	Role Expectations		
	Expectations for Cooperating Teacher	Expectations for Student	Expectations for College Supervisor
Areas of Conflict			
Areas of Ambiguity			

variety of ways. Some college supervisors ask the students assigned to them to identify their expectations prior to the clinical experience. If the student has done this, she may welcome the opportunity to share her expectations during the three-way conference. If the student has not previously identified her expectations, and seems uncomfortable about doing so spontaneously at this conference, both cooperating teacher and college supervisor can encourage the student to discuss her expectations on an ongoing basis throughout the weeks ahead. Of course, the student will be encouraged, during this conference, to ask questions that reflect her immediate concerns regarding expectations for her role.

The process of exploring role definitions probably will not be completed at the initial three-way conference. Communication regarding role expectations will no doubt need to take place on a continuing basis as different areas of concern arise. The initial conference can serve, however, to reduce the anxieties of the participants and provide direction for the initial stage of the clinical experience.

FACTORS AFFECTING COMMUNICATION AMONG ROLE OCCUPANTS

When cooperating teacher, student, and college supervisor meet to discuss expectations for their roles, they initiate a process of communication that will continue throughout the clinical experience. The nature of their communication will be a major influence in determining whether the experience is mutually satisfying and beneficial or fraught with misunderstanding and unresolved conflict. Because effective communication is so essential in establishing and maintaining viable relationships in clinical experiences, it is important to examine both those factors that decrease and those that increase the probability of achieving this critical objective.

Achieving effective communication is a complex and often difficult process. Inherent in the nature of the clinical experience are factors that can make this process especially difficult. First, each participant approaches the clinical experience from a different perspective. The student views it as one step toward achieving the goal of completing a teacher education program. The cooperating teacher, while viewing the experience as an opportunity to participate in the process of preparing teachers, still maintains a focus on the larger context of his responsibilities to the children in his classroom. The college supervisor approaches the experience from the perspective of the college's overall teacher education program and her own previous work with students. Thus, each comes with expectations derived from a different frame of reference. Identifying and clarifying these expectations represents a complex task in communication, but an essential one.

A second factor that can affect communication in the clinical experience is the level of anxiety the role occupants experience. That students, college supervisors, and cooperating teachers frequently have many anxieties as they approach the clinical experience has been discussed. If high levels of anxiety are experienced by role occupants, they may find it difficult, initially, to communicate effectively. Failure to persist in the process of attempting to understand each other, however, may actually result in an increase in anxiety. As Manera (1979) points out: "Many times the very factors that cause us stress have arisen from poor communication. Everyone can remember a time when our stress level went drastically high due to misunderstanding, lack of communication, or some block in our communication system" (p. 38).

Galloway (1979) makes a similar point concerning the relationship between anxiety and communication: "Under conditions of uncertainty and with an absence of information, human beings fear the worst. If you don't provide full information, I fear the worst. . . . In human terms, if I don't know how you feel about me and you don't provide the information, I'm going to have a tendency, even though I'm a whole, healthy person, to guess badly or negatively" (p. 19).

It is essential, then, that role occupants in clinical experiences communicate sufficiently to provide each other with information that will help alleviate their feelings of anxiety. The kinds of information that can be useful in reducing anxiety levels are discussed in Chapter 5.

Other elements can interfere with communication in clinical experiences, just as they can in any interpersonal setting. Hennings (1975) suggests three elements that can become barriers to effective communication: (1) masking, (2) filtering, and (3) wandering.

According to Hennings, both words and nonverbal signs can be used to *mask* an individual's real thoughts and feelings. Agreeing to participate in an activity when we would prefer not to do so is one example of masking with which many people probably can identify. Appearing to be interested in a speaker's message, through the use of facial expressions and gestures, is another example of masking that may be familiar. Hennings suggests that these and other masking techniques are used to help others maintain the images they are projecting, to gain the acceptance of others, or to avoid potentially offensive situations. She also suggests that a person is more likely to use masking behaviors in situations in which he feels threatened than in situations in which he feels comfortable and secure.

Hennings raises the question whether an individual is right in masking his real feelings. She points out that making a judgment about the rightness of masking behavior can be difficult in situations that are more complex than the examples given here: "Where do we draw the line between an unconscionable hypocrisy and a social amenity?" (p. 36). She concludes that while masking can be a barrier to communication, each individual must judge for himself the rightness of using this behavior in a given situation.

Hennings identifies several *filters* that individuals use to view the messages they are receiving. One of these filters is the set of attitudes, values, and likes and dislikes a person brings to a situation. These preferences, perceptions of self, and biases determine the way the person interprets the messages he receives. For instance, a feeling of personal insecurity can lead a person to interpret a message as a threat when, in fact, no threat was intended.

The dialectal[3] differences that exist within a language can also affect the way in which people interpret messages. Regional and social language variations produce dialectal differences in vocabulary, pronunciation, and grammatical structure. The failure of speakers of different dialects to understand the differences in their speech can result in faulty communication. An even more serious consequence of a failure to understand dialects is that it frequently results in a judgment by the speaker of one dialect that his dialect is "correct" and that the dialects spoken by others are "incorrect."

Lastly, Hennings suggests that people filter the communication they receive through their interpretation of various nonverbal signals and that these nonverbal expressions can be interpreted as differently as verbal ones. She points out that cultural groups frequently differ in their interpretation of gestures and facial expressions and in their response to physical contact and distance in human interaction. This can result in misinterpretation when people from different cultures communicate. Hennings reminds us, moreover, that this can occur even within our own culture: "Even among Americans there are differences in the way groups of people interpret not only distance and physical contact but also gestures, facial expressions, and posture or stance. These differences can become barriers to communication" (p. 40).

Hennings uses the term *wandering* to refer to a third set of behaviors that can block effective communication. One form of wandering occurs when a listener's personal problems and concerns interfere with his ability to focus on what is being said. As his attention shifts back and forth between his problems and the discussion at hand, he may miss elements of the speaker's message that are essential to accurate understanding. Wandering behavior also takes the form of anticipating. Anticipators are listeners who think they know what the speaker is going to say before he says it because they have heard the topic discussed on other occasions. As a result, they feel that they need not give their full attention to the speaker. Another form of wandering is mental waiting. Here listeners are involved in formulating their own ideas rather than in attending to the speaker. Hennings says that these listeners have put themselves in a "holding position" until they have the opportunity to speak. Finally, listeners can let their minds go completely blank and become nonreceivers. Such factors as an overly warm room, the drone of the speaker's voice, or fatigue can cause listeners to fail to receive messages.

Wandering can affect speakers as well as listeners. Verbal messages are often less well organized than written messages. Speakers can begin talking about one topic, shift to another, and perhaps to yet another, without ever completing the original thought. When this happens, listeners can find it very difficult to comprehend the speaker's message.

Each participant in a clinical experience must contribute to the process of achieving effective communication by attempting to overcome the communication barriers. It has been suggested, however, that the cooperating teacher

---

[3]"A dialect is a pattern of speech used and understood by members of a subgroup within a large speech community. A dialect is a complete, adequate system of language and is simply a variant of a more widespread speech system or of the language of the country." Nebraska Curriculum Development Center. *A curriculum for English: Language explorations for the elementary grades.* Lincoln, NE: University of Nebraska Press, 1966, pp. 7, 163.

must bear the heaviest responsibility in this process (Lang, Quick, and Johnson 1975). The cooperating teacher, therefore, will want to assess his communication frequently in order to determine the extent to which he is successful in (1) avoiding those behaviors that can interfere with communication and (2) creating an atmosphere in which other participants are secure enough not to feel the need to engage in behaviors that block communication. The following questions can help the cooperating teacher analyze his participation in the communication process. If he can respond to these points in positive ways, he can feel assured that he is increasing the probability that communication will be effective.

- Do I express my real feelings, thereby encouraging other participants to communicate openly?
- Am I consistent in efforts to prevent my attitudes and values from determining my interpretation of others' messages?
- Do I communicate respect for personal characteristics, such as speech and attire, that differ from my own?
- Do I attempt to understand the effect of my nonverbal behavior on others as well as the nonverbal messages that others are sending?
- Do I avoid permitting personal problems to interfere with my attention when others are communicating?
- Are my verbal messages concise and well-organized?

REFERENCES

Castillo, Jovito B. The role expectations of cooperating teachers as viewed by student teachers, college supervisors, and cooperating teachers. (Doctoral dissertation, The University of Rochester, 1971). *Dissertation Abstracts,* 1971, 32, 1374. (University Microfilms No. 71–22, 329).

Coates, Thomas J., and Thoresen, Carl E. Teacher anxiety: A review with recommendations. *Review of Educational Research,* Spring 1976, 46 (2), 159–84.

Corrigan, Dean, and Garland, Colden. *Studying role relationships* (AST Research Bulletin 6). Cedar Falls, IA: Association for Student Teaching, 1966.

Galloway, Charles M. Improving nonverbal communication. In Walter S. Foster and Charles A. Sloan (Eds.), *Improving communication in teacher education: Proceedings of the ATE summer workshop—1978.* DeKalb, IL: Association of Teacher Educators and Northern Illinois University, 1979.

Garland, Colden B. An exploration of role expectations for student teachers: Views of prospective student teachers, cooperating teachers, and college supervisors. (Doctoral dissertation, The University of Rochester, 1964). *Dissertation Abstracts,* 1965, 26, 1497–98. (University Microfilms No. 65-8557).

Gross, Neal; Mason, Ward S.; and McEachern, Alexander. *Explorations in role analysis: Studies of the school superintendency role.* New York: Wiley, 1958.

Hennings, Dorothy Grant. *Mastering classroom communication—What interaction analysis tells the teacher.* Pacific Palisades, CA: Goodyear Publishing, 1975.

Howey, Kenneth H.; Yarger, Sam J.; and Joyce, Bruce R. *Improving teacher education.* Palo Alto, CA: Association of Teacher Educators, 1978.

Kaplan, Leonard. An investigation of the role expectations for college supervisors of student teaching as viewed by student teachers, supervising teachers, and college supervisors. (Doctoral dissertation, The University of Rochester, 1967). *Dissertation Abstracts,* 1967, 28, 517. (University Microfilms No. 67-8985).

Karmos, Ann H., and Jacko, Carol M. The role of significant others during the student teaching experience. *Journal of Teacher Education,* September-October 1977, *28* (5), 51–55.

Lang, Duaine C.; Quick, Alan F.; and Johnson, James A. *A partnership for the supervision of student teachers.* Mt. Pleasant, MI: Great Lakes Publishing, 1975.

Manera, Elizabeth S. Stress: Its effect on communication. In Walter S. Foster and Charles A. Sloan (Eds.), *Improving communication in teacher education: Proceedings of the ATE summer workshop—1978.* DeKalb, IL: Association of Teacher Educators and Northern Illinois University, 1979.

Pfeiffer, Robert T. Common concerns of college supervisors. In *The college supervisor: Conflict and challenge.* The Forty-third Yearbook of the Association for Student Teaching. Dubuque, IA: Wm. C. Brown, 1964.

Sarbin, Theodore R. Role theory. In Gardner Lindzey (Ed.), *Handbook of Social Psychology* (Vol. 1). Reading, MA: Addison-Wesley, 1954.

Sorenson, G., and Halpert, R. Stress in student teaching. In J. A. Johnson and F. Perry (Eds.), *Readings in student teaching for those who work with student teachers* (2nd ed.). Dubuque, IA: Kendall-Hunt, 1969.

Thompson, Michael L. Identifying anxieties experienced by student teachers. *Journal of Teacher Education,* December 1963, *14,* 435–39.

Twyman, J. Paschal, and Biddle, Bruce J. Role conflict of public school teachers. *Journal of Psychology,* January 1963, *55,* 183–98.

PART 3

the dimensions of clinical experiences

It would be difficult to overemphasize the significance of the first days of a clinical experience. A cooperating teacher who establishes a comfortable relationship with the student during this period and provides appropriate initial experiences for involving the student in the classroom program is creating the basis for a clinical experience from which he, the student, and the pupils they teach can derive the maximum benefit. The value of a satisfying beginning makes careful preparation for this stage of the clinical experience well worth the effort involved.

Identifying and clarifying role expectations, through the process described in Chapter 4, is essential in reducing the anxieties of role occupants at the beginning of a clinical

CHAPTER 5 PREPARING FOR AND INITIATING clinical EXPERIENCES

experience. In addition, role occupants can provide information that will be useful in gaining an understanding of each other and of the setting in which they will interact. As each role occupant communicates relevant information to the others, he is helping to ensure that the initial period of the clinical experience will be satisfying and productive.

A STRATEGY FOR PREPARING FOR CLINICAL EXPERIENCES

The cooperating teacher can take several important steps in preparing for the preservice student's initial experiences in his classroom. First, he can provide information that will enable the student to understand and adjust to new relationships and surroundings. Second, he can identify the background data concerning the student that he will need in order to plan meaningful initial experiences. Third, he can request that the college supervisor provide information concerning the student's overall professional program and her previous experiences in the program.

Identifying Information the Cooperating Teacher Can Provide for the Student

A wide range of questions will occur to the student who is beginning a clinical experience. These questions will reflect the student's interest in learning about the cooperating teacher, the pupils and the classroom, the school, and the community. By providing information in these areas, the cooperating teacher will demonstrate his awareness of the student's concerns and contribute to the student's sense of security in approaching this experience.

Questions about the cooperating teacher undoubtedly will be uppermost in the mind of the student. Because she knows that she will work closely with the cooperating teacher, the student will be anxious to learn about him, both as a person and as a professional. What are his interests, likes, dislikes? How does he feel about sharing his classroom with a student? What are the major characteristics of his approach to teaching? What are the cooperating teacher's goals? How does he define *effective* teaching? Communicating information of this nature will help the student begin to know the cooperating teacher and his frame of reference for viewing the teaching process.

The student also will have many questions about the pupils with whom she will be working. Of particular concern will be the student's relationship with the pupils. In Thompson's study (see Chapter 4), for example, the following were among those questions identified by students as anxieties experienced before their internship: Will the pupils like me and respond to my guidance? How will the students be likely "to try me out"? How informal or formal should I be with students? What will the students do if I make a mistake? Providing an overall description of the pupils, and the management procedures to which they are accustomed, will serve to reduce these anxieties and help the student begin the experience with confidence.

The student will, of course, need to gain much additional information about the pupils in order to plan appropriate learning experiences for them. Information concerning individual needs, interests, and capabilities will be acquired through observation, conferences with the cooperating teacher, and the examination of cumulative records. While it is essential that the student obtain this information, she may feel overwhelmed if she is presented with a great deal of data at the outset. To avoid this situation, the cooperating teacher may find it effective to focus initially on the concerns identified in the preceding paragraph. Once this information helps the student feel secure in her new situation, she can begin to acquire the additional information.

The student will have questions concerning school personnel, organization, and policies. Again, the cooperating teacher will want to select carefully the information that will be communicated to the student initially. A detailed account of the procedure for admitting new pupils, for example, is probably of little value to the student whose attention is focused on trying to remember how to go from the instructional materials center to the cafeteria without getting lost. As a guide in selecting information about the school to give to the student initially, the cooperating teacher can consider this question: What information will the student need in order to function comfortably and effectively during her first days in this school? When the student feels oriented to the overall school setting, she can begin to explore more specific concerns, such as the availability of audiovisual and other materials, procedures for the use of equipment, and the services provided by the nurse, counselor, reading teacher, and other resource personnel.

Finally, the student will have questions regarding the community in which the school is located. Many of these questions will be answered as she walks or drives through the neighborhood. The cooperating teacher can assist the student in becoming acquainted with the area surrounding the school by accompanying her in order to point out important and interesting features of the neighborhood. If accompanying the student proves difficult to arrange, the cooperating teacher can identify the educational and recreational facilities, agencies, and businesses to which the student will want to direct her attention.

The student will gain additional information about the community as she works with the children and has contacts with their parents. The cooperating teacher can be helpful here by making the student aware of the formal and informal ways in which parents are encouraged to become part of the work of the school and by including the student in as many of these experiences as possible.

A final point needs to be made with regard to the importance of helping students learn about the communities in which their clinical experiences are taking place. During the 1960s, this dimension of the clinical experience began to receive increased attention as large numbers of white, middle-class preservice students were placed in schools in inner-city neighborhoods. Helping these students learn about communities different from their own and develop an awareness of the damaging effects of stereotyping and overgeneralizing became an objective of high priority in virtually every urban teacher education program. This objective should indeed receive attention in preparing students for experiences in inner-city schools, but it must also receive attention in preparing students for clinical experiences in other areas. Stereotypes about ethnic neighborhoods, suburbs, and rural areas can be just as prevalent as misconceptions about inner-city communities. Many students, for example, would be incredulous at learning that the school to which they have just been assigned, located in a suburb of white, upper-middle-class residents, recently was closed for several days because of a problem with head lice that reached near-epidemic proportions!

The preceding discussion of the cooperating teacher's role in helping students feel comfortable at the beginning of a clinical experience has suggested that students will have questions regarding (1) the cooperating teacher, (2) the pupils and the classroom, (3) the school, and (4) the community. Information in the first two areas will need to be provided by cooperating teachers on an individual basis. Information concerning the school and the community can be provided by groups of cooperating teachers. Frequently, in schools in which preservice students are placed regularly, cooperating teachers develop handbooks that include relevant school and community information. These handbooks are mailed to students before their arrival or given to them on the first day of their placement. Figure 5.1, taken from handbooks prepared by cooperating teachers in one school, illustrates the way in which useful information can be provided for students.

Figure 5.1 Information That the Cooperating Teacher Can Provide for the Student

Community Information

Bensalem Township is in the extreme southern corner of Bucks County. It is conveniently located near major transportation arteries such as the Pennsylvania Turnpike and Interstate 95. Public transportation is also available by train, via the Reading Railroad (Conrail) 215-387-6600, or the Penn Central Railroad 215-972-3000; by bus, contact Septa Bus Lines 215-969-0900, or Philadelphia International Airport 215-492-3000.

Housing is available in numerous apartment complexes or by contacting one of our local real estate agents. Bensalem Township has many places of worship to meet almost any religious affiliation. Lower Bucks County offers numerous shopping complexes such as the Neshaminy, Oxford Valley, and Bucks County Malls. Local hospitals include St. Mary's in Langhorne 215-752-0511, Lower Bucks County in Bristol 215-245-2200.

Local libraries are plentiful. Some nearby are the Free Libraries of Bucks County in Langhorne 215-757-2510 and Levittown 215-949-2323, the Grundy Library in Bristol 215-355-1183, and of course, Valley School's Library.

Information about Bucks County's parks and recreational facilities can be obtained by contacting the Bucks County Department of Parks and Recreation, Core Creek Park, R. D. 1, Langhorne, PA 19047, 215-757-0571.

Information on the numerous places to visit and events happening in Bucks County and Philadelphia can be obtained from the Historical Tourist Commission, Main and Locust Streets, Fallsington, PA 19054, 215-295-5450, the Philadelphia Convention and Tourist Bureau, 1525 John F. Kennedy Boulevard, Philadelphia, PA 19120, 215-864-1976, or from the Mayor's Office, 143 City Hall, Philadelphia, PA 215-686-2250. Ask for Packet S if obtaining the information by mail.

A street and road map of Lower Bucks County can be obtained by contacting the Lower Bucks County Chamber of Commerce at 409 Hood Boulevard, Fairless Hills, PA 19030, 215-943-7400.

Any other information can most likely be obtained in the Lower Bucks County or Philadelphia phone book, yellow pages, or by contacting a local newspaper such as the Bucks County Courier Times, 215-943-1000, the Bulletin, 215-382-7000, or the Philadelphia Inquirier, 215-854-2000.

SOURCE: Debbie Bernstein, Jackie Blaswick, and Deanann Padgeon. *Welcome! third grade student teachers*. Valley Elementary School, Bensalem Township School District, Cornwells Heights, PA, 1979, pp. 1–2. Reprinted with permission.

Helpful Hints

School Standards

On a school wide basis, we have set up some "common sense" standards: No running, no loud talking, no gum chewing, treating things carefully, remembering our manners when we are listening or wish to speak, etc. We consider all the children in the school each teacher's responsibility. So if you see a child misbehaving, take a moment to remind him of the standards.

Lesson Plans

Most of the time you will be required to submit a lesson plan to your cooperating teacher. Below is a simple and useful format to follow. It is recommended that you make use of the format.

    I   Objectives (stated behaviorally)

    II   Materials

    III   Procedure

        a. Introduction (motivation)

        b. Development

        c. Conclusion/Closing

    IV   Follow up

    V   Evaluation

        a. For students

        b. Of lesson

You will be required to write behavioral objectives for your lesson plans. A very helpful reference book is *Preparing Instructional Objectives* by Robert F. Mager, Fearon Publishers.

Books

We use two basal reading series here in Valley. We use the Scott Foresman Open Highways Reading Series and the 1974 and new edition of the Houghton Mifflin Reading Series. We are also blessed with many supplemental programs and series. Try to become familiar with all the various reading materials; you'll find it useful and interesting.

We also use the Houghton Mifflin Math Book school wide. Each pod has a unique math program developed for its own use. Become familiar with your own pod's program. If you have some "extra" time, check out the other pods' programs!

● Exchange phone numbers and addresses with your cooperating teacher. If anything should happen, it's a good idea to get in touch with him or her.

● There is a public telephone located near the office, down the hall to the right. It can be used for all personal calls you may need to make.

There is also a phone located in the faculty room which can be used for interschool calls or for school-related business.

● It's a good idea to get to know the school personnel including: custodians, aides, cafeteria ladies, etc. They can be helpful to a teacher in need!

● We have a teachers resource room—it's located in the back of the teacher's lounge! There are

Helpful Hints

a variety of resource books and materials to be used. The books can be signed out and returned. The laminator, thermofax machine, paper cutter, typewriter, and ditto machines are also located there.

- Find out how to operate the machines we have:
    - *a.* A laminator
    - *b.* A thermofax copier
    - *c.* Electric ditto machines
    - *d.* Regular ditto machines

These machines are all available for your use! But please ask for instructions on how to operate them if you aren't familiar with them.

We also have a variety of audiovisual equipment:
- *a.* Slide projectors
- *b.* Filmstrip projectors
- *c.* Film projectors
- *d.* Tape recorders
- *e.* Systems 80 machines
- *f.* Viewers
- *g.* Overhead projectors

Again, we urge you to become familiar with and learn to operate all the equipment!

1st to 5th

In general, you will be asked to fulfill a variety of requirements. In most pods, you will begin with a gradual take over of the teacher's routine, such as morning exercises, dismissals, culminating in a full week or so of complete classroom instruction (including duties).

In most pods you will be required to:
- plan and implement a unit of study other than one planned by the team.
- prepare detailed lesson plans for each lesson taught.
    NOTE: refer to Helpful Hints for information on behavioral objectives and a lesson plan format.
- conference with your cooperating teacher at designated times (occasionally before or after school).

SOURCE: Lynne Benedict, Anne Evans, Carol Henderson, and Marsha Messinger. *Student teacher handbook.* Valley Elementary School, Bensalem Township School District, Cornwells Heights, PA, 1979, pp. 3–5. Reprinted with permission.

Activity 3   Using Analysis Guide 3, identify the information about yourself, your pupils, and your classroom that you would want to provide before a student begins a clinical experience with you. Next, if your school does not have a handbook for preservice students, identify the school and community information you would want to provide. Complete the analysis guide by including additional information that would be needed in order to understand your particular setting. When you have recorded your information, exchange analysis guides with another group member who is participating in this activity. Provide feedback for each other by responding to the following questions. On the basis of the feedback you receive, revise your analysis guide, if this seems appropriate, by adding or deleting information.

1. Does the information recorded seem to provide a sufficient orientation to each area included on the analysis guide?
2. Is information provided that a student might find more useful following the initial stage of the clinical experience?

Analysis Guide 3   Identifying Information the Cooperating Teacher Can Provide for the Student

Areas of Interest	*Information*
Personal and Professional Background	
Pupils and the Classroom	
School Policies and Procedures	
Community	
Additional Areas	

Identifying Information the Student Can Provide for the Cooperating Teacher

The student also can provide information that will help the cooperating teacher prepare for the initial stage of the clinical experience. Many colleges ask students to supply background data at the time they make application for the clinical experience, and these data are then made available to cooperating teachers. If the cooperating teacher finds that the college with which he is working does not follow this procedure, he will want to request background information directly from the student. A consideration of the information typically included by colleges that use an information record can serve as a basis for identifying the data to be requested from the student.

Students are usually asked to provide both personal and professional information. Personal information frequently concerns general health, the communities in which the student has lived, and the student's current living arrangements (i.e., whether he lives on- or off-campus). Additional questions may ask the student to identify the extent of her home or work responsibilities. Finally, the student is usually encouraged to list special interests or abilities that she feels will contribute to her effectiveness in the clinical experience. This background information can be useful to the cooperating teacher in providing a basis for his initial efforts in establishing a satisfying relationship with the student.

One item of professional information that is typically requested concerns the nature and extent of the student's previous experiences with children or young people. It is important for the cooperating teacher to have this information when he plans for the student's initial involvement in the classroom. The experiences planned for the student who has had pre-student teaching assignments or has worked as a classroom aide will differ considerably from those planned for the student who is approaching her first encounter with children or youth.

Another item of professional information often explored is the nature of the student's community contacts. This information can be useful to the cooperating teacher in determining the amount of help the student will need in becoming acquainted with the school community. The student who has volunteered or worked part-time at one or more community agencies may be able to explore the school community relatively independently, for example, while the student who has had no community contacts will need specific guidance.

Activity 4   Using Analysis Guide 4, identify the information concerning a student that you would find useful in planning her initial experiences in your classroom. Add areas or questions that have particular relevance in your school setting. When you have completed the guide, compare your analysis with one completed by another participant in the group. As you discuss the information each of you has identified, revise your analysis guide, if this seems appropriate, by adding or deleting information.

Identifying Information the College Supervisor Can Provide for the Cooperating Teacher

While the student can describe certain aspects of her professional background, there is additional information needed by the cooperating teacher that the college supervisor can provide. The cooperating teacher will want to know, first, the overall orientation of the student's professional program. For example, is it a competency-based approach to teacher education, a program with a humanistic orientation, or one that reflects an eclectic approach to teacher preparation? Within the framework of the overall approach, it is important that the cooperating teacher know which courses in her professional sequence the student will have taken prior to her clinical experience in his

Analysis Guide 4   Identifying Information the Student Can Provide for the Cooperating Teacher

Areas of Interest	Information
Personal Background	
Previous Experiences with Children or Youth	
Previous Community Experiences	
Additional Areas	

classroom. Knowing that the student will not have had the required course in reading education, for example, will help the cooperating teacher in planning the nature of the student's involvement in that area of the curriculum. Lastly, it is important that the cooperating teacher understand the relationship between the clinical experience that the student is about to begin and other clinical experiences. An understanding of the nature and objectives of a particular clinical experience is essential to the effective planning of the student's initial experiences and her overall sequence of involvement.

Activity 5   On Analysis Guide 5, identify the information you would want to obtain from the college supervisor prior to the beginning of a student's experience in your classroom. Include questions regarding the college's program and procedures, in addition to those suggested here, that you would need to ask the college supervisor in order to plan for the student's involvement in your particular classroom, school, and school community. When you have completed the analysis guide, compare the information you have identified with the information identified by others who are participating in this activity. On the basis of your discussions, make revisions in your analysis if you feel they are needed.

Analysis Guide 5   Identifying Information the College Supervisor Can Provide for the Cooperating Teacher

Areas of Interest	Information
Nature of the Student's Professional Program	
Aspects of the Professional Sequence that Support the Clinical Experience	
Objectives of the Clinical Experience	
Additional Areas	

Communicating Information Needed by Role Occupants

The information to be provided by student, cooperating teacher, and college supervisor can be communicated in several ways. If the cooperating teacher is working with a college that asks students to supply background information, a copy of this information no doubt will be sent to him prior to the beginning of the student's assignment in his classroom. The cooperating teacher can respond to this information by sending the student the background data he has prepared for her. If possible, it would be useful to follow this exchange with a preassignment conference during which the shared information can be discussed. If the college does not provide background information concerning the student, but does supply the student's name and address, the cooperating teacher can contact her directly to arrange for this exchange of information. Unfortunately, in some situations students are not assigned to specific classrooms until the day the clinical experience begins. When this situation occurs, the cooperating teacher should schedule time on the first day for a conference during which he and the student can begin to share background information.

One responsibility often associated with the role of the college supervisor is that of meeting with cooperating teachers, individually or as a group, prior to the beginning of clinical experiences. Materials that describe the college's teacher education programs are frequently distributed and discussed at this time. If the college supervisor arranges a meeting with the cooperating teachers in a school, they can use this opportunity to obtain the information they will want to consider as they begin to plan their students' experiences. If the college supervisor does not arrange a meeting, cooperating teachers should not hesitate to contact her and request such a meeting.

A STRATEGY FOR INITIATING CLINICAL EXPERIENCES

Planning the Student's First Day

The importance of arranging a preassignment conference for the purpose of sharing background information and clarifying expectations has been emphasized in this chapter and in Chapter 4. A preassignment conference also enables the cooperating teacher to involve the student in planning her initial experiences in the classroom. Based on her feelings of competence and security, the student can suggest, or select from the cooperating teacher's suggestions, activities in which she feels she can participate comfortably and effectively. If the cooperating teacher will not have the opportunity to meet with the student prior to her first day, he will want to consider carefully the information he has been able to obtain in order to plan experiences that are appropriate in terms of the student's background. In either situation, Stratemeyer and Lindsey (1958) suggest three major guides that should serve as a framework in planning the student's first day in the classroom.

First, the student should be introduced in a way that gives her the status of a colleague. Preparing pupils for the student's arrival by discussing with them the benefits of having another teacher in the classroom is an important first step toward this objective. Providing an appropriate desk for the student's use will also help to establish her position as that of co-worker.

The cooperating teacher's introduction of the student will reinforce these preparations if he includes ways in which the student will be able to contribute to the interests or ongoing activities of the class. The following are illustrations of introductions made by cooperating teachers:

> Boys and girls, I would like to introduce Mr. Touni, who will be teaching in our class every Tuesday and Thursday morning. We may have to rearrange our schedule so that he will be able to participate in as many activities as possible. Everyone will also have to remember to tell Mr. Touni everything that happens when he is not here. On Monday, Wednesday, and Friday he attends college and perhaps one day he will tell us about the things he does there. Mr. Touni is also the coach of a softball team. Perhaps he will help our room's softball team practice during recess.

> Today, we are going to meet Mrs. Staerk. She is a teacher who will be in our classroom until December. Mrs. Staerk has designed the scenery for many plays at college and she has promised to help us build and paint the scenery for our play. I'm sure that everyone will enjoy having two teachers in our room.

The second guide is that the cooperating teacher should plan to involve the student in the activities of the classroom beginning with her first day. Stratemeyer and Lindsey identify three reasons for their emphasis on early involvement in the classroom program. First, by giving the student specific responsibilities, the cooperating teacher will help her feel secure in her new situation. The high level of anxiety that results from not knowing when and how to become involved in the work of a busy classroom can be avoided if the student is given tasks for which she will be responsible at given times throughout the day. As the student carries out her responsibilities, she will begin to feel that she is a participant in the activity of the classroom, rather than an outsider who has no part to play.

The second reason for early involvement is that having responsibilities will help the student focus on, and begin to learn about, specific elements of the teaching-learning situation. As Stratemeyer and Lindsey point out, a classroom is a complex setting, and the process of deriving meaning from observation can be difficult, even for the experienced observer. It is doubtful, then, that a student who is beginning a clinical experience will profit significantly from an extended period of observation. Rather, they suggest, by interacting with specific aspects of the classroom in the initial stage of the experience, the student will develop understandings that will make observing at later stages much more meaningful.

Lastly, by having the student assume responsibility immediately, the cooperating teacher will establish the concept that there are now two teachers, working together, in the classroom. Stratemeyer and Lindsey point out the importance of this concept at a later stage in the experience when the student is assuming the major teaching responsibility and the cooperating teacher is assisting. Since the children have experienced co-teaching from the outset, the cooperating teacher will have the freedom to ask questions, offer suggestions, and provide help as the student needs it without conveying the impression that the student is inadequate.

In their third guide concerning the student's first day in the classroom, Stratemeyer and Lindsey stress the importance of providing time, at the end of the day, for a discussion of the student's reactions. No doubt she will have many questions to ask, and the cooperating teacher's responses will help the student feel that she is beginning to understand the classroom. Furthermore, as he listens to her questions and comments, the cooperating teacher will gain insight into the student's readiness for subsequent experiences. Following this discussion, the cooperating teacher will want to share with the student the plans for the next day's activities.

Activity 6   Using the guidelines suggested by Stratemeyer and Lindsey, develop a plan for a student's first day in your classroom. On Analysis Guide 6, record the day's schedule of activities, indicating your responsibilities, those of the student, and those of any additional personnel (aide, tutor) who will be present. While the activities you select for a student will reflect your particular situation, you may find it helpful to consider the following suggestions:

- working with small groups of pupils
- preparing materials for class use

- helping individuals who are doing independent work
- working with pupils preparing a bulletin board
- reading a story to a small group of pupils
- accompanying pupils to music or physical education class
- helping pupils care for classroom pets
- accompanying the cooperating teacher as he assumes responsibility for lunch, recess, and similar activities

When you have completed Analysis Guide 6, exchange guides with another group member. Provide feedback for each other by responding to the following questions. On the basis of the feedback you receive, make revisions in your schedule if you feel they are needed.

1. Does the schedule provide time for introducing the student to the class?
2. Do the activities identified for the student seem to provide varied opportunities for interaction with the pupils?
3. Does the schedule include a conference with the student at the end of the day?

Stratemeyer and Lindsey conclude their discussion of the first day of a clinical experience by identifying what they consider "the essentials of a good beginning" (p. 164). Several points they make, adapted here in question form,

Analysis Guide 6   Planning the Student's First Day

Time Schedule	Responsibilities of Participants		
	Cooperating Teacher	Student	Other Personnel

are listed below. The cooperating teacher may find it useful to ask himself these questions at the end of the student's first day. His responses will provide direction for the next steps to be taken in fulfilling the role of cooperating teacher.

- Did we approach each other with trust, confidence, and respect for what each of us can bring to the experience?
- Did we view our work together as a cooperative effort to provide meaningful learning experiences for children?
- Did I communicate a respect for differences in thinking and a willingness to be experimental in my approach to teaching?
- Did I provide for the student's involvement in both teaching and planning?
- Did the teaching activities in which the student participated seem to match her level of readiness?
- Did I provide sufficient time for the student to ask questions?
- Did my responses seem to help the student understand the principles underlying my actions?

REFERENCES

Stratemeyer, Florence B., and Lindsey, Margaret. *Working with student teachers.* New York: Teachers College, 1958.

If cooperating teacher, student, and college supervisor participate as fully as possible in identifying role expectations and preparing for the student's arrival, the initial stage of the clinical experience will be comfortable and productive for each role occupant. Once this stage has been completed, the student is ready to become increasingly involved in planning and implementing the classroom instructional program. As she begins this process, the student will need the cooperating teacher's guidance in assessing pupils' learning needs, developing alternative teaching strategies, selecting appropriate resources, and evaluating pupil progress. The quality of this guidance is critical in determining the extent of the student's progress toward teaching competence.

CHAPTER 6 PROVIDING GUIDANCE IN PLANNING AND IN ASSUMING TEACHING RESPONSIBILITY

AN INTERACTIVE TEACHING FUNCTIONS FRAMEWORK

As the student considers the responsibilities she will assume in the classroom, she is confronted simultaneously by all the complexities of teaching. By providing her with a framework for viewing the major components of teaching, the cooperating teacher can help the student analyze this complex process. Figure 6.1, developed by Spanjer (1972), presents five dimensions of the teaching act: (1) managing classroom behavior, (2) asking questions, (3) interacting verbally, (4) communicating nonverbally, and (5) reinforcing pupil behavior. Spanjer suggests that while this framework may be limited in scope, it does distinguish some important components of classroom instruction. He proposes that an understanding of these dimensions can improve the ability of teachers to perform rationally and deliberately by increasing their self-awareness of the teaching act.

How can cooperating teacher and teacher education student use Spanjer's framework of teaching functions? First, an analysis of the components of the framework can help the cooperating teacher identify areas in which the student is likely to need the most guidance, particularly in the early stages of the

Figure 6.1   Interactive Teaching Functions

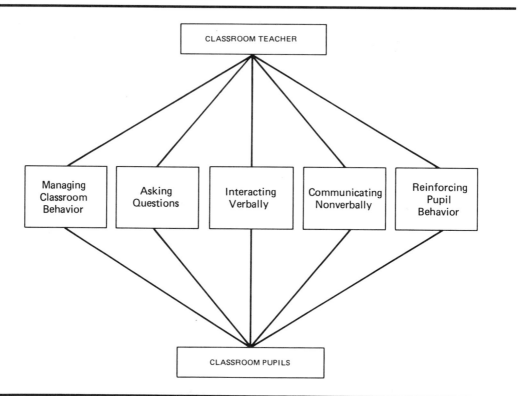

SOURCE: From R. Allan Spanjer, *Teacher preparation: Supervision and performance* (Washington, DC: Association of Teacher Educators, 1972), p. 10. Reprinted with permission.

clinical experience. Second, the framework can help the student focus on the major dimensions of teaching that she will need to consider as she plans for the responsibilities she is assuming. Third, cooperating teacher and student can use the framework as a basis for diagnosing problems that the student may encounter and designing strategies for overcoming them. The following discussion, in which ways of looking at the components of Spanjer's framework are suggested, may serve as a starting point for cooperating teacher and student in using the framework for these and additional purposes.

Managing Classroom Behavior

Studies of the anxieties expressed by teacher education students prior to and during clinical experiences indicate consistently that a major concern of students is their ability to manage classroom behavior. In Thompson's (1963) study, for example, interns expressed anxiety about the behaviors they could expect from pupils, maintaining desired standards of behavior, and whether they would be allowed to discipline pupils. It is important, then, for cooperating teachers to help students examine the causes of common management problems and to plan specific techniques that will prevent their occurrence.

In a recent book, Charlotte Epstein (1979) identifies specific management problems that can occur in classrooms and proposes strategies to prevent them. The problems Epstein describes are those frequently encountered by students in clinical experiences. It is worthwhile, therefore, to abstract from her analysis a set of guidelines that can help teacher education students develop an approach to classroom management that will reduce their anxieties and enhance the quality of their interaction with children. The following discussion is based on Epstein's examination of three dimensions of classroom management: (1) management of the physical setting, (2) management of time, and (3) management and the curriculum.

Management of the Physical Setting. The relationship between the objectives of a particular lesson and the arrangement of seats and other classroom furniture is well understood by the experienced teacher. A science demonstration at the front of the room will result in little learning for those seated too far away to see what is happening; similarly, pupils cannot participate in a discussion while they are seated in rows staring at the backs of one another's heads. Epstein suggests that this relationship may not be equally clear to teacher education students. She contends that while students typically develop lesson plans in their professional methods courses, they rarely are asked to include in these plans seating arrangements that are consistent with lesson objectives. If a cooperating teacher finds that the student with whom he is working lacks experience in analyzing classroom arrangements, he will want to provide guidance in helping her to devise seating arrangements that are appropriate for the lessons she is going to teach. Providing this guidance will enable the student to avoid the confusion, disruptive behavior, and other problems that naturally occur in an inappropriate physical setting.

Epstein looks at another aspect of the relationship between objectives and classroom arrangement in discussing what she terms "a universal seating error." This error exists when the classroom is arranged in such a way that pupils are seated far from each other and from the teacher; an arrangement that in her opinion interferes with orderly classroom interaction. She illustrates this by reminding us of two important objectives we hold as teachers: (1) to teach pupils to cooperate with one another and to care about one another's problems and (2) to facilitate learning in the classroom. It is clear that pupils cannot acquire the behaviors associated with cooperation when they are seated too far apart to interact naturally and easily. And it is evident that learning is not facilitated when pupils must move some distance, or talk loudly, in order to communicate; when these behaviors occur, attention quickly shifts from learning to problems of interaction.

To avoid the problems that occur when communication cannot take place easily, Epstein suggests changing the seating arrangement of the traditional classroom so that productive interaction is encouraged. One approach to this is through the use of learning, or activity, centers.[1] As pupils at each center work together to solve a problem or complete a task, they can talk without disturbing groups in other parts of the room and at the same time begin to acquire skill in small-group cooperation. While the pupils are working, the teacher can move from center to center, giving help as needed. Thus, in this arrangement, both pupil-pupil and pupil-teacher interactions are facilitated.

In recent years, the use of learning centers has become associated with "open space" school design. This association is unfortunate if it leads to the belief, particularly on the part of teacher education students, that learning centers "won't work" in self-contained classrooms. As many teachers have demonstrated, the learning center concept is workable in all physical settings. It is hoped that cooperating teachers will explore the concept of learning centers with students and provide guidance in developing and using them.

Management of Time. The management of time is a major factor in determining the incidence of disruptive and nonproductive classroom behaviors. Because of her inexperience in organizing and managing an entire teaching day, the teacher education student can find herself encountering periods of confusion or disruption. The cooperating teacher can help the student avoid these anxiety-producing occurrences by directing her attention to specific situations in which the management of time is particularly important in determining pupils' behavior.

One of these situations occurs when pupils arrive in the classroom. The student will create the potential for problem behavior if she becomes involved in such routines as taking attendance and collecting lunch money without providing activities in which pupils can engage independently. The cooperating teacher can help the student learn to manage this time period in two ways: (1) suggest that she note the procedures he uses during this period, and the activities he provides; and (2) suggest alternative activities the student may want to develop and use with pupils.

[1]Howard E. Blake's *Creating a learning centered classroom: A practical guide for teachers.* New York: Hart Publishing, 1977 is an excellent resource for teachers interested in developing learning centers.

Another potential problem situation is created when the student makes an abrupt transition from one activity to another before pupils are ready for the change. Stopping a discussion on pollution in which pupils are actively participating because the daily schedule calls for math at this time can be very frustrating to them and may make it difficult to focus their attention on the math lesson. The cooperating teacher's attitude toward the daily routine can be a major factor in a student's understanding of the need for flexibility in following a schedule. If the student observes that the cooperating teacher adjusts the routine at times, according to the readiness, interests, or special needs of the class, she will feel that she, too, can make adjustments without fearing criticism. Admittedly, a flexible attitude toward scheduling may be easier to implement in an elementary school than in a middle school or secondary school. Even when they are working within the constraints of specified periods of time, however, teachers can provide for flexibility if they are willing to make adjustments in their long-range planning.

A third situation that prospective teachers often encounter is the problem behavior that can occur when some pupils finish an activity sooner than others. If those who finish first do not know what to do next, disruptive behavior can arise. In teacher-pupil planning sessions, the cooperating teacher can help the student avoid this situation by demonstrating ways in which the teacher and the class decide on a sequence of activities and plan the options that are available during free time. The cooperating teacher can further help the student by directing her attention to the importance of including in her plans specific procedures for the transition from one activity to another.

Management and Curriculum.   Certainly, teacher education students learn about the importance of considering readiness, interest, and relevance in planning effective learning experiences for pupils. That they may still need guidance in applying this knowledge in specific situations is illustrated in the following anecdote: A student teacher was observed teaching reading to a small group of fifth graders in a school in Philadelphia. The story for the day involved a series of incidents in the life of Betsy Ross. The student introduced the selection by asking, "What is history?" She then proceeded to introduce new vocabulary and set purposes for silent reading. When the children had finished reading, the student discussed the content of the selection with them, and the lesson ended. At no time did it occur to the student to ask whether the children knew that the Betsy Ross House was located a short distance from their school, determine if any of them had visited it, or raise the possibility of planning a field trip to this historic site! While it can be hoped that this illustration is extreme, it does suggest that without guidance from cooperating teachers, students can overlook opportunities to make children's learning experiences relevant and interesting.

There are several ways in which the cooperating teacher can help the student plan learning experiences that will minimize the occurrence of those behaviors that arise when learners are bored, find no meaning in the work they are doing, or lack the skills needed to complete an assignment. First, the cooperating teacher will want to provide the student with information concerning the pupils' levels of skill development and the special learning needs of particular pupils. He can also suggest that the student administer an inventory to determine both group and individual interests. Finally, as the cooperating teacher discusses the student's plans with her, he will have many opportunities to offer suggestions and alternatives for designing meaningful learning experiences.

In concluding this discussion of classroom management, it is important to address the belief held by some teachers and teacher education students that the management problems encountered in urban or inner-city schools are somehow different from those encountered in schools in other settings and therefore require different management techniques. Epstein argues that this belief is untenable. She supports her position in the following statement, taken from the introduction to her text:

> What I am trying to do here is to identify those *human* problems that arise in a specific setting: the classroom. These are not problems experienced by teachers of inner-city children, or teachers of middle class children; teachers of Black children or white children; Native American, Puerto Rican, or Chicano children. They are problems faced by teachers of children whoever and wherever they are. Given certain contingencies, certain consequences, certain common behaviors appear. With some children, these behaviors may appear more quickly. They may last longer and be more resistent to extinction. But, given the same contingencies, we will see the same behaviors.
>
> Because certain contingencies obtain more frequently in urban schools, we may get more frequent behaviors of certain kinds. But it is a matter of frequency, not kind. That is, urban and suburban children do not respond differently to the education situation; it is just that the different behaviors appear with greater or lesser frequency in the urban or suburban setting. It is the causes and the reinforcing factors of the various behaviors that are the keys to dealing with them effectively. (pp. xiv–xv)

Epstein's position represents the only responsible approach to helping teacher education students develop the competence they will need as teachers in order to interact with children, in any setting, in ways that are mutually beneficial.

Asking Questions

The frequency with which questions are used in teaching suggests that teacher education students need specific guidance in developing effective questioning techniques. In discussing this dimension of his teaching functions framework, Spanjer identifies three factors that affect the quality of questions and the responses they elicit. A brief examination of these factors is presented here.

Patterns of Questioning. The use of certain patterns in questioning can limit the ability of pupils to respond appropriately. One pattern is asking questions that are unclear or incomplete, such as, "What about pollution?" and "Are these words alike or different?" The lack of focus in these questions can prevent pupils from providing the intended response.

A second pattern involves asking a series of questions without allowing time between questions for pupil response: "How can we make this word plural?" "Will this change the meaning?" "What will the word mean when it is plural?" The result of such a sequence is confusion on the part of pupils as they try to determine to which question they are expected to respond.

A third pattern is asking run-on questions with intervening information. Spanjer provides this example: "If you had, assuming this was possible, though it probably isn't, all the grains of sand in the world stacked up, it would be quite a pile, I guess; could you, if you had time which would be more than a person usually has, count the grains?" (p. 14). Undoubtedly, pupils would find it difficult to respond to this confusing question.

Teacher education students who have had only limited experience in developing questions may exhibit one or more of these three questioning patterns. Cooperating teachers will need to help them gain skill in developing clear, precise questions that will enable pupils to respond appropriately.

Eliciting Pupil Response. Spanjer points out that the ways in which teachers elicit pupil responses affect the quality of discussion and learning in the classroom. He suggests that the five types of pupil response discussed by Harris (1963) provide a useful guide for analyzing teaching behavior intended to elicit responses.

> *Solitary response.* The teacher designates a pupil to respond and then asks a question. Total class attention is not required, since only the pupil named needs to think about the question.
> *Controlled response.* The teacher first asks a question and then designates a pupil to respond. When this technique is used, it can be expected that at least several pupils will be thinking about the question. This technique does not encourage creativity or spontaneity, however.
> *Uncontrolled response.* The teacher asks a question without designating a pupil to respond. This procedure encourages free discussion, and the pupils assume more responsibility for contributing to the discussion.
> *Spontaneous response.* The teacher neither asks a question nor designates a respondent. With this procedure, a pupil can volunteer a question or make a comment that is not preceded by a teacher question that would require the response. Spontaneous responses from other pupils may then follow. Only in this setting, according to Harris, can there be a genuine discussion.
> *Mass response.* The use of this technique involves asking a number of pupils to respond simultaneously. Teachers frequently use this technique in connection with rote-learning activities. Harris raises the question of how well the teacher can assess pupils' ability when many are responding simultaneously.

The Harris categories provide a simple means of recording and analyzing pupil responses. The cooperating teacher may want to suggest that the student analyze her behavior to determine the patterns of pupil responses she is eliciting. Cooperating teacher and student can then discuss the effects of these patterns in achieving specific objectives and decide whether changes are indicated.

The Thought Level of Questions. In recent years teachers have been urged to broaden their questioning techniques to include a greater number of questions at levels beyond that of recall or recognition of literal information. The rationale for this emphasis on higher-level questioning is that learners will not develop the ability to think critically and creatively unless they are presented with questions that call for such thinking. Spache and Spache (1973) summarize this position in considering the relationship between teachers' questions and reading comprehension:

> It appears that what the reader retains while reading reflects such influences as: (1) his purpose in reading or what he intends to retain; (2) the instructions he is given before reading, which may lead him to find only the precise answers to specific questions or to secure a broader comprehension if the questions are more general. Comprehension is affected even more, however, by the pattern of questions the child learns to anticipate. He learns to read with only those types of thinking that the teacher's questions demand. Since teachers' questions appear to be limited in type and depth, children's thinking (or comprehension) tends to be superficial and stereotyped, and lacks critical thinking. (p. 542)

Medley (1979) and Rosenshine (1979) report that in the studies they reviewed, effective teachers asked lower-level, rather than higher-level, cognitive questions (see Chapter 1). Do these findings imply that we need not be concerned with asking higher-level questions? Rosenshine identifies an important dimension of this research that needs to be considered in attempting to answer this question. The studies reviewed by Medley and Rosenshine were limited to the measurement of achievement in reading and mathematics. As Rosenshine points out, since higher-level questions simply do not appear on standardized achievement tests, it makes sense to expect that practice in answering lower-level questions would be positively related to achievement gains, whereas practice in answering other kinds of questions would not develop the skills required for these tests. Thus, if we are concerned only that learners develop the kinds of thinking necessary to performing well on standardized achievement tests, we can limit the questions we ask to those in lower-level categories. However, if our objective is to help learners develop the ability to think critically and creatively as well, we will need to ask higher-level questions that stimulate such thinking.

Efforts to help teachers improve their questioning techniques have resulted in the development of a variety of systems for classifying questions. Some are designed for use in specific curricular areas, while others can be used to categorize questions in any subject. One useful system that has been widely used is the model developed by Sanders (1966). This model, based on Bloom's (1956) *Taxonomy of Educational Objectives: The Cognitive Domain,* includes seven categories into which questions can be classified: memory, translation, interpretation, application, analysis, synthesis, and evaluation. Sanders' taxonomy is organized in a hierarchy, beginning with the memory level. Each subsequent level of thinking includes some form of all the preceding levels. Definitions of the seven categories in Sanders' taxonomy are presented here:

Memory: Questions in the memory category ask the student to recognize or recall information.

Translation: Questions in the translation category ask the student to change ideas in a communication into parallel forms (e.g., charts, graphs, outlines, summaries).

Interpretation: Questions in the interpretation category ask the student to discover or use relationships among two or more ideas.

Application: Questions in the application category ask the student to use principles, definitions, values, and skills studied previously in new contexts.

Analysis: Questions in the analysis category ask the student to solve problems in the light of conscious knowledge of the parts and processes of reasoning.

Synthesis: Questions in the synthesis category encourage the student to engage in divergent thinking. This type of thinking starts from a problem that offers a variety of possibilities radiating out to many satisfactory solutions.

Evaluation: Questions in the evaluation category ask the student to set up standards or values and then determine how closely an idea or object meets these standards or values.

Sanders discusses ways in which teachers can use the categories of the taxonomy to classify, over a period of time, the kinds of questions they are asking to determine whether they are overemphasizing certain categories and excluding others. If they find that this is happening, teachers can then use the taxonomy, in daily and long-range planning, as a basis for developing a wider range of questions.

Sanders suggests that the taxonomy also provides a useful tool for evaluating instructional materials. He points out that many textbooks offer only recall questions. If teachers find that the texts they are using overemphasize questions in the recall category, they can use the taxonomy as a guide either in developing questions in additional categories or in selecting materials that include a wider variety of questions.

The significance of questioning in the development of pupils' thinking ability makes it essential that the cooperating teacher work with the preservice student in examining the questions she uses. This guidance will be particularly necessary for the student who lacks experience in designing higher-level questions. Through the use of the Sanders classification system, the cooperating teacher can help the student (1) analyze the questions in her plans and (2) evaluate the questions in instructional materials. As the student implements these suggestions, she will grow in her ability to provide questions that stimulate pupils' thinking.

Interacting Verbally

Cooperating teachers have always recognized the importance of helping preservice students analyze the nature of their verbal interaction with pupils. In recent years, however, this dimension of teaching has received increased attention. In the sections that follow, we consider how cooperating teachers can guide preservice students (1) by encouraging them to examine the overall patterns of their verbal interaction, and (2) by helping them analyze the specific verbal behaviors they employ.

Teacher-talk Formats.   Teachers employ a variety of talk formats in their verbal interaction with pupils. Hennings (1975) describes four such formats that are widely used. The first, the one-teacher/individual-student model, is used by the teacher for helping students who are working independently and for diagnosing and remediating individual problems. This model is found frequently in open classrooms.

When the teacher divides the class into groups or subclasses, he is employing Hennings' second talk format, the one-teacher/subclass model. This format is frequently used for working with pupils who have common needs or interests. As Hennings points out, this communication pattern is often used for teaching reading in elementary schools.

The teacher may use a third pattern, the one-teacher/total class format, to introduce an activity, conduct discussions, and present subject matter. An advantage of this format is that everyone receives the same information at the same time. In addition, in discussions, the range of ideas and opinions that can occur is increased. This format can also increase the range of ability represented by the students, a disadvantage that may result in the inability of some class members to deal with the content of the lesson. A second disadvantage is that this format limits the number of contributions by each student.

The fourth verbal interaction format described by Hennings is the one-teacher/superclass model. This format occurs when one teacher is responsible for two or more classes. Activities conducted with a superclass often include giving directions, preparing students for a film, or introducing a speaker. The one-teacher/superclass format may be used in team teaching when several classes are going to participate in the same activity.

Hennings points out that the selection of a talk format depends on the objectives of a particular lesson or activity. The cooperating teacher may want to discuss these formats with the student during planning sessions in order to provide guidance in selecting appropriate talk formats. When the lessons have been taught, cooperating teacher and student can discuss the strengths and limitations of the formats selected.

Classifying Teacher-Pupil Verbal Behaviors.   As teachers and learners interact, they employ a variety of verbal behaviors. Cooperating teachers should guide students in learning to analyze these verbal behaviors and in assessing their relationship to the achievement of specific objectives.

Many systems for coding teacher-pupil verbal interaction have been developed in recent years. The well-known Flanders coding system is reprinted as Figure 2.1 in Chapter 2. An adaptation of this sytem, the McRel Interaction Analysis instrument, developed by the Mid-continent Regional Educational Laboratory, is shown in Figure 6.2.

Figure 6.2   McRel Interaction Analysis Categories

Teacher Talk

Indirect Influence

1. *Teacher Accepts Feeling:* The teacher accepts and clarifies the feeling of a pupil in a nonthreatening manner. Feelings may be positive or negative. Predicting or recalling feelings is included.

2. *Teacher Praises or Encourages:* The teacher praises or encourages pupil action or behavior. Jokes that release tension, but not at the expense of another individual; nodding head, or saying "um hum?" or "go on" are included.

3. *Teacher Accepts or Uses Ideas of Pupils:* The teacher accepts, clarifies and/or incorporates into on-going activity the ideas suggested by a pupil; as the teacher brings more of his own ideas into play, category five (5) is recorded.

4. *Teacher Asks Recall Questions:* The teacher asks a question about who, where, when or what.

4_1. *Teacher Asks Probing Questions:* The teacher asks for further amplification or asks indirectly for further explanation. It would include questions asking to describe, explain or interpret (how and why).

Direct Influence

5. *Teacher Gives Information:* The teacher gives facts or opinions about content or procedures, lectures, expressions of his own ideas and the asking of rhetorical questions are included; also included are orienting, demonstrating and modeling behaviors.

6. *Teacher Gives Directions:* The teacher gives a direction, command or order with the intent that a pupil comply.

7. *Teacher Criticizes or Justifies Authority:* The teacher makes statements intended to change pupil behavior to what the teacher feels is a more acceptable pattern; criticizes pupil behavior, not necessarily negative criticism, states why he's doing what he's doing; engages in extreme self-reference.

Student Talk

8. *Pupil Response:* Talk by a pupil in response to the teacher; the teacher initiates the contact or solicits the pupil's statement.

8_1. *Pupil Reading:* Pupil reading (or singing) aloud if it is associated with a teacher assignment. If it is an original or "research" report he is reading, record a nine (9).

9. *Pupil Initiates Talk:* Talk by a pupil which indicates his own ideas, suggestions, opinions or criticisms that do not appear to be solicited by the teacher and/or changes the frame of reference established by the teacher, may include questions about procedures.

10. *Constructive Activity* without distinct observable verbal interaction.

11. *Disruptive Silence or Confusion:* Does not direct activity to an acceptable learning objective.

97

Figure 6.2 McRel Interaction Analysis Categories *(continued).*

12. Indicates different pupil talking following a first pupil speaker (to indicate an exchange between pupils).

There is NO scale implied by these numbers. Each number is classificatory, it designates a particular kind of communication event. To write these numbers down during observation is to enumerate, not to judge a position on a scale.

SOURCE: From Grant Clothier and Elizabeth Kingsley, *Enriching student teaching relationships* (Shawnee Mission, KS: Midwest Educational Training and Research Organization, 1973), p. 51. Reprinted with permission.

The McRel instrument includes several categories not found in the Flanders system. Clothier and Kingsley (1973) indicate that its development was an attempt to give increased attention to inquiry or problem-solving behaviors. This resulted in the division of the Flanders category *Asks Questions* into two categories: *Teacher Asks Recall Questions* (4) and *Teacher Asks Probing Questions* (4_1). The category *Pupil Reading* (8_1) was added to differentiate reading (or singing) aloud from talk by a pupil that is either in response to the teacher or initiated by the pupil to express his own ideas. The categories *Constructive Activity* (10) and *Disruptive Silence or Confusion* (11) are divisions of the Flanders category *Silence or Confusion.* Finally, a category (12) was added to denote pupils talking to each other.

Clothier and Kingsley point out that using the McRel instrument requires considerable practice to achieve reliability in recording behavior at three-second intervals, as recommended by Flanders. They suggest, as an alternative to this procedure, that the observer record only the number of times the teacher and pupil behaviors occur, instead of trying to identify these behaviors at specified time intervals.

The McRel instrument provides a useful tool for examining classroom verbal interaction. The cooperating teacher may want to record the interaction taking place while the student is teaching or may suggest that the student tape lessons and record the behaviors. Also, the student may record the teacher's interaction as he demonstrates certain verbal behaviors or patterns of behaviors. When data have been collected, both cooperating teacher and student can analyze them to determine the extent to which different teacher and pupil verbal behaviors facilitate or inhibit progress toward specific outcomes.

Communicating Nonverbally

Teachers are constantly involved in interpreting the nonverbal cues expressed by their pupils. They are aware of the potential consequences of failure to attend to this important dimension of classroom interaction. Are they equally aware of the effect that *their* nonverbal behavior has on pupils? Charles Galloway (1968), a leading researcher in the field of nonverbal communication, suggests that they are not.

In a psychological sense, teacher-pupil contacts are distinguished by spontaneity and immediate response. Therefore, nonverbal reactions are unwitting responses.

Not only are teachers quite likely to be unaware of their own behavior, but they can unwittingly reveal feelings to students that are not in their own best interests. Teachers must be on the alert to discover these possibilities after they occur, for the probability of preventing their occurrence is quite difficult. To increase an awareness of the psychological consequences of what is ordinarily out-of-awareness is a step in the right direction. Attitudinal displays and emotional reactions are not peculiar to classrooms, but the need to be open to the meaning of their appearance is greater than imagined. (p. 173)

In a recent address in which he focused on improving nonverbal communication, Galloway (1979) reported the results of research conducted for the purpose of determining how pupils respond to the nonverbal behaviors of their teachers.

> For the last four or five years I've been trying to devise instruments and measures to give to kids to find out what they see; their experiences in terms of the teacher and the classroom. We just finished a three-year study of high-school kids and found out what we have known for so long: the kids really do care whether the teacher smiles or not. They keep choosing smiling as an indication of how much the teacher enjoys the work, the students, etc. Secondly, they chose a sense of humor that comes through. The third important sign was encouragement from the teacher. This is more than just praise.
>
> All of this comes from nonverbal sources. Nonverbal signs and signals create contexts for contact. These are contexts of communicative exchange between teacher and student. Besides being able to smile, having a sense of humor, and encouraging kids, it is important to share yourself and to let yourself go. Kids know when you are going beyond your role, and they really appreciate it. (p. 21)

Teachers who want to improve their nonverbal communication can begin by analyzing their current nonverbal behaviors. Galloway has designed a seven-category system that is useful for recording and classifying teachers' nonverbal acts. Three of the categories are considered as encouraging communication and three as inhibiting communication. The category of pro forma is considered as neither encouraging nor inhibiting. When an observer using this system notes the occurrence of a particular behavior, he records the number representing that category of behavior in Galloway's (1962) system. The categories included in this system are presented here:

ENCOURAGING COMMUNICATION

1. *Enthusiastic Support.* A nonverbal expression implying enthusiastic support of a pupil's behavior, pupil interaction, or both. An expression that manifests enthusiastic approval, unusual warmth, or emotional support; being strongly pleased. An expression that exhibits strong encouragement to pupil. Examples of nonverbal determinants are as follows:
   a. *Facial expression.* Any expression that implies support or approval of some behavior or interaction occurring in the classroom. . . .
   b. *Action.* Any movement or action that portrays enthusiastic approval and active acceptance in an approving way, e.g., a pat on the back, or a warm greeting of praise. . . .
   c. *Vocal language.* Any voice quality indicating pleasure or warm acceptance. . . .

2. *Helping.* A responsive act that relates to modifications in the teacher's behavior which suggest a detection of expressed feelings, needs, urgencies, problems, etc., in the pupil. A communicative act that performs a function which helps a pupil or answers a need. An act that meets a pupil's request; a nurturant act. . . . intellectually supporting or problem-centered. Examples of nonverbal determinants:

   a. *Facial expression.* An expression that implies "I understand" or "I know what you mean," which is followed up by some kind of appropriate action. . . .

   b. *Action.* A movement or action that is intended to help or perform a function for the pupil. . . .

   c. *Vocal language.* A vocal utterance that is acceptant and understanding. . . .

3. *Receptivity.* A nonverbal expression that implies a willingness to listen with patience and interest to pupil talk. . . . Such a nonverbal expression implies to the pupil that "lines of communication are open."

   a. *Facial expression.* Maintains eye contact . . . indicates patience and attention . . . a readiness to listen or an attempt at trying to understand.

   b. *Action.* The teacher's demeanor suggests attentiveness by the way the total body is presented and movements used. . . .

   c. *Vocal language.* A vocal utterance or vocalization that augments pupil talk or that encourages the pupil to continue. . . .

4. *Pro Forma.* A communicative act that is a matter of form. Thus, the nature of the act, whether it is a facial expression, action, or vocal language, conveys little or no encouraging or inhibiting communicative significance in the contextual situation; a routine act. When the pupil is involved in a consummatory act, or when it is appropriate or unnecessary for the teacher to listen or respond, pro forma applies.

INHIBITING COMMUNICATION

5. *Inattentive.* A nonverbal expression that implies an unwillingness or inability to engage attentively in the communicative process, thus, indicating disinterest or impatience with pupil talk. . . .

   a. *Facial expression.* Avoids eye contact to the point of not maintaining attention; exhibits apparent disinterest or impatience with pupil by showing an unwillingness to listen.

   b. *Action.* An expressional pose of movement that indicates disinterest, boredom, or inattention. A demeanor suggesting slouchy or unalert posture. . . .

   c. *Vocal language.* A vocal utterance that indicates impatience, or "I want you to stop talking."

6. *Unresponsiveness.* A communicative act that openly ignores a pupil's need, or that is insensitive to pupil's feeling; tangential response. . . .

   a. *Facial expression.* . . . an expression that threatens or cajoles pupils; a condescending expression; an unsympathetic expression; or an impatient expression.

   b. *Action.* Any action that is unresponsive to or withdrawing from a request or expressed need on the part of the pupil. . . .

   c. *Vocal language.* A vocalization that interferes with or interrupts ongoing process of communication between pupils, or from pupil to teacher. . . .

7. *Disapproval.* . . . An expression that indicates strong negative overtones, disparagement, or strong dissatisfaction.

a. *Facial expression.* The expression may be one of frowning, scowling, threatening glances. Derisive, sarcastic, or disdainful expression may occur. . . .
b. *Action.* Any action that indicates physical attack or aggressiveness, e.g., a blow, slap, or pinch. Any act that censures or reprimands a pupil. A pointed finger that pokes fun, belittles, or threatens pupils.
c. *Vocal language.* Any vocal tone that is hostile, cross, irritated, or antagonistic to the pupil.[2]

Teacher education students participating in clinical experiences focus on the verbal dimension of their interaction with children. They are concerned with their ability to explain new material, ask questions, and provide directions in ways that prevent confusion and the occurrence of management problems. As a result, they are perhaps even less likely than experienced teachers to be aware of what they are communicating nonverbally. Cooperating teachers can help students develop an awareness of the effect of their nonverbal behavior through the use of Galloway's system of categories. If videotaping equipment is available, cooperating teacher and student can view a segment of the student's teaching and record the student's nonverbal behavior. Following this, they can analyze the behavior and plan strategies for increasing or reducing particular behaviors that seem to encourage or inhibit communication. If videotaping equipment is not available, the student and the cooperating teacher can arrange a time during which the cooperating teacher can observe and record the student's nonverbal behavior. The cooperating teacher, in turn, may want to ask the student to observe and record his nonverbal behavior for a period of time in order to check the accuracy of his perception of his own nonverbal communication.

Reinforcing Pupil Behavior

Belkin and Gray (1977) define *reinforcement* as follows: "An effect on a person that increases the probability of a response reoccurring. The effect results from a reinforcer" (p. 650). The authors suggest that *positive reinforcement* (providing a reward for positive behavior) is perhaps the most widely used behavioral technique in school settings. Certainly classroom teachers have always engaged in reinforcing some behaviors and not others—consistently or inconsistently, consciously or unconsciously. In recent years, however, a great deal of attention has been paid to the development of systematic techniques for providing reinforcement in connection with behavior modification programs. Because of the current interest, this section examines the general procedure for establishing a behavior modification program.

Belkin and Gray identify the following sequence of steps in establishing a behavior modification program:

[2]Charles M. Galloway. *An exploratory study of observational procedures for determining teacher nonverbal communication.* Unpublished doctoral dissertation, University of Florida, 1962, pp. 65, 67–68, 146–49. Reprinted with permission.

1. *Establishing baseline data.* The teacher records on index cards the kinds and frequency of positive and negative behaviors exhibited by children in his classroom. After doing this for two to three weeks, the teacher has a thorough inventory of behaviors, both those to be strengthened and those to be weakened.
2. *Selecting reinforcers.* Once baseline data have been established, the teacher must decide what reinforcers to use. Gray and Belkin point out that while reinforcers are often thought of in terms of tokens or other tangible rewards, research has demonstrated that attention, praise, and peer approval can be used equally well. The teacher will need to assess his resources, and use his knowledge of individual pupils, to determine the most effective reinforcers.
3. *Implementing the program.* In the first part of program implementation, the teacher establishes with the pupils a verbal or written contract that states the roles, contingencies, and consequences of a variety of behaviors. Gray and Belkin emphasize that the contract should identify specific behaviors that will be rewarded and punished and the rewards and punishments that will be consequent to each behavior. Once the contract has been established, the program can be implemented by carrying out the terms of the contract.
4. *Evaluating the program.* While the program is being implemented, the teacher will want to assess which aspects of the program are working well and which are not. By continuing to tally appropriate and inappropriate behaviors on the original index cards, he can determine the extent to which specific parts of the program are effective. After several weeks of recording, the teacher may decide to develop a new contract if he sees that there are new positive behaviors to be strengthened or new negative behaviors to be weakened.

Whether or not the cooperating teacher is using specific behavior modification techniques in his classroom, he will want to help the student analyze the ways in which she is reinforcing pupil behaviors and the behaviors she reinforces most often. The cooperating teacher will also want to make the student aware of any reinforcement techniques he has been using with the pupils. On the basis of these discussions, cooperating teacher and student can plan a reinforcement program in which they are consistent with each other in their efforts to strengthen the positive behaviors and weaken the negative behaviors exhibited in their classroom.

A STRATEGY FOR PROVIDING GUIDANCE IN PLANNING

An examination of the components of Spanjer's teaching functions framework reminds us of the wide range of decisions teachers make as they engage in planning. What seating arrangement will be most appropriate for a particular activity? Which questions will be effective in stimulating discussion of a given topic? How can a new skill be introduced so that learners see its relationship to previously learned skills? Once the many planning decisions have been made and implemented, their effectiveness must be assessed. This assessment provides the basis for further decision making as the planning process continues.

Teacher education students typically have opportunities to become involved in planning as they progress through their professional education program. There can be considerable variation among opportunities for planning, however. In some programs, students develop plans as a part of course requirements but never actually teach the lessons planned. In other instances, students write plans and implement them in peer teaching situations. In still other programs, in which a range of clinical experiences is provided, students plan lessons that they then carry out with groups of children in one or more classroom settings prior to their final student teaching or internship. Because of this variation in planning opportunities, the cooperating teacher will want to determine the nature of the student's involvement with planning prior to her work in his classroom. This knowledge will enable the cooperating teacher to plan the guidance he will need to provide to help the student develop competence in planning systematically and effectively.

Dimensions of the Planning Process

Teachers approach specific aspects of planning in a variety of ways. With regard to the overall process, however, teachers make decisions regarding (1) objectives, (2) instructional strategies, and (3) means of assessment. Since cooperating teachers have the responsibility of providing guidance for students in these dimensions of planning, we will examine them briefly before turning to the more detailed aspects of involving students in the planning process.

Identifying Objectives.   While the preservice student no doubt will have encountered discussions of educational objectives prior to her clinical experience, these discussions may have dealt with objectives in rather broad terms. As a result, she may be unaware of the importance of stating objectives in terms of pupil behavior or performance.

In his text on preparing instructional objectives, Robert Mager (1975) emphasizes the importance of defining objectives in behavioral terms in order to have a sound basis for (1) designing instructional strategies, (2) evaluating the success of the instruction, and (3) organizing the pupils' own efforts. The cooperating teacher may need to help the student become aware of these reasons for stating objectives behaviorally, perhaps through discussions of his own objectives at first, and then in discussions of objectives for the plans that she will develop.

Teacher education students typically learn very quickly to write precise objectives that express *cognitive* outcomes. For example, students have little or no problem learning to write objectives such as the following:

Area	Objective
Reading	Given a list of 20 words, the learner will be able to circle the consonant blend in each word.

Area	Objective
Mathematics	Given 20 long-division problems, the learner will be able to correctly compute and write the solutions for 18 problems.

However, when faced with the task of writing objectives in *affective* areas, such as intergroup relations or self-concept development, students frequently fall back on such phrases as "to become aware of" or "to appreciate." If this situation occurs, the cooperating teacher will want to help the student think through the activity she is planning, identify what she views as the important outcomes of the activity, and define the pupil behaviors that will indicate that the outcomes have been achieved. The following are examples of behaviorally stated objectives in two affective areas:

Area	Objective
Intergroup relations	The pupils will say how they feel about Black people.[3]
Self-concept development	The pupils will voluntarily describe themselves in positive ways.

Each subsequent aspect of the planning process depends on the objectives developed at the outset of the process. For this reason, it is essential that objectives be stated in clear, precise terms. By giving the student specific guidance in learning to identify precise objectives, the cooperating teacher will provide her with the foundation on which to develop the additional planning skills she needs.

Designing Instructional Strategies. Once clearly defined objectives have been identified, decisions regarding appropriate instructional strategies can be made. Morine (1973) makes two points in exploring the concept of *variety of instruction* that can serve as a useful starting point for helping the preservice student develop skill in making decisions regarding instructional strategies. Morine first states that there is evidence that "*variation* of instructional activities is more effective than constant *repetition* of instructional activities" (p. 135). She supports this statement by citing studies that demonstrate that variety of instruction contributes to several factors: (1) increased pupil interest and attention, (2) increased task-directed behavior, and (3) higher achievement and more positive pupil attitudes. Morine's second point is that planning for variety of instruction is essential because interactive events are characterized by a quality of unpredictability.

[3]Before they can begin to try to solve problems, children need opportunities to get their feelings out in the open. The small-group affective discussion is an activity that encourages children to put their feelings into words, compare emotional experiences, and learn to see their peers as more than just reciters of facts.

The objective identified here is appropriate for a group made up of white children only. If the affective discussion is conducted in a region where the intergroup problems occur between Indian and white children, or between Mexican and Anglo children, or between Japanese-American and whites, then the discussion will reflect concern with the groups involved.

No lesson ever proceeds exactly as the teacher planned it. The more pupil partici-pation is encouraged, the more this unpredictable quality increases. The teacher who has considered a number of alternative routes before the lesson begins has more instructional moves available at his fingertips when unpredicted events sud-denly occur. (p. 135)

Morine's two points make clear the importance of focusing the attention of teacher education students on planning for variety of instruction, both as a means of capitalizing on the factors related to variation in instructional ac-tivities and as a way of helping them develop the ability to respond successfully to the unpredictability of teaching.

One way in which the cooperating teacher can help the student think about alternative instructional strategies is to have her observe the variety of instructional activities he employs. Perhaps he will suggest that she select several areas of the curriculum and record, over a period of time, the range of activities he provides in each area. As he discusses with the student, in sub-sequent conferences, the reasons for selecting particular strategies, she will begin to develop insight into the relationship between variety of instruction and the factors cited by Morine.

Morine identifies a second way in which teacher education students can develop skill in planning for variety of instruction. She suggests that students engage in the process of developing more than one plan for a given situation. While it does not seem feasible for students to develop more than one *written* plan in the context of a field experience, it is possible for them to think through alternative teaching strategies before deciding which one will be the basis for the final written plan.

Initially, the cooperating teacher probably will want to discuss alternative strategies in planning conferences. As the student gains experience in generat-ing alternatives, she can continue this process independently. In both stages, the student may find it helpful to use the components of Spanjer's teaching functions framework as a basis for developing alternative strategies. The com-ponents of the framework suggest questions to which the student can respond as she engages in the planning process:

> What seating arrangement could be used for this activity?
> Which kinds of questions would be appropriate?
> In what ways can the questions be sequenced?
> In what ways can pupil responses be elicited?
> How can positive pupil behaviors be reinforced?

As she responds to these questions, the student will become involved in generating alternative strategies and in identifying the factors that need to be considered as a basis for selecting among them.

Evaluating the Outcomes of Instruction. Selecting the means of evaluating pupil learning is the final dimension of the planning process in which the student will need guidance. There are several aspects of evaluation that the cooperating teacher will want to emphasize in helping the student develop skill in assessing pupil learning. First, the student needs to have a clear understanding of the relationship between evaluation and objectives. Objectives state the desired learning outcomes. The assessment of learning, then, must enable pupils to engage in the behaviors identified in the objectives. For example, if an objective calls for pupils to select the most appropriate title for a story, given three possible titles, the assessment of their progress toward this objective must provide them with the opportunity to exhibit this behavior; it cannot call for a different behavior, such as writing a title for the story in their own words. The use of materials that include criterion-referenced measurement will, of course, ensure this correspondence between objectives and evaluation. However, even if the student will have the opportunity to use some of this material in the classroom, it is unlikely that such material will be available in every area in which she will teach. For this reason, it is important that she develop an understanding of the need for relating evaluation to objectives in her planning.

A second point on which the cooperating teacher will want to focus is that effective evaluation involves the continuous collection of a variety of data using a range of techniques. If the student's previous experience in planning is limited, she may be at the stage of equating evaluating with administering a paper-and-pencil test at the conclusion of a lesson or unit. If this is the case, the teacher will want to provide her with opportunities to learn about the many evaluative techniques that can be used to collect information concerning pupil progress. She will then need guidance in learning to select the appropriate techniques for given situations. Developing an understanding of the following sources of evaluative data will provide the student with a basis for planning for effective evaluation:

- teacher-made tests
- daily written work
- observation
- individual conferences
- anecdotal records
- criterion-referenced tests
- standardized achievement tests

Lastly, the cooperating teacher will want to guide the student in deciding how she will analyze the evaluative data she collects. It is important that this analysis be carried out in such a way that the results provide clear direction for the next steps in the instructional sequence. For example, if the student merely counts the number of correct and incorrect solutions achieved by a group of pupils in solving a set of problems in long division, she will learn only that some pupils are having more difficulty than others. It would be much more useful to determine at what point in the sequence of problem solving those pupils who are experiencing difficulty seem to lack the skill or understanding they need to continue the sequence successfully. With this information, the student can plan much more precisely for further instruction. As the cooperating teacher guides the student in making precise analyses of evaluation data, he will help her develop an understanding of the significance of evaluation in the overall planning process.

Cooperative Planning of Daily Lessons

Teacher education students frequently have concerns about planning as they enter a clinical experience. In Thompson's (1963) study of the anxieties of student teachers, for example, the following concerns were identified as those the students had experienced both prior to and during their internship: Will I be required to turn in my lesson plans, and who will evaluate them? Can I deviate from the plan of work as outlined? What should I do if my material has been covered and there is extra time? Will the critic teacher allow me to use my own initiative? Do I really know my subject matter? In addition, students frequently express anxiety about possible conflict between cooperating teacher and college supervisor regarding expectations for the planning format to be used, the amount of detail to be included, and the criteria that will be used to evaluate their plans. In order to reduce the student's level of anxiety, it is essential that the cooperating teacher schedule a conference to discuss planning as soon as possible after the student arrives.

Several outcomes should be achieved during this initial conference on planning. In order to establish a basis for guiding the student, the cooperating teacher will first want to discuss the student's previous experiences in planning. As the student provides this information, the cooperating teacher can decide how to begin working with her in this area.

Second, it is important that the cooperating teacher help the student develop an understanding of what the pupils are currently learning in the various curricular areas. In addition, he will want to share his overall long-range plans. This information will give the student the background she needs to begin her work in the classroom. It will also enable her to identify areas in which she feels she would like to participate initially.

A third outcome of this conference should be the clarification of the cooperating teacher's expectations regarding planning. The student will want to know whether there is a format the cooperating teacher prefers, and how much detail she should include. As one way of clarifying these expectations, the cooperating teacher can bring to the conference a plan that he has developed illustrating a format he finds workable and that includes the amount and kind of detail he feels the student should include in her plans initially. Providing the student with this sample plan will (1) give her a useful framework for planning, (2) reduce her anxiety, and (3) prevent the occurrence of problems that can result from a lack of understanding of the cooperating teacher's expectations.

Following this first planning conference, the student can begin to develop her initial plans. The cooperating teacher can facilitate this process, and contribute to the student's sense of security, by developing these plans with the student. A sequence for implementing cooperative planning is identified here. In addition to engaging in this process at the outset of the student's experience, the cooperating teacher may find it useful to follow this procedure in guiding the student's initial planning in each new area for which she assumes responsibility.

1. Cooperating teacher and student select the area in which the student will plan her initial lessons (e.g., reading, social studies).

Figure 6.3 Cooperative Planning of Daily Lessons

1. Area: Reading Readiness

2. Cooperating Teacher Input
   Activity
   - prepare a lesson for the "Tigers" group that provides practice in determining sequence.

   Information about Children
   - The Tigers are midway through the readiness program. They have completed exercises that required them to discriminate among various shapes, objects, and letters and have completed a large number of listening activities. Also, they have begun to develop quite a vocabulary! Recently, I introduced the concept of sequence; however, they need additional practice.
   - *Kay* is very shy and needs to be encouraged to participate in the lesson. She is very interested in reading and completes all exercises quickly and accurately.
   - *Bert* seems to be having some trouble with sequence. He works very well with the group and has had few problems with preceding exercises.
   - *Karen* is having a great deal of trouble keeping up with the group. We may want to move her to another group. Let me know what you think after the lesson. She enjoys listening to stories and creating her own.
   - *Hal* understands and completes the lessons with little trouble; however, he enjoys telling stories and will monopolize lesson time if you are not careful.

   Suggestions
   - All of the children enjoy the comic books on the shelves. You might want to utilize them in your lesson.
   - This group has not completed all the pages from their workbook dealing with sequence.
   - Keep them busy! They love it!

3. Student Input
   Behavioral Objective
   - The children will be able to place a series of pictures in logical sequence.

   Procedure
   - *Introduction*—I think I will use comic strips and introduce the lesson by talking about comics. I will ask how many like comics and which are their favorites.
   - *Development*—I will give each child a comic strip that has been cut into four panels. After putting the panels in the correct sequence, he will paste them onto a piece of oaktag. Each child will then tell the story that his pictures illustrate.
     - How is this group at pasting?
     - I think this lesson will last 30 minutes. Is that too long? How will that length of time fit into your schedule?
     - Will I meet with the group in the classroom or move to another room?
     - Will I have access to a blackboard, feltboard, etc.?
     - Is there an opaque projector in the school? I might want to enlarge some of the smaller comics.
     - Would it be a good idea to reinforce the lesson by completing some pages from their workbooks? I will need the numbers of the pages they have completed.
   - *Conclusion*—Will I continue to meet with this group? I would like the children to make up their own comic strips, cut them up, exchange them, and put them in the correct order. If I am going to meet with this group again, I can ask them to draw some at home and bring them in to exchange.
   - *Evaluation*—If the children are able to put the pictures in a logical sequence, they will have met the objective.

108

4. Final Plan

I. Behavioral Objectives
  A. The children will be able to place a series of pictures in a logical sequence.
  B. The children will be able to complete correctly pages 25 and 26 of their workbook.
II. Procedure
  A. Introduction
    1. How many of you have read some of the comic books on the shelves?
    2. Has anyone ever read the comics in the newspaper to you?
    3. What are some of your favorite comics?
    4. Today we are going to make some comics of our own.
  B. Development
    1. Place a three-panel comic strip on the feltboard in the wrong order. Do these three pictures tell a funny story? What is wrong with them? How would you change them? Have a student come to the board and rearrange the panels. Is this better? Review each panel to make sure that the students understand what happened first, second, and last.
    2. Give each child a package of four panels and a piece of oaktag. Look at the four pictures in front of you, and decide which picture shows what happened first, second, third, and last.
    3. When you have the pictures in order, paste them on your piece of oaktag.
    4. Have each child then tell a story that explains his sequence of pictures.
  C. Conclusion
    1. Let's look at page 25 in our workbook. What is wrong with the four pictures at the top of the page? (They are in the wrong order.) Which picture should be first? Put a 1 under that picture. Continue until the pictures are in the correct order. Ask one of the children to tell the story that the pictures show.
    2. Have the children follow the same procedure for the three remaining stories on pages 25 and 26.
    3. Tonight you might want to draw a comic strip yourself. Cut it into pieces and tomorrow we will see if we can put your comic strip in the right order.
III. Evaluation
  A. If the children are able to present the stories in a logical sequence, the objective will be met.
  B. If the children correctly complete workbook pages 25 and 26, the objective will be met.

2. The cooperating teacher provides information and suggestions that the student can use as a basis for developing her first plan.
3. Using the cooperating teacher's input, the student prepares an outline of the plan that includes her ideas and any questions that she has.
4. Cooperating teacher and student schedule a conference to discuss the student's ideas and questions. They then develop the final plan together.

Figure 6.3 illustrates the cooperative planning process implemented by one cooperating teacher and student. Several points about the cooperating teacher's input seem particularly important:

- The cooperating teacher suggests that the student begin her teaching by providing practice in a skill already introduced, rather than attempt to introduce a new skill or concept.
- The information about the children not only identifies the skill level of the group but also acquaints the student with individual differences.
- As the cooperating teacher continues to give the student information about one group of children at a time, he provides the student with a gradual introduction to the total class.

Activity 7   In preparation for role-playing the cooperative planning process, select an area you feel would be appropriate for a student's initial teaching efforts in your classroom. Then, on Analysis Guide 7, under the heading *Cooperating Teacher Input*, identify the information the student would need to develop a plan for a lesson in this area. When you have completed this section of the analysis guide, continue with the next steps in the cooperative planning process by working with another group member who is participating in this activity:

1. Exchange analysis guides. Assume the role of the student and develop an outline for a lesson plan, under the heading *Student Input*, based on the information provided on your partner's analysis guide.
2. When the plans have been outlined, discuss cooperating teacher and student input for each plan, assuming the appropriate roles, and provide whatever additional information is needed. Following these discussions, develop a final plan for each lesson.
3. Provide feedback for each other regarding your perceptions of the usefulness of the cooperating teacher's input as you role-played the student and attempted to outline a plan.
4. Provide feedback for each other regarding your perceptions of the effectiveness of the cooperating teacher both in providing guidance for you as the student and in encouraging you to try your own ideas.

Cooperative Weekly Planning

Since the cooperating teacher will be involving the student in the classroom program from the outset, it is important that cooperating teacher and student begin cooperative weekly planning at the earliest time possible. If a preassignment conference is held, part of the conference can be used to plan for the student's first week. If no preassignment conference is scheduled, the cooperating teacher will need to plan the student's first week himself. Soon after the student arrives, he can share his planning with her and make revisions where they seem appropriate.

There are several important outcomes of cooperative weekly planning. First, it provides for continuity in the instructional program by ensuring the

Analysis Guide 7   Cooperative Planning of Daily Lessons

1. Area:

2. Cooperating Teacher Input	3. Student Input

4. Final Plan

coordination of responsibilities. This coordination is particularly necessary, though often not as easily achieved, if (1) the student is working in the classroom on a part-time basis or (2) additional personnel (aide, parent, volunteer, tutor) assume responsibility for aspects of the program. Of course, the cooperating teacher will want to include auxiliary personnel in sessions held for the purpose of overall planning to the extent that this is feasible.

A second outcome of weekly planning is that it gives the student the lead time she needs to plan thoroughly. In the initial stage of the experience particularly, the student will want to spend a considerable amount of time studying curriculum guides and instructional materials, acquainting herself with the school library and other resource centers, and acquiring information about pupils as she prepares for specific involvement in the instructional program.

Third, cooperative weekly planning provides a means of assuring the inclusion, on a regular basis, of specific times for conferences. These conferences, requiring varying amounts of time, will be needed for discussing the student's plans, providing feedback concerning her teaching, and sharing evaluations of pupil progress. While both cooperating teachers and students recognize the importance of holding conferences, it is frequently difficult to find the necessary time unless the conferences are scheduled in advance.

The sample plan for a student's first week (see Figure 6.4) was developed by one cooperating teacher prior to his student's arrival and was shared with the student on her first day in the classroom. The schedule provides for an effective introduction of the student to the classroom through attention to several points previously discussed:

- The student is involved in the classroom program beginning with her first day.
- The coordination of the responsibilities of cooperating teacher, student, and reading aide is clearly identified.
- The student becomes acquainted with pupils gradually through her work with individuals and with small groups.
- Specific conference periods are identified in advance.

Activity 8 Using Analysis Guide 8, plan a schedule for a student's first week in your classroom. Then exchange the completed schedule with another group member who has completed Analysis Guide 8. Provide feedback for each other by considering the following elements of each schedule:

1. The appropriateness of the kinds of responsibilities to be assumed by the student.
2. The clarity of the coordination of teaching responsibilities.
3. The adequacy of the number of planned conference periods.

Providing Feedback in the Planning Process

Several factors underscore the need to give the student feedback regarding planning. First, as the cooperating teacher raises questions and offers suggestions, he is helping to ensure that the student's teaching experiences will be successful. This is critical in the initial stage of independent planning, a period during which the student's anxiety level can be quite high. If she encounters success in her initial teaching efforts, the student will be encouraged to approach increased responsibility with confidence. Feedback is necessary also because discussion of the student's plans serves as the basis for the cooperating teacher's observation and analysis of the student's teaching. These dimensions of the cooperating teacher's role are discussed in Chapter 7. Finally, reviewing the student's plans with her helps ensure that the pupils derive the maximum benefit from their experiences with the student and that the continuity of their learning is maintained.

In providing feedback concerning the student's plans, the cooperating teacher must communicate clearly the basis for the comments he makes and the questions he raises. The use of Spanjer's framework of teaching functions, discussed in the first section of this chapter, in reviewing the student's plans is one approach to establishing a clear basis for the cooperating teacher's feedback. In subsequent discussions with the student, as the cooperating teacher relates specific aspects of the student's plans to one or more dimensions of the

Analysis Guide 8 Planning the Student's First Week

Time Schedule	Monday	Tuesday	Wednesday	Thursday	Friday

Figure 6.4 Plan for a Student's First Week

Time Schedule	Monday	Tuesday	Wednesday	Thursday	Friday
9:00-9:15	Opening Activities —CT* introduces S*	Opening Activities —CT facilitates —S observes	Opening Activities —S facilitates —CT observes	Opening Activities —S facilitates —CT observes	Opening Activities —S facilitates —CT observes
9:15-10:00	Math —The two groups alternate between working with the CT and working at the math learning center with the S.	Social Studies —Students are out of the classroom. CT and S Conference: —Pre-observation conference for Wednesday's lesson	Math —Same as Monday's Schedule	Physical Education —Students are out of the classroom. S accompanies the students to the gym.	Math —Same as Monday's Schedule
10:00-10:15	Recess —CT facilitates —S observes	Recess —CT facilitates —S observes	Recess —S facilitates —CT, RA*, S Planning Conference	Recess —S facilitates —CT observes	Recess —S facilitates —CT observes
10:15-12:00	Reading —The three groups alternate working with the CT, at the learning center with the RA, and on their own. The S observes the CT's lessons.	Reading —Same as Monday's Schedule	Reading —The S assumes responsibility for planning for one group.	Reading —Same as Wednesday's Schedule	Reading —Same as Wednesday's Schedule
12:00-1:00	Lunch —CT facilitates —S observes	Lunch —CT facilitates —S observes	Lunch —S facilitates —CT observes	Lunch —S facilitates —CT observes	Lunch —S facilitates —CT observes

Time	Monday	Tuesday	Wednesday	Thursday	Friday
1:10-1:30	Spelling —S administers pre-test	Spelling —CT facilitates	Spelling —Same as Tuesday's Schedule	Spelling —Same as Tuesday's Schedule	Spelling —S administers post-test
1:30-2:15	Music —Students are out of the classroom. CT and S Conference: —Planning Conference	Math —Same as Monday's Schedule	Science —Students are out of the classroom. CT and S Conference: —Planning	Math —The S assumes responsibility for planning for one group.	Art —Students are out of the classroom. CT and S Conference: —Planning for Week II
2:15-2:50	Language Arts —CT facilitates —S observes	Language Arts —CT facilitates —S observes	Language Arts —S teaches creative writing lesson —CT observes	Language Arts —S continues creative writing lesson —CT observes	Language Arts —S teaches handwriting lesson & reads a story —CT observes
2:50-3:00	Dismissal —CT facilitates —S observes	Dismissal —S facilitates —CT observes	Dismissal —S facilitates —CT observes	Dismissal —S facilitates —CT observes	Dismissal —S facilitates —CT observes
3:00-3:15	CT and S Conference: —Planning conference		CT and S Conference: —Post-observation conference	CT and S Conference: —Post-observation conference	CT and S Conference: —Post-observation conference

*CT = Cooperating Teacher
S = Student
RA = Reading Aide

framework, the student will become aware of the reasons that underlie the teacher's comments and questions. This will help the student view the feedback as positive and supportive rather than as negative and critical.

Another responsibility of the cooperating teacher in providing feedback is to encourage the student to develop and implement her own ideas, rather than rely entirely on the cooperating teacher's techniques. The attitude toward trying new ideas expressed by the cooperating teacher will directly affect the student's perception of the value of experimentation. If the cooperating teacher responds positively to the student's ideas, and experiments in his own teaching, he will communicate his belief in the importance of continually searching for more effective teaching strategies.

Typically, teacher education students are eager to try out new ideas and respond with enthusiasm to the opportunity to become part of a classroom in which creativity and initiative are valued. Occasionally, however, the cooperating teacher may encounter a student who seems overly dependent on his guidance. The student who is reluctant to move toward increasing independence in developing new ideas will need to be actively encouraged to locate resources that can serve as a basis for expanding her repertoire of teaching strategies. Overreliance on the cooperating teacher as a source of alternative approaches will severely limit her ability to function in the future.

The cooperating teacher also needs to think through the procedure that will be followed in providing feedback. One area of concern here is how far in advance of her teaching the student will give the teacher her plans to review. The amount of time needed for this step in the feedback process will vary, of course, with the planning involved. For example, the cooperating teacher will need more lead time for considering unit or other long-range plans than he will for plans involving relatively brief activities. The feedback process also must provide time to permit the student to revise her plans when this is indicated. If the student receives feedback only minutes before she is to begin teaching, she will find it highly anxiety-producing to attempt to make suggested changes.

A second consideration in providing feedback is the form in which it will be given. Both the length and complexity of the plans, and the extent of the student's experience, can provide a basis for deciding whether feedback should be given orally or in writing. In the initial stage of developing daily plans, the student will probably find it useful to receive feedback in writing. She can then refer to the cooperating teacher's comments and suggestions in planning subsequent lessons. As the student gains experience and skill in planning, much of the feedback concerning her daily plans probably can be given orally during conferences. When the student is involved in more complex planning, such as that required for the development of units or learning centers, she will, of course, need written feedback. Attempting to remember oral feedback for the purpose of revising such plans would prove a difficult task.

The cooperating teacher's written feedback can be presented to the student in a variety of ways. The format shown in Figure 6.5 is one approach to recording the cooperating teacher's responses to a student's plan. After the cooperating teacher has provided feedback, the plan can be revised by the cooperating teacher and student during a conference or returned to the student for independent revision.

Figure 6.5   Providing Feedback in the Planning Process

Lesson: Phonic Analysis

Student's Plan	*Cooperating Teacher's Feedback*

I. Behavioral Objectives
  A. The children should be able to state the following generalization: When the letter *c* is followed by *o* or *a*, the sound of *k* is likely to be heard.

  B. The children should be able to use this generalization to pronounce unfamiliar words to which it applies.

Very good behavioral objectives. It is important that the children be able to apply the rule to new words.

II. Procedure
  A. Introduction
     Today we are going to learn a rule that will help you read new words. However, I am not going to tell you the rule. You must find out what this rule is yourselves.

Good idea! You will increase their involvement by having them discover the rule. Have you used the inductive approach in areas other than phonic analysis?

  B. Development
     1. Put these words on the board.

        came   come
        call   corn
        can   cold

How will you arrange the group for this lesson? You will want everyone to be able to see the board.

     2. Let's say these words together. With what consonant does each word begin? *(c)* What sound does the consonant have? *(k)* Do all these words begin with the *k* sound?

     3. What letter comes after the *c* in each word in the first column? *(a)* What letter comes after the *c* in each word in the second column? *(o)*

Would it be a good idea to underline the second letter in each word when you come to it? This will focus their attention on those vowels.
The nature of the questions is critical in using the inductive approach. Let's talk about questions that could be added to help them see the relationship between steps 3 and 4 more clearly. Can you reword the second question in step 5 so that it will encourage each of them to say the rule?

     4. What consonant sound will we hear if the letter *c* is followed by the letter *a* or *o*? *(k)*

     5. Who can say this in a sentence? Would anyone else like to say our rule?

     6. Let's look at the sentences on the board. Will our new rule help us say the underlined words?
        a. Blue is the *color* of the sky.
        b. Eric *caught* a *cod* fish.
        c. The horse pulled the *cart*.

This group is familiar with the word *color*. You might use the word *cot* instead.
How long do you think this lesson will last?

117

Figure 6.5   Providing Feedback in the Planning Process *(continued)*.

Lesson: Phonic Analysis

Student's Plan	*Cooperating Teacher's Feedback*
7. Discuss the meanings of the new words.	Don't feel that you have to rush them. It is important that each one understand the generalization, and our schedule is flexible.
C. Conclusion Today you have taught yourselves a rule that will help you to read some words that are new to you. Can you think of other words that fit our rule?	As a follow-up activity, the group could go through their word cards and pick out the words to which the rule applies.
III. Evaluation If the children can state the rule and pronounce the new words, they will have met the objectives.	I think the children will achieve the objectives and enjoy the lesson. I have never used the inductive approach in teaching phonics, but I look forward to trying it in the future.

Activity 9   A sample plan for a lesson designed to teach outlining skills is shown in Analysis Guide 9. Assume that the plan was developed by a student who has recently begun her student teaching experience and has had no pre-student teaching field experiences. Analyze the plan, using Spanjer's framework of teaching functions, and on the analysis guide, record the feedback you would provide for this student. When you have completed your evaluation of the plan, exchange analysis guides with another group member who is participating in this activity. Provide feedback for each other by responding to the following questions:

1. Are the reasons for the comments and suggestions clearly identified?
2. Do the comments reflect a positive attitude toward the student's efforts in developing the plan?
3. Does the feedback communicate a flexible approach to teaching?

THE ROLE OF THE COLLEGE SUPERVISOR IN THE PLANNING PROCESS

The quality of the student's planning directly affects the nature of the learning achieved by the pupils with whom she interacts. Since providing for maximum learning is the cooperating teacher's primary responsibility, it is the cooperating teacher who assumes the major role, on a daily basis, in guiding the student's development in planning. While the college supervisor cannot provide daily help in planning, there are significant ways in which she can provide support, both for the student and for the cooperating teacher.

An important responsibility of the college supervisor is to ensure that the student is not faced with conflicting expectations concerning planning. By clarifying expectations in a preassignment conference or at the beginning of the assignment, the college supervisor and the cooperating teacher can reach

Lesson: Outlining

Student's Plan	*Cooperating Teacher's Feedback*

I. Behavioral Objectives
  A. The learners will be able to arrange the parts of a story in correct outline form.
  B. Given the major headings of a selection, the learners will be able to complete the outline.

II. Procedure
  A. Introduction
     Very often when we are reading, we want to remember important information. Today we are going to select the important ideas from a passage and place them in correct order so that we will not forget them.
  B. Development
     1. Everyone should silently read the story I just gave out.
     2. Now open your envelope, and you will find the important parts of the story on strips of paper. Select the three strips that tell the most important ideas in the story. Find the two strips that fit under each of the main ideas.
     3. Once the learners have correctly formed the outline, put the outline on the board. Point out the differences between the major headings and the subheadings. Refer the learners to the story to check the accuracy of the outline.
     4. Hand out another short passage and ask the learners to read it. Put the major points of the story on the board in outline form. Ask the group to supply the subheadings.
  C. Conclusion
     We have talked about using an outline as a good way to remember important parts of a story. What other

Lesson: Outlining

Student's Plan	Cooperating Teacher's Feedback
ways can we use an outline? (studying, writing a paper, preparing a speech, etc.) III. Evaluation If the learners are able to arrange the outline in correct order and complete the outline of a second passage, they have achieved the objectives.	

agreement about the planning format that will be used, the amount of detail to be included for particular plans, and any additional aspects of planning for which either of them has expectations. For example, if the college supervisor is going to ask the student to submit plans at regular intervals or write unit plans in particular curricular areas, these expectations should be made clear to the cooperating teacher and the student.

The college supervisor also must provide guidance in planning whenever that help is requested by student or cooperating teacher. When one or more students in the same school seem to need help with a specific dimension of planning, such as writing behavioral objectives, the college supervisor can supplement the efforts of cooperating teachers in helping students acquire the necessary competency through individual conferences or in group seminars.

A third way in which the college supervisor can contribute to the overall planning process is by helping the student locate background information, materials, and other resources. The experienced college supervisor will be acquainted with a variety of sources of curriculum guides, audiovisuals, kits, and other teacher aids to which she can direct the student. This extends the student's resources beyond the school in which she is teaching and provides her with increased opportunities to plan creative experiences for children.

A STRATEGY FOR PROVIDING GUIDANCE IN ASSUMING TEACHING RESPONSIBILITY

Closely related to the cooperating teacher's responsibility for guiding the student's development of skill in planning is his role in providing an appropriate sequence of experiences through which the student can assume increasing responsibility within the classroom and the school. A central concern of cooperating teachers is the pace at which students should move through this sequence. "Am I asking my student to assume responsibility too rapidly or not rapidly enough?" is a question that is frequently raised.

The overall objective of the particular clinical experience in which the student is involved will provide one guide for the cooperating teacher in determining the nature and sequence of the student's induction into the teaching role. For example, if the student is engaged in a pre-student teaching experience that involves being in a classroom one morning a week, her responsibility probably will be limited to working with a small group of children in one or two curricular areas. However, if the student has completed her sequence of professional courses and is involved in a full-time student teaching or internship experience, she will want to work toward the goal of assuming total responsibility for the classroom. Since providing guidance for a student having a full-time experience is more complex than it is for a student having a limited experience, this discussion focuses on the student who is in the classroom full-time.

Decisions regarding the sequence of the student's experiences also must be based on the readiness of the student. As the student demonstrates competence in one skill or set of skills, she evidences her readiness to acquire new skills. Shumsky (1968) stresses the readiness of the individual student as the main criterion to follow in attempting to achieve a balance between (1) moving the student into independent teaching too quickly and (2) failing to help the student make steady progress toward independence. Of these two conditions, Shumsky suggests that while students are critical of cooperating teachers who plunge them too early into taking over, there are actually more complaints about cooperating teachers who are slow in letting students take over.

The focus, thus far, has been on the cooperating teacher's assessment of the student's readiness to move from one stage to another in assuming responsibilities throughout her clinical experience. It is important that the student also actively participate in the process of assessing her readiness. As cooperating teacher and student share their perceptions of the student's readiness to move into new areas, they will have the basis for designing a sequence of experiences that corresponds to the student's growth toward the goal of independent teaching.

Planning the Student's Induction into the Teaching Role

The actual time sequence through which each student moves toward independence in teaching will be determined by her capabilities and by the unique characteristics of the classroom setting. It does not seem useful, therefore, to attempt to identify specific time intervals for students' movement from one level to another. What can be suggested is a sequence that provides a framework for planning the student's induction into the teaching role. As cooperating teacher and student plan the student's experiences, they can consider the sequence identified here and make modifications that seem appropriate in their particular situation:

1. The student assumes initial responsibilities (see Chapter 5) and observes the cooperating teacher in the instructional area in which the student will begin his teaching.
2. Student and cooperating teacher co-teach in the instructional area in which the student has been observing. The student observes in a sec-

ond instructional area and begins to assume responsibility for facilitating classroom routines.

3. The student assumes full responsibility for the area in which she began her teaching and co-teaches in the second area. The student observes in a third area and assumes increased responsibility for classroom management.

4. The student continues to assume responsibility for additional instructional areas and classroom routines until she is responsible for the overall planning and coordination of the classroom program. This includes planning with the cooperating teacher and paraprofessionals for their responsibilities. The length of time for this stage ranges from several days to one or more weeks.

5. As the conclusion of the experience nears, the responsibilities of the cooperating teacher increase, while the responsibilities of the student decrease. Through this process, the cooperating teacher becomes ready once again to assume responsibility for the classroom program.

Figure 6.6, a plan for the induction of a student into the teaching role, uses the above procedure. Included are the first, third, and sixth weeks of a seven-week full-time student teaching experience. The plan provides for a gradual, continuous increase in responsibility for the classroom program. As has been pointed out, each student must progress at her own pace in achieving independence in teaching. Accordingly, there is no intent in providing this illustration to suggest that every student be expected to follow the time sequence planned for this particular student.

While the sequence of experiences presented in the plan focuses on induction into teaching in a self-contained classroom, it can easily be adapted for use in departmentalized settings in middle and secondary schools. In these settings, students can progress through the stages of observing, co-teaching, and assuming full responsibility in each of the classes for which their cooperating teachers are responsible until they are carrying out the cooperating teacher's entire teaching assignment.

Activity 10 Working with another member of the group, role-play the process of planning a student's induction into teaching. Alternate roles so that each participant has the opportunity to play the role of student and of cooperating teacher. The person assuming the student role in each situation can contribute initially by describing her "background of experience." For example, one student may indicate that she has completed her methods courses but has had no previous clinical experiences, while another may describe the responsibilities she assumed during the two part-time field experiences she had the preceding year. Using Analysis Guide 10, develop a plan for helping each student move toward independent teaching. Consider both the student's readiness and the characteristics of the cooperating teacher's classroom in developing each plan. When the plans have been completed, identify their similarities and differences. In what ways does each plan reflect the unique combination of student's characteristics and cooperating teacher's classroom?

Figure 6.6 Plan for a Student's Induction into the Teaching Role

Week I	Monday	Tuesday	Wednesday	Thursday	Friday
CT's* Responsibilities	—introduces S				
	—facilitates planning, pre-observation, and post-observation conferences —				
			—observes the S facilitate all classroom routines —		
			—observes all language arts lessons —		
S's* Responsibilities	—observes classroom routines —	—facilitates dismissal	—facilitates all classroom routines —		
		—works with students at the math learning center —		—co-teaches math activities with one group	
		—administers spelling pre-test —	—works with students independently in spelling —	—administers post-test	
		—observes and co-teaches language arts lessons — teaches creative writing lessons —		—teaches handwriting lesson and reads a story —	

Week III	Monday	Tuesday	Wednesday	Thursday	Friday
CT's Responsibilities	—facilitates planning, pre-observation, and post-observation conferences —				
	—helps S plan to assume responsibility for the entire math program for the 4th week —				
	—observes all language arts lessons —				
S's Responsibilities	—facilitates all classroom routines —				
	—assumes responsibility for planning and teaching the language arts program —				
	—begins to plan math lessons for the entire class for the 4th week —				
	—continues to plan reading activities for one group —				

Week VI	Monday	Tuesday	Wednesday	Thursday	Friday
CT's Responsibilities	—facilitates planning, pre-observation, and post-observation conferences —				
	—prepares to resume, gradually, responsibility for the class during the 7th week —				
S's Responsibilities	—assumes responsibility for overall planning and coordination of the classroom program —				

*CT = Cooperating Teacher
S = Student

Analysis Guide 10   Planning the Student's Induction into the Teaching Role

Week I	Monday	Tuesday	Wednesday	Thursday	Friday
Cooperating Teacher's Responsibilities					
Student's Responsibilities					
Week III	Monday	Tuesday	Wednesday	Thursday	Friday
Cooperating Teacher's Responsibilities					
Student's Responsibilities					
Week VI	Monday	Tuesday	Wednesday	Thursday	Friday
Cooperating Teacher's Responsibilities					
Student's Responsibilities					

THE ROLE OF THE COLLEGE SUPERVISOR IN GUIDING THE STUDENT'S INDUCTION INTO TEACHING

While the major responsibility for guiding the student's induction into teaching lies with the cooperating teacher, the college supervisor can contribute to this process. At the beginning of the assignment, the college supervisor can provide the cooperating teacher with information concerning the objectives of the particular experience the student will be having. This will enable the cooperating teacher to know whether he is expected to provide the student with opportunities to assume only a limited range of teaching responsibilities or to guide the student toward assuming full responsibility for the classroom program. The college supervisor also can give the cooperating teacher information concerning any previous clinical experience that the student has had. Information such as the length of previous experiences, the ages of the children with whom the student has worked, and the extent of the student's involvement in teaching will be useful to the cooperating teacher in judging how the student can build on her previous experiences in this new assignment.

The college supervisor will want to participate in the process both of helping the student and the cooperating teacher plan an appropriate sequence of experiences for the student and of helping the student assess her progress as she moves through the sequence. Three-way conferences can provide for this participation. If the scheduling of frequent three-way conferences presents a problem, the college supervisor can share in this process through her individual conferences with the student and with the cooperating teacher. Whether through three-way conferences or a combination of two- and three-way conferences, it is important that the college supervisor maintain her involvement in the student's induction into teaching in order to ensure, at each stage in the sequence, that there is agreement among the participants that the student is making continuous progress.

REFERENCES

Belkin, Gary S., and Gray, Jerry L. *Educational psychology.* Dubuque, IA: Wm. C. Brown, 1977.

Bloom, Benjamin S. (Ed.). *Taxonomy of educational objectives: The cognitive domain.* New York: Longman Inc., 1977.

Clothier, Grant, and Kingsley, Elizabeth. *Enriching student teaching relationships* (Supervising teacher ed.). Shawnee Mission, KS: Midwest Educational Training and Research Organization, 1973.

Epstein, Charlotte. *Classroom management and teaching: Persistent problems and rational solutions.* Reston, VA: Reston Publishing, 1979.

Galloway, Charles M. *An exploratory study of observational procedures for determining teacher nonverbal communication.* Unpublished doctoral dissertation, University of Florida, 1962.

Galloway, Charles M. Nonverbal communication in teaching. *Theory into Practice,* December 1968, *7,* 172–75.

Galloway, Charles M. Improving nonverbal communication. In Walter S. Foster and Charles A. Sloan (Eds.), *Improving communication in teacher education: Proceedings of the ATF summer workshop—1978*. DeKalb, IL: Association of Teacher Educators and Northern Illinois University, 1979.

Harris, Ben M. *Supervisory behavior in education*. Englewood Cliffs, NJ: Prentice-Hall, 1963.

Hennings, Dorothy Grant. *Mastering classroom communication—What interaction analysis tells the teacher*. Pacific Palisades, CA: Goodyear Publishing, 1975.

Mager, Robert F. *Preparing instructional objectives* (2nd ed.). Belmont, CA: Fearon, 1975.

Medley, Donald M. The effectiveness of teachers. In Penelope L. Peterson and Herbert J. Walberg (Eds.), *Research on teaching: Concepts, findings, and implications*. Berkeley, CA: McCutchan, 1979.

Morine, Greta. Planning skills: Paradox and Parodies. *Journal of Teacher Education*, Summer 1973, *24* (2), 135–41.

Rosenshine, Barak V. Content, time and direct instruction. In Penelope L. Peterson and Herbert J. Walberg (Eds.), *Research on teaching: Concepts, findings, and implications*. Berkeley, CA: McCutchan, 1979.

Sanders, Norris M. *Classroom questions*. New York: Harper & Row, 1966.

Shumsky, Abraham. *In search of teaching style*. New York: Appleton-Century-Crofts, 1968.

Spache, George D., and Spache, Evelyn B. *Reading in the elementary school* (3rd ed.). Boston: Allyn & Bacon, 1973.

Spanjer, R. Allan. *Teacher preparation: Supervision and performance*. Washington, DC: Association of Teacher Educators, 1972.

Thompson, Michael L. Identifying anxieties experienced by student teachers. *Journal of Teacher Education*, December 1963, *14*, 435–39.

Much of the guidance needed by teacher education students during their induction into the role of teacher is provided through their participation in observation and conferencing. Recognition of the significance of these two components in determining the overall quality of clinical experiences could well suggest that each deserves treatment in a separate chapter. The rationale for treating observation and conferencing in a single chapter is the interrelatedness of these two components of clinical experiences. Experiences in which students are the observers need to be preceded and followed by conferences if students are to derive the maximum benefit from them. Conversely, cooperating teachers and college supervisors recognize that observa-

CHAPTER **7** PROVIDING GUIDANCE THROUGH OBSERVATION AND CONFERENCING

tions of students' teaching must include conferences in order to provide feed-back for students.

OBSERVATION EXPERIENCES

Observation experiences in which teacher education students participate can be divided into two categories: (1) those in which students are the observers and (2) those in which students are observed as they interact with pupils. This section discusses observation experiences in the first category; those in the second category are considered later in this chapter when the application of the *clinical supervision cycle* to teacher education is examined.

Lang, Quick, and Johnson (1975) suggest that students should participate as observers in two kinds of experiences: (1) instruction-related observations and (2) activity-related observations. They give the following examples of these observation experiences:

Instruction-Related Observations
- Of the cooperating teacher
- Of other teachers (same grade level or subject area; other grade levels or subject areas)
- Of other teacher education students
- Of self

Activity-Related Observations
- Of pupils (clubs, organizations, lunch, playground, etc.)
- Of teachers (meetings, organizations, lounge, etc.)
- Of administrators, counselors, custodians, nurses, etc.
- Of community groups and agencies, parents, school board, etc.

Observing the cooperating teacher is the most common instruction-related observation experience. Lang, Quick, and Johnson point out, however, that students need to observe other teachers also. Observing teachers in different settings provides students with opportunities to develop skill in analyzing a variety of approaches and teaching styles. Today's cooperating teachers recognize the importance of giving students opportunities to observe approaches to teaching other than their own and typically assume responsibility for helping students arrange a series of these experiences.

New techniques for observing and analyzing teaching behavior began to appear in the 1960s as the Office of Education teacher education models were developed. The use of these techniques enables students to observe classroom teachers systematically and to collect data that can be analyzed later with the guidance of cooperating teachers or college supervisors.

In many teacher education programs, students also use these techniques to observe and record the teaching of their peers. Following the observations, they provide feedback for each other using the data they have collected. When these techniques are combined with audiotaping or videotaping, they can be used by individual students for self-analysis. The addition of peer and self-analysis procedures to programs of teacher education has greatly expanded the observation opportunities available to preservice teachers.

Whether teacher education students are observing experienced teachers, analyzing each other's teaching, or engaging in self-analysis, it is essential that each observation situation have a clearly defined purpose. Providing students with a purpose prior to an observation enables them to focus on a specific aspect of the teaching-learning situation and record interactions that can be analyzed systematically at a later time. Without a clear objective, students will shift their attention from one kind of interaction to another, and at the conclusion of the observation will find that the data they have collected cannot be analyzed in any meaningful way.

Various frameworks for viewing the teaching process have been developed in the search for useful ways of analyzing teaching. Each framework identifies a set of variables that provides a basis for defining objectives for instruction-related observations. For example, Spanjer's interactive teaching functions framework, discussed in Chapter 6, includes five dimensions of the teaching process. Each dimension can serve as the focus of an observation or series of observations.

Once the dimension of teaching that will serve as the focus of a particular observation has been decided upon, it becomes possible to select the recording system that will be used to collect observation data. If, for example, the focus of the observation is verbal interaction, a system such as the Flanders categories for interaction analysis can be used to record the statements, questions, and responses that take place. If the observers are going to focus on nonverbal communication, they may select Galloway's categories of nonverbal behavior as their tool. Regardless of the dimension of teaching selected for analysis or the system chosen for recording data, the point to be emphasized is that clearly defining the objective of each observation is prerequisite to obtaining meaningful and useful results.

In discussing activity-related observations, Lang, Quick, and Johnson point out that the potential value in this category of observations is frequently overlooked. They are not suggesting that students do not observe pupils, teachers, and administrators in a variety of settings. What they suggest is that these observations typically are not planned and carried out in the way that instruction-related observations are, with the result that students can fail to derive the maximum benefit from them. Students need clearly defined purposes when they participate in activity-related observations just as they do when they engage in instruction-related observations. In fact, since the activities students observe may be less structured than teaching episodes, it is even more important that students have purposes that can help them focus on specific dimensions of the activities.

In addition to needing purposes for activity-related observations, students also need guidance in analyzing the events that have taken place. When cooperating teacher and student observe activities together, the cooperating teacher can help the student understand the relationship of the activities to the overall structure of the school or community. Without this guidance, the student may view these observations as "interesting," but unrelated to the process of "learning how to teach." Through planning and analyzing a sequence of activity-related observations with his student, the cooperating teacher can help her learn that the teacher's role includes dimensions and relationships beyond those that exist in the classroom.

CONFERENCES

The importance of maintaining communication among the participants in clinical experiences has been discussed previously. While many factors contribute to the success of clinical experiences, and effective communication alone does not guarantee success, it would be difficult to imagine a clinical experience being judged productive and satisfying in the absence of effective communcation. The communication needed in clinical experiences ranges from spontaneous interaction between cooperating teacher and student as they move through each day's activities to scheduled conferences that have been planned to meet specific objectives.

The approach to examining the conferences that occur in clinical experiences taken here is to integrate the discussion of each kind of conference with the phase of the experience to which it is related. In previous chapters, the following conferences have been considered: (1) preassignment conferences, (2) conferences in which students' plans are discussed, and (3) weekly planning conferences. This chapter focuses on those conferences associated with students' observation experiences. In the preceding section of the chapter, conferences in connection with observations in which students are the observers were discussed. The following sections consider those conferences that are needed when students are being observed.

A STRATEGY FOR IMPLEMENTING THE ANALYTICAL DIMENSION OF OBSERVATION AND CONFERENCING

One of the most important expectations held for cooperating teachers is that they will systematically observe their students when they are teaching and provide feedback concerning their performance. In meeting this expectation, cooperating teachers help students increase the effectiveness of their teaching and gain skill in self-analysis. Frequently, however, cooperating teachers encounter difficulty as they attempt to provide guidance for students through observations and conferences. The source of the difficulty is suggested by Copeland and Boyan (1975):

> Many of these [cooperating] teachers, who are excellent performers themselves, have difficulty exercising direct influence of a beneficial nature on student teachers. They find it difficult, for example, to conduct fruitful conferences for the purpose of improving the student teacher's teaching skills. They often can not provide meaningful feedback about teaching performance to the student teacher because of their own lack of skills needed for effective observation and analysis of teaching encounters (p. 29)

Copeland and Boyan further suggest that teacher education institutions have failed to provide adequate assistance to cooperating teachers in the development of the skills they need to conduct observations and conferences. This section presents a procedure that will help cooperating teachers implement these essential dimensions of their role.

In Chapter 3, a supervisory process known as the *clinical supervision cycle* was introduced. Developed by Morris Cogan, Robert Anderson, and Robert Goldhammer, this process is the result of efforts to improve supervision by making it more analytical and objective. The cycle consists of the following five-step sequence:

1. Preobservation Conference
2. Observation
3. Analysis and Strategy
4. Postobservation Conference
5. Postconference Analysis

Several writers (Copeland and Boyan 1975; Lang, Quick, and Johnson 1975; McNeil 1971) have discussed the application of this supervisory cycle to clinical experiences in teacher education. These authors propose that this cycle can be used as effectively in guiding teacher education students as in supervising experienced teachers. Copeland and Boyan, for example, point out that when student teachers are experiencing instructional problems, they often are unable to define the specific behaviors that should be changed. As a basis for identifying the needed changes, it is necessary that they develop an increased awareness of the teaching-learning behaviors that actually exist in their classrooms. This can be achieved by collecting data through systematic observation. Since students cannot systematically observe their own classrooms while they are teaching, it is the responsibility of cooperating teachers to observe and to provide deliberate feedback based on data obtained from the observations. This process of systematically observing and providing feedback is the focus of the clinical supervision cycle.

In describing their applications of the clinical supervision cycle to teacher education, the writers use the terms *instructional supervision* (Copeland and Boyan) and *supervision by objectives* (Lang, Quick, and Johnson; McNeil). The processes they describe, however, contain essentially the same components as those included in the cycle proposed by Cogan, Anderson, and Goldhammer. In presenting the sequence for observation and conferencing that follows, no attempt is made to associate specific steps with a particular writer or group of writers. Rather, the discussion identifies a sequence that has come to be recognized as a process directed toward increasing teacher effectiveness through the systematic analysis of teaching behavior.

Preobservation Conference

In this initial step in the clinical supervision cycle, cooperating teacher and student meet to agree, first, on the objectives of the lesson the student is going to teach. When the cooperating teacher and student agree that the objectives clearly define the desired learning outcomes, they then come to an agreement concerning the ways in which achievement of the outcomes will be demonstrated. For example, will oral responses be accepted as evidence of achievement, or will the learners be expected to respond in writing to questions or problems? Coming to an agreement on objectives and the means of their assessment ensures that cooperating teacher and student have the same focus, both during the observation and in the subsequent analysis of the lesson.

Cooperating teacher and student next review the development of the student's plan. As they do this, they may decide that revisions of portions of the plan are necessary. For this reason, it is typically recommended that the preobservation conference not immediately precede the observation. One factor that can help to determine how far in advance to schedule the preobservation conference is the student's level of skill in planning. As the student's skill increases, and her plans require fewer revisions, less time will be needed between the preobservation conference and teaching the lesson.

The cooperating teacher and student also may want to state one or more objectives for the student's behavior on which to focus during the observation. For example, one student may have been trying recently to increase the number of higher-level questions she asks. She may want the cooperating teacher to categorize her questions during the lesson as a means of assessing her progress toward this objective. Another student may have become concerned that she seems to focus on the same few pupils in accepting responses to questions. She may ask the cooperating teacher to record the names of those pupils who respond during the lesson as she attempts to increase pupil participation. Whatever student behavior is focused on during the observation, it is essential that cooperating teacher and student formulate a clear statement of the objective to be attained.

Once the objective has been defined, the cooperating teacher and student decide on a means of collecting data relative to that objective. That a wide range of published systems for collecting classroom interaction data is available has been discussed previously. In *Mirrors for Behavior III* (1974), generally considered the most complete source available, ninety-nine systems are described and analyzed. The categories of these systems are grouped in seven major classes: (1) Affective, (2) Cognitive, (3) Psychomotor, (4) Activity, (5) Content (what is being talked about), (6) Sociological Structure (who is talking to whom and in what roles), and (7) Physical Environment. One of the systems described in this work, the Flanders categories for interaction analysis, is reprinted in Chapter 2.

These systems have made it possible to develop descriptions of classroom interaction that are much more precise and analytical than those of earlier times. Cooperating teachers and teacher education students can benefit from examining particular systems and applying selected ones to their teaching situations. Two factors, however, need to be taken into account by cooperating teachers and students in considering the use of these systems. First, it is essential that cooperating teachers and students acquire a thorough understanding of the objectives, components, and data recording procedures of a system before they attempt to use it as a basis for analyzing the student's teaching behavior. This suggests that they use the system in a series of practice sessions until they feel that they have sufficient skill to record data accurately and easily. Without this ability, the focus of the observer will be on the use of the instrument, rather than on the interaction that is taking place. The second factor concerns the location of a system that is appropriate for meeting the objectives of a particular situation. Even when a cooperating teacher and student have several systems available to them, they may fail to find one that addresses the specific concern on which they have decided to focus.

Because of the amount of time involved in learning to use observation systems and the frequent unavailability of appropriate ones, cooperating teachers and students often design their own observation instruments. The first step in constructing an observation instrument is to identify the specific behaviors that will need to be recorded to meet the objectives of the observation. The second step involves selecting an instrument format that will enable the observer to record the information.

Boyan and Copeland (1978) describe a variety of formats that can be used in constructing observation instruments. As they point out, no one format is appropriate for every observation. The selection of a format is determined by the amount and kind of information wanted. Brief descriptions, and examples, of the instrument formats identified by Boyan and Copeland are presented here.

1. *Category system.* A set of categories, dealing with one type of behavior, is developed. The set must include all possible behaviors of the type to be recorded. That is, if the behavior to be observed is teacher-pupil verbal interaction, there must be a category into which each kind of verbal interaction can be placed. The categories also must be mutually exclusive so that when a behavior of the type being observed occurs, it clearly falls into one, and only one, category.

An example of a category system is the Flanders system of interaction analysis (see p. 25). This system meets both criteria identified above. There is a category for each type of verbal interaction, and the categories are mutually exclusive.

2. *Sign system.* Behaviors that may or may not occur during the observation are identified. The observer does not try to determine prior to the observation what behaviors might occur. He merely lists those behaviors he wants to count if they occur. He makes a notation on the instrument only at the occurrence of those behaviors.

Examples of behaviors in a sign system might be "pupil asks a question" or "pupil contributes to discussion."

3. *Frequency count system.* The observer identifies the behavior that will be the focus of the observation. He then makes a record, or frequency count, of the number of times the behavior occurs during a specified period.

Examples of behaviors in a frequency count system might be "teacher uses speech mannerism 'you know'" or "teacher blocks pupils' view of chalkboard."

4. *Sequential record system.* The use of a sequential record system produces more information than the use of a frequency count system. The observer employing this system records the behaviors to be observed in the order in which they occur. Recording behaviors in this way yields both their frequency and the pattern of their occurrence.

For example, a sequential system might direct the observer to record both the frequency of teacher positive and negative responses to pupil statements and the sequence in which the two types of responses occur.

5. *Time-dependent system.* A time-dependent system requires the observer to record behaviors at stated time intervals or to measure and record the amount of time covered by certain behaviors.

The Flanders system is an example of a category system that is time-dependent. Every three seconds the observer writes down the category number of the interaction he has just observed. The observer does not wait for a change in the interaction to take place before recording successive category numbers. He records a number every three seconds, even though he may record the same number several times in succession.

Sign systems can also be time-dependent. A time-dependent sign system, for example, might direct the observer to record the amount of time the teacher spends working with small groups of pupils during a specified period.

6. *Event-dependent system.* An event-dependent system requires the observer to record each occurrence of the behaviors being observed. An event-dependent system is not concerned with how long an event lasts or when it occurs.

An example of a behavior that could be recorded using an event-dependent system is "teacher interrupts pupil statement/question."

The formats identified by Boyan and Copeland are not mutually exclusive. A cooperating teacher and student might decide, for example, that for a particular observation an event-dependent sequential record system will best provide the information they want. For another observation, the use of a time-dependent category system may be the most appropriate means of obtaining the desired data. When the objectives of the observation are clear, selecting a format and designing a simple instrument are not difficult tasks.

The preobservation conference ends when the cooperating teacher and student have identified (1) the objectives of the lesson, (2) the means by which the learners' achievement of the objectives will be assessed, (3) the dimension of the student's teaching behavior that will be the focus of the observation, and (4) the system that will be used to collect data relative to that dimension of behavior.

A brief summary of a preobservation conference is given in Figure 7.1. Following the summary are the outcomes of the conference recorded by the cooperating teacher and student. These outcomes include objectives for the learners, means of evaluating learners' progress toward objectives, objectives for the student, and the instrument to be used by the cooperating teacher during the observation. This instrument was designed by the cooperating teacher and student and has the following characteristics: (1) It is a category system, (2) it provides for a sequential record of the behavior being observed, and (3) it is event-dependent in that the observer records each occurrence of the behavior.

Activity 11 As a means of increasing your understanding of how a cooperating teacher and student plan an observation, role-play a preobservation conference with another group member. Use the format shown in Analysis

Guide 11 to record the outcomes of the conference. Complete the following procedure for this preobservation conference:

1. Identify the lesson to be taught (e.g., a phonics lesson dealing with the CVC generalization, a lesson introducing decimal fractions, a social studies discussion of pollution).
2. Write behavioral objectives for the learners.
3. Determine the means by which achievement of the objectives will be evaluated.
4. Identify *(a)* the dimension of the student's teaching behavior that will be the focus of the observation and *(b)* the data to be collected relative to that behavior.
5. Select an appropriate observation system format and design an instrument to use in collecting the data.

Observation

While the student is teaching, the cooperating teacher collects data that can be used to assess achievement of the objectives agreed upon in the preobservation conference. Since the cooperating teacher and student have previously determined the means by which the data will be collected, the student can focus her full attention on the lesson. She will not be distracted by anxious thoughts about what the cooperating teacher is doing. In addition, the student knows that the data will be made available to her later. This should further serve to prevent feelings of anxiety from arising.

It is important to emphasize that throughout the observation the cooperating teacher's role is to record *objective* information concerning the interaction that takes place. It is not his role to record what he *thinks* or *feels* about what is happening. If the cooperating teacher records his interpretation of the events that are taking place, rather than the events themselves, the student will be denied the opportunity to develop skill in analyzing her teaching on the basis of objective data. The use of audiotaping or videotaping equipment can help ensure the objectivity of the data collected. Since it is unlikely, however, that every lesson will be audiotaped or videotaped, the major responsibility for providing the student with objective data lies with the cooperating teacher.

Figure 7.1   Outcomes of a Preobservation Conference

Summary of the Preobservation Conference

The student brought to the preobservation conference a plan for a social studies lesson in which a unit on Japan's environment would be reviewed. The lesson was designed for a group of eight pupils. The cooperating teacher and student reviewed the objectives and means of evaluation and agreed that they were appropriately defined.

The cooperating teacher and student discussed their concern with the lack of pupil participation during previous group discussions that the student had held. They decided that the stu-

Figure 7.1 **Outcomes of a Preobservation Conference** *(continued).*

Summary of the Preobservation Conference

dent would attempt, in this lesson, to increase participation by eliciting uncontrolled and spontaneous responses rather than solitary, controlled, or mass responses. (See reference to Harris (1963) in Chapter 6.)

Behavioral Objectives for Learners	*Evaluation of the Learners*
1. The learners will be able to describe five ways in which the Japanese people have adapted to their environment.	1. The learners will orally describe the five ways of adapting.
2. The learners will be able to name four advantages and three disadvantages of farming in Japan.	2. The learners will orally name the four advantages and the three disadvantages of farming.
3. The learners will be able to infer the effects that living on an island have had on the Japanese people.	3. The learners will infer the effects of living on an island and state them orally.

Behavioral Objectives for the Student

1. The student will include in the lesson at least 12 questions/statements that are designed to elicit learner responses.
2. The student will elicit uncontrolled and spontaneous responses 90% of the time.

Observation Instrument

Directions: Categorize learners' responses, in order of occurrence, by placing a √ under the appropriate heading.

Response Number	Solitary	Controlled	Uncontrolled	Spontaneous	Mass
1					
2					
3					
4					
5					
6					
—					
—					

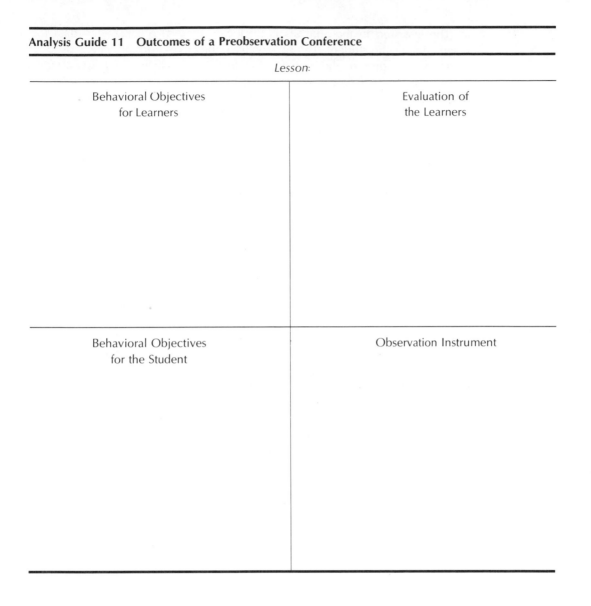

Lesson:

Behavioral Objectives for Learners	Evaluation of the Learners
Behavioral Objectives for the Student	Observation Instrument

Analysis of Observation Data

When the observation period has ended, the data are analyzed. While the majority of writers describing the clinical supervision cycle recommend that the observer analyze the data independently, Clothier and Kingsley (1973) suggest that the cooperating teacher and student may want to complete this step jointly. An advantage in a joint analysis is that the student is given the opportunity to learn how to implement this stage of the cycle. Thus, while this stage is described here in terms of the cooperating teacher's independent analysis of the data, there is no intent to imply that the cooperating teacher should not carry out this procedure with the student.

The first step in the analysis is to decide how to organize the data for presentation to the student. The observation objectives and the means used to collect the data provide the basis for this decision. For example, the cooperating teacher may have categorized the questions asked by the student during the lesson because the student wants to increase the number of higher-level questions she asks. The cooperating teacher can organize the observation results by tabulating the number of questions that occurred in each category or by computing the percentage of higher-level questions asked. In this step the cooperating teacher is not interpreting data; he is simply organizing material in order to make it readily understandable.

In the next step, the cooperating teacher compares the observation results with the objectives identified in the preobservation conference. He does this to assess the extent to which the objectives, those for the learners and those for the student, were achieved. If some objectives were not achieved, he attempts to determine what prevented the learners or the student from achieving them. He notes these factors for use at the postobservation conference. He next describes strategies that could be used to bring about achievement of these objectives. With regard to achieved objectives, the cooperating teacher identifies the teaching behaviors that seemed to facilitate their achievement. He notes these as behaviors to be maintained or increased.

In the final step of the data analysis, the cooperating teacher develops a plan for the postobservation conference. In doing this, he considers the sequence in which he will present the observation data to the student and the questions he will ask as he guides the student's analysis of these data.

The material in Figure 7.2 illustrates the sequence of steps in analyzing observation data just described. The objectives of the observation, and the means of assessment, appear in Figure 7.1.

Activity 12   On Analysis Guide 12 are shown the outcomes of a preobservation conference developed by a cooperating teacher and student. Following the outcomes of the conference are the data collected by the cooperating teacher during the observation. Using the information provided on the analysis guide, complete the sequence for analyzing observation data as indicated. Keep the information recorded on Analysis Guide 12 for use with Activity 13.

Postobservation Conference

The cooperating teacher's major role in the postobservation conference is that of facilitating the student's analysis of the lesson. Since the focus is on helping the student develop skill in self-analysis, the cooperating teacher does not begin the conference by presenting his analysis of the lesson. Instead, he presents the organized observation data and asks questions that guide the student in drawing inferences concerning the reasons for the congruence or lack of congruence between the data and the observation objectives.

Figure 7.2   Analysis of Observation Data

Summary of Data	Congruence of Data with Objectives
Learners	*Learners*
1. Five ways in which the Japanese have adapted to their environment were described.	1. The objective was met.
2. The learners named four advantages and four disadvantages of farming in Japan.	2. The objective was met; in fact, they named an additional disadvantage.
3. The learners inferred and described six effects that living on an island have had on the Japanese people.	3. The objective was met; however, several learners did not participate in the discussion.
Student	*Student*
1. The student included in the lesson 12 questions/statements that elicited learner responses.	1. The objective was met.

Response Number	Solitary	Controlled	Uncontrolled	Spontaneous	Mass
1	✓				
2		✓			
3		✓			
4			✓		
5			✓		
6			✓		
7			✓		
8			✓		
9				✓	
10				✓	
11			✓		
12				✓	

139

Figure 7.2   Analysis of Observation Data *(continued).*

2. Learner Responses:
    Solitary—1
    Controlled—2
    Uncontrolled—6
    Spontaneous—3
    Mass—0
Sequence of Responses:
    Solitary—1
    Controlled—2
    Uncontrolled—5
    Spontaneous—2
    Uncontrolled—1
    Spontaneous—1
Percentage of Uncontrolled and Spontaneous Responses: 75%
	2. The student did not achieve 90% uncontrolled and spontaneous responses.

Plan for the Postobservation Conference*

1. Share the data summary with the student.
2. Guide the student in analyzing the relationship of the data to the objectives and in generating alternative strategies using these questions:
   - Did the learners meet the objectives?
   - What do you think enabled the learners to make the inferences you asked for?
   - Why do you think your questions/statements did not elicit uncontrolled or spontaneous responses as often as you wanted?
   - What strategy do you think you could use next time to increase the frequency of uncontrolled and spontaneous responses?
3. Provide feedback from my own analysis where appropriate:
   - The student asked questions that helped the learners to make inferences. This is a skill that they have not had much experience with. Since the student has the ability to ask good inference questions, she should continue to work with the learners in this area.
   - It seemed that the student became nervous when the learners did not respond immediately. This could have caused her to elicit controlled responses and a solitary response. We will need to discuss ways of overcoming this problem.
4. Plan the next observation with the student.

*If the cooperating teacher and student are completing the data analysis jointly, this analysis leads naturally into the postobservation conference. A plan is unnecessary; however, it is important to include in the conference all of the steps shown in this plan.

       As the student analyzes the data, the cooperating teacher encourages her to generate alternative strategies for reaching unattained objectives. During the process, the cooperating teacher shares his analysis when appropriate. On the basis of their analysis of the lesson, the cooperating teacher and student modify existing objectives or identify new objectives, both for the pupils and for the student. They then develop strategies for reaching these objectives. In addition, they may make plans for the next observation. As several writers have pointed out, the postobservation conference for one observation frequently leads into the planning conference for the next observation.

The outcomes of a postobservation conference are shown in Figure 7.3. The conference is based on the analysis of observation data shown in Figure 7.2.

Activity 13 In order to complete the observation and conference cycle, role-play two postobservation conferences with another group member. Use the data analysis and plan for a postobservation conference recorded by each participant on Analysis Guide 12 as the basis for the conferences. Use the format shown in Analysis Guide 13 to record the outcomes of the conferences. Audiotape the conferences for use with Activity 14. When the conferences have been completed, compare them in order (1) to identify the similarities and differences in the data analyses and plans for the postobservation conference and (2) to determine the reasons for the differences where they occur.

Postconference Analysis

In this final step of the supervisory cycle, the cooperating teacher reviews his performance and plans ways of increasing his effectiveness in implementing this sequence for observation and conferencing. Because of the significance of communication in determining the quality of supervisory conferences, the cooperating teacher will want to assess carefully, in reviewing the cycle, the verbal interaction that has taken place. This dimension of conferencing is examined in the following section of this chapter. A procedure for helping cooperating teachers analyze conference verbal interaction is included in that section.

At the conclusion of the cooperating teacher's initial efforts in implementing the supervisory cycle, he undoubtedly will want to assess, also, the success with which the individual steps were implemented. This analysis can be undertaken with the student so that they can compare their perceptions of any problems encountered. On the basis of their analysis of the completed cycle, cooperating teacher and student may identify specific points that will need increased attention, or modification, in the next cycle they carry out.

A STRATEGY FOR FACILITATING THE INTERPERSONAL DIMENSION OF CONFERENCING

In Chapter 3, the point was made that the supervisory process cannot be effective unless attention is given to both dimensions of supervision: the analytical and the interpersonal. In the preceding sections of this chapter, we examined the clinical supervision approach to implementing the analytical dimension of observation and conferencing. In this section, we examine the cooperating teacher's role in facilitating the interpersonal dimension of conferencing.

Outcomes of a Preobservation Conference

Lesson: Directed Reading Lesson
Group of Six

Behavioral Objectives for Learners	*Evaluation of the Learners*
1. The learners will be able to infer reasons why Pedro met some friends before Tina did. (Inference)	1. The learners will give reasons based on inference rather than recall.
2. The learners will be able to demonstrate their appreciation of Tina's feelings by describing how she felt because she had no friends. (Appreciation)	2. The learners will describe how Tina felt because she had no friends.

Behavioral Objective for the Student

1. The student will ask only questions which require the learners to draw inferences and to appreciate the feelings of a story character.

Observation Instrument

Directions: For each question, (1) locate the row in the matrix that indicates the type of question asked, and (2) record learner response in the appropriate column(s) of that row.

Type of Question Asked	Type of Learner Response				
	Literal	*Reorganization*	*Inference*	*Evaluation*	*Appreciation*
Literal					
Reorganization					
Inference					
Evaluation					
Appreciation					

Data Recorded

Type of Question Asked	Type of Learner Response				
	Literal	Reorganization	Inference	Evaluation	Appreciation
Literal	√ √				
Reorganization					
Inference	√ √ √		√		
Evaluation					
Appreciation				√	√ √

Analysis of Observation Data

Summary of Data	Congruence of Data with Objectives
Learners 1. 2. *Student* 1.	*Learners* 1. 2. *Student* 1.

Plan for the Postobservation Conference

Factors Affecting the Quality of Interpersonal Relationships

The work of Carl Rogers has produced a significant body of knowledge concerning human relationships. While his focus has been the relationship between therapist and client in psychotherapy, Rogers proposes that his research findings are applicable to every kind of *helping relationship.* Rogers (1961) defines "helping relationship" to mean "a relationship in which at least one of the parties has the intent of promoting the growth, development, maturity, improved functioning, improved coping with life of the other" (pp. 39–40). Since the objectives of Rogers' *helping relationship* correspond to the objectives of cooperating teachers as they work with teacher education students, it is important to consider Rogers' findings and their application in clinical experiences.

Rogers has identified three conditions that facilitate the growth of the individual being helped when they occur in the person whose intent it is to help him. The more these conditions occur, the greater the likelihood that the

Figure 7.3   Outcomes of a Postobservation Conference

Analysis of Observation Data

Student's Analysis	*Cooperating Teacher's Input*
The student indicated that the objectives for the lesson had been met. She felt that her questions clearly indicated the need for inferring rather than recalling, and that this enabled the learners to make the inferences.	The cooperating teacher agreed with the student that the learners' objectives had been met. He expressed his feeling that the student did appear nervous when the learners did not respond immediately. He assured her that this is a very common reaction for beginning teachers. He suggested that they develop a strategy to help her overcome this anxiety.
The student said that she became nervous when questions were not answered immediately. When this happened, she called on individuals and, therefore elicited several controlled responses and a solitary response. She also noted that only five of the eight members of the group participated in the discussion.	The cooperating teacher also thought that they should identify those learners who seldom participate in discussions, and plan for increasing their involvement.

Development of Objectives and Teaching Strategies

During the next lesson the student will continue to try to elicit uncontrolled and spontaneous responses. She will try to control her nervousness by mentally counting to five after she asks a question. If she does not receive a response, she will reword the question before calling on an individual.

The student and cooperating teacher will observe the patterns of participation in group discussions during the next several lessons. They will then discuss ways of increasing participation.

Cooperating teacher and student identified overall objectives for the next week's social studies lessons. While the student is teaching the lessons, the cooperating teacher will observe.

helping relationship will be successful. The terms Rogers uses to describe these conditions are defined here:

1. *Congruence.* An individual is expressing congruence when others sense that he is being what he is, that they are dealing with the person himself, not with a "front." The more genuine an individual, the higher the degree of congruence.
2. *Unconditional positive regard.* An individual is evidencing unconditional positive regard when he expresses a positive, acceptant attitude toward another, without reservations or evaluations.
3. *Empathic understanding.* An individual is expressing empathic understanding when he senses the feelings and personal meanings being experienced by another, and is successful in communicating this understanding to him.

Analysis Guide 13 Outcomes of a Postobservation Conference

Analysis of Observation Data

Student's Analysis	Cooperating Teacher's Input

Development of Objectives and Teaching Strategies

The Quality of Interpersonal Relationships and the Outcomes of Conferences

Gilles Dussault (1970) has applied the conditions described by Rogers to teacher education. Specifically, Dussault proposes a theory of supervision in teacher education based on the theory of therapy and personality change developed by Rogers (1959). Dussault explains that there are similarities between a number of the variables of the teaching function of supervision and a number of the variables in Rogers' view of therapy and that this was the factor that led him to use Rogers' theory as a model in developing his own.

Dussault identifies three delimitations of his theory. The first is that his theory is concerned only with the *teaching* function of supervision. The second is that his focus is the *supervisory conference* in student teaching and other professional laboratory experiences. The third is that his theory deals only with the *affective* meanings of the supervisory conference.

On the basis of his analysis of the supervisory conference in clinical experiences, Dussault proposes that ". . . the relationships between the affective meanings and the outcomes of the supervisory conference are similar to those that exist between the conditions and outcomes of therapy" (pp. 171–72). He contends, moreover, that the appearance of perceptual psychology, particularly that of Rogers, in the literature of teacher education lends additional support to his conclusion that ". . . the outcomes of therapy and the outcomes of the supervisory conference are in many respects really—semantically—similar" (p. 164).

Dussault's theory consists of two parts, which correspond to the two parts of Rogers' theory. In the first part, Dussault states the conditions that must exist in the supervisory conference if the outcomes in the second part of his theory are to be achieved. In the second part, he identifies the outcomes of the supervisory conference that are predicted to occur when the conditions stated in the first part are met.

Dussault states that the following conditions must be met in the supervisory conference if the predicted outcomes are to occur:

1. The supervisor and the supervisee are in contact.
2. The supervisor is congruent in his relationship with the supervisee.
3. The supervisor experiences unconditional positive regard toward the supervisee.
4. The supervisor experiences an empathic understanding of the supervisee's internal frame of reference.
5. The supervisee perceives, at least to a minimal degree, conditions 3 and 4, the unconditional positive regard of the supervisor for him and the empathic understanding of the supervisor.[1]

Dussault explains that this set of conditions is similar to the set of conditions in the first part of Rogers' theory with two exceptions: (1) The terms "supervisor" and "supervisee" have been substituted for "therapist" and "client" and (2) one item in Rogers' set of conditions, dealing with the client's incongruence and anxiety, has been omitted. He explains, further, that the requirement in the first condition that the supervisor and supervisee be in contact refers to psychological contact. As defined by Rogers (1959), two persons are in psychological contact when each makes a difference in the expe-

---

[1] Gilles Dussault. *A theory of supervision in teacher education.* New York: Teachers College Press, 1970, p. 180. Reprinted with permission.

riential field of the other. Lastly, Dussault points out that conditions 2 through 5 are not all-or-none elements. What his theory really asserts, says Dussault, is that the more marked the presence of these conditions, the greater the observable changes in the supervisee's personality and behavior.

In the second part of his theory, Dussault lists those changes that will be observed in the supervisee at the end of the professional laboratory experience if the foregoing conditions are met during supervisory conferences:

1. The supervisee is more congruent (or, equivalently, more open to his experience, less defensive) than he was at the beginning of the period of supervised laboratory experiences;
2. His psychological adjustment is improved, being closer to the optimum;
3. He perceives his own professional activities and teaching performances more objectively, more realistically;
4. His perception of his ideal teaching-self is more realistic and more achievable;
5. His perception of his ideal self is more realistic and more achievable;
6. His teaching-self is more congruent with his ideal teaching-self;
7. His self is more congruent with his ideal self;
8. His professional fears and apprehensions are reduced;
9. His anxiety is reduced;
10. He has an increased degree of positive regard for himself as a teacher;
11. He has an increased degree of positive self-regard;
12. He perceives the other persons in his professional environment more realistically and accurately;
13. He experiences more acceptance of the other persons in his professional environment, having in particular more positive attitudes toward pupils;
14. He experiences more acceptance of others in general;
15. In making and evaluating his professional decisions and choices, he resorts more often than he did before to the evidence he is provided with by his experiences and less often than before to the judgments and values of other members of the profession;
16. His teaching behavior changes in various ways, in a direction away from the imitation of his supervisor's practices and methods and toward a more idiosyncratic style;
17. His teaching behavior is more creative, more flexible, more uniquely adaptive to each new situation and each new problem.[2]

Dussault classifies these 17 outcomes in two broad categories: (1) Ten are "professional" changes and (2) seven are "personal" changes. He suggests that this numerical distribution may reflect the predominance of professional over personal concerns during the supervisory conference, a time when both supervisor and supervisee are giving more of their attention to the professional

[2]Gilles Dussault. *A theory of supervision in teacher education.* New York: Teachers College Press, 1970, pp. 190–91. Reprinted with permission.

growth of the supervisee than to his psychological adjustment. While the "personal" dimensions of the supervisee's self usually are not the focus of supervisory conferences, Dussault hypothesizes that changes in the supervisee's personality will occur if the conditions in the first part of the theory are met. He bases this hypothesis on a conception of the self as a whole pattern, which changes when one of its aspects is changed. Therefore, when changes occur in the professional aspects of the supervisee's self, changes in the whole pattern of his self can be predicted.

Analyzing Communication in Conferences

Certainly cooperating teachers want to establish and maintain effective relationships in their interaction with teacher education students. An understanding of the concepts of congruence, unconditional positive regard, and empathy as conditions that facilitate helping relationships provides direction for cooperating teachers as they interact with students in conference settings. With this framework in mind, they can make a conscious effort to communicate genuineness, empathy, and unconditional positive regard. A problem arises, however, when the individual who is attempting to fulfill these conditions asks, How can I know to what extent I am expressing these qualities? What is needed is a means by which cooperating teachers can assess the nature of their communication with students in conferences.

Dussault points out that the Barrett-Lennard Relationship Inventory (1962) is an appropriate instrument to use in measuring empathic understanding, congruence, and unconditionality of regard. Blumberg (1980) employed the Barrett-Lennard Relationship inventory, in his studies of supervisor-teacher relationships, to assess teachers' perceptions of the quality of their relationships with supervisors. On the basis of his findings, Blumberg identified a set of supervisory behaviors associated with positive evaluations by teachers of their relationships with supervisors (see Chapter 3). Using these behaviors, he constructed a scale that supervisors can use to assess the nature of their interaction with teachers. Elizabeth Kingsley has adapted Blumberg's rating scale for use in clinical experiences. Kingsley designed two scales for cooperating teachers to use in assessing verbal interaction with students in conferences. These scales, adapted and modified for our purposes, can be seen in Analysis Guide 14.

The cooperating teacher interested in assessing his interpersonal communication skills can use the Kingsley scales in a variety of ways. Following conferences that have been taped, he can play the tapes and categorize his verbal behaviors as he perceives them. After one or more conferences, he can identify those behaviors he wants to (1) maintain, (2) increase, or (3) decrease. If the cooperating teacher categorizes his perceptions of the student's behavior, also, he can begin to assess the effect of changes in his behavior on that of the student. For example, does increasing the emphasis placed on asking for the student's opinion result in an increase in the emphasis the student places on offering suggestions on her own?

Another way of using the Kingsley scales is to modify one or both of them so that other information can be obtained. Additional categories of behavior that the cooperating teacher is interested in assessing can be added to the scales, for example. Tallying the number of times the behaviors occur, rather than rating the emphasis placed on them, is a modification that also might prove useful. As the scales are used, no doubt other modifications will occur to cooperating teachers.

The discussion of the Kingsley scales thus far has emphasized the cooperating teacher's independent use of the scales. This focus was selected because of the significance of the cooperating teacher's behavior in facilitating the helping relationship. This in no way implies that the scales should not be used by cooperating teacher and student together. If both complete the scales, they will have a means for assessing the accuracy of their perceptions of their verbal behavior. As Kingsley points out, they also will have a basis for discussing ways of making their conferences more productive.

Activity 14   As a means of learning to use the Kingsley scales, analyze the verbal interaction that occurred in the audiotaped postobservation conference you role-played in Activity 13. Complete the following procedure:

1. Analyze *(a)* your verbal behavior in the conference in which you assumed the role of cooperating teacher and *(b)* the verbal behavior of the person who role-played the student in that conference. Record your perceptions of the verbal interaction on the conference rating scales shown on Analysis Guide 14.
2. When you have completed the scales, record under the appropriate headings *(a)* the verbal behaviors for which you would want to maintain the same amount of emphasis and those for which you would want to change the amount of emphasis by increasing or decreasing it and *(b)* the verbal behaviors of the student for which you think the amount of emphasis should be maintained or changed.
3. When you have completed Analysis Guide 14, you and your role-playing partner may want to replay the tapes and compare your perceptions of the verbal interaction that took place in the conferences.

THE ROLE OF THE COLLEGE SUPERVISOR IN OBSERVATION AND CONFERENCING

A major responsibility of the college supervisor is to observe the student's teaching and participate in conferences, both those held in connection with the observations and those in which the student's overall progress is assessed. The importance of these dimensions of the college supervisor's role cannot be stressed too strongly. Students and cooperating teachers are understandably critical of college supervisors who observe students only once or twice during an assignment of several weeks' duration and then present them with a grade or written evaluation. Evaluating students' competence on the basis of limited data is unjustifiable. With regard to conferences, it is clear that when adequate communication is not maintained, misunderstandings can arise, and the in-

Analysis Guide 14 Analyzing Conference Verbal Interaction

Supervising Teacher Perceptions of Student Teacher Behavior

In completing this questionnaire, please respond to the questions according to how you *perceive* your contacts with your student teacher, not how you feel they should be.

Listed below are a number of ways that you might have behaved during conference. Your concern should be the emphasis you placed on particular behaviors. Please place an X in the position you think designates the degree to which a behavior was used.

The categories for rating your behavior usage are (1) very heavy emphasis, (2) fairly heavy emphasis, (3) moderate emphasis, (4) very little emphasis, and (5) no emphasis.

Behaviors	Categories				
	1	2	3	4	5
1. Asked for student teacher's opinion					
2. Asked for clarification of ideas					
3. Accepted student teacher's ideas					
4. Praised student teacher					
5. Gave constructive suggestions about teaching					
6. Gave objective information about teaching behaviors					

Supervising Teacher Perceptions of Own Behavior

In completing this questionnaire, please respond to the questions according to your perceptions of your student teacher's behavior during the conference.

Listed below are a number of ways that your student teacher might have behaved during conference. Your concern should be the emphasis placed on particular behaviors. Please place an X in the position you think designates the degree to which a behavior was used.

The categories for rating [student teacher] behavior usage are (1) very heavy emphasis, (2) fairly heavy emphasis, (3) moderate emphasis, (4) very little emphasis, and (5) no emphasis.

Behaviors	Categories				
	1	2	3	4	5
1. Accepted supervising teacher's ideas and suggestions					
2. Offered suggestions and ideas					

151

	Categories				
Behaviors	1	2	3	4	5
3. Clarified own ideas and actions					
4. Assessed own teaching performance					
5. Asked for supervising teacher's opinion and ideas					
6. Asked for clarification of ideas					

Supervising Teacher Behavior		Student Behavior	
Maintain Amount of Emphasis	Change Amount of Emphasis	Maintain Amount of Emphasis	Change Amount of Emphasis
_____	_____	_____	_____
_____	_____	_____	_____
_____	_____	_____	_____

SOURCE: Grant Clothier and Elizabeth Kingsley. *Enriching student teacher relationships: Supervising teacher edition.* Shawnee Mission, KS: Midwest Educational Training and Research Organization, 1973, pp. 40–41. Reprinted with permission.

adequate communication can be perceived as lack of interest on the part of supervisors. Cooperating teachers and students cannot build effective relationships with supervisors they rarely see, and then for only brief periods of time.

College supervisors would agree that observation and conferencing are important. They differ considerably, however, in the success they achieve in fulfilling these responsibilities. Some supervisors maintain a schedule of observing and conferencing on a weekly or biweekly basis. Others, because of the number of students they have or the location of the schools in which the students are placed, visit each student less frequently. One university sets as a goal for its supervisors one observation cycle per week with each student teacher. Recognizing that at times a supervisor may have difficulty attaining this goal, the university further specifies that a minimum of three observations (including pre- and postobservation conferences) during each seven-week placement is required. It would not seem unrealistic to add to this requirement that the supervisor should hold at least that number of three-way conferences during the student's placement.

The frequency with which the college supervisor is able to engage in observing and conferencing affects the content and quality of the process. If the supervisor's visits are infrequent, the time may have to be spent in clarifying expectations and procedural matters. With frequent visits there will be time to provide guidance in specific aspects of the student's teaching and increase her effectiveness in self-analysis. In addition, frequent visits enable the college supervisor and cooperating teacher to build a relationship characterized by mutual understanding and support. The college supervisor who works closely with the student and cooperating teacher in a clinical experience can contribute significantly to the quality of the outcomes of that experience.

REFERENCES

Barrett-Lennard, G. *Dimensions of therapist response as causal factors in therapeutic change.* (Psychological Monograph 562). Washington, DC: American Psychological Association, 1962.

Blumberg, Arthur. *Supervisors and teachers: A private cold war* (2nd ed.). Berkeley, CA: McCutchan, 1980.

Boyan, Norman J., and Copeland, Willis D. *Instructional supervision training program.* Columbus, OH: Merrill, 1978.

Copeland, Willis D., and Boyan, Norman J. Training in instructional supervision: Improving the influence of the cooperating teacher. In Ruth Heidelbach (Ed.), *Developing supervisory practice.* Washington, DC: Association of Teacher Educators, 1975.

Dussault, Gilles. *A theory of supervision in teacher education.* New York: Teachers College Press, 1970.

Lang, Duaine C.; Quick, Alan F.; and Johnson, James A. *A partnership for the supervision of student teachers.* Mt. Pleasant, MI: Great Lakes Publishing, 1975.

McNeil, John D. *Toward accountable teachers: Their appraisal and improvement.* New York: Holt, Rinehart and Winston, 1971.

Rogers, Carl R. A theory of therapy, personality, and interpersonal relationships, as developed in the client-centered framework. *Psychology: A study of a science* (Vol. III). In Sigmund Koch (Ed.), *Formulations of the person and the social context.* New York: McGraw-Hill, 1959.

Rogers, Carl R. *On becoming a person.* Boston: Houghton Mifflin, 1961.

Simon, Anita, and Boyer, E. Gil (Eds.). *Mirrors for behavior III.* Wyncote, PA: Communication Materials Center, 1974.

Dussault (1970) identifies two major functions of supervision in professional laboratory experiences: a teaching function and an evaluating function. He describes the evaluating function in this way: "When viewed in the perspective of its evaluating function, supervision may be described as a process through which the prospective teacher is assessed or judged with regard to anything from his skill in a particular performance to his overall readiness to assume the responsibilities of professional teaching" (p. 3).

In fulfilling the teaching function of supervision, the supervisor of course evaluates the supervisee and his performance on a continuous basis. This evaluative aspect has

CHAPTER **8** THE
EVALUATION
PROCESS

been discussed in Chapters 6 and 7. Dussault suggests that the evaluation provided by the supervisor when he is fulfilling his teaching function is different from that provided when he is fulfilling his evaluating function. The former is evaluation as feedback and guidance; the latter is evaluation as judgmental assessment.

Teacher education students would no doubt agree with Dussault that these two kinds of evaluation are significantly different. While students in clinical experiences are concerned with the feedback they receive on a day-to-day basis, they frequently experience a particularly high level of anxiety as they anticipate receiving the final evaluation of cooperating teachers and college supervisors. This anxiety is understandable. For students in the initial stages of their professional program, satisfactory completion of a particular clinical experience may be a prerequisite for moving to the next stage of the program. For students nearing the completion of their professional program, the evaluation of the last, and probably the most extensive, clinical experience may determine whether the student completes the degree toward which she has been working, receives certification, or secures a teaching position. The importance, to students, of the evaluating function of supervision suggests the seriousness with which cooperating teachers and college supervisors need to consider their responsibilities in fulfilling this dimension of their role.

Cooperating teachers, as well as the students with whom they work, also frequently feel apprehensive about the final evaluation of a clinical experience. Lang, Quick, and Johnson (1975) describe the view of this responsibility held by many cooperating teachers:

> . . . Most classroom teachers enjoy working with prospective teachers in a clinical environment but when the time arrives for final evaluation it frequently has a traumatic effect. If one surveyed those responsible for the classroom supervision of student teachers, and rated what they disliked about supervision the most—the task of evaluating would win handily. (p. 139)

Perhaps cooperating teachers dislike the evaluation function of their role because they are aware that students view this function with apprehension. Perhaps, too, cooperating teachers find the evaluation function difficult because they recognize the problems that are inherent in attempting to assess the competence of preservice teachers.

This chapter first examines current efforts to address the overall problem of assessing the competence of preservice teachers. Following this, we consider the specific problems that can occur in implementing the evaluation process in clinical experiences. Lastly, a strategy is identified through which cooperating teachers, teacher education students, and college supervisors can work together in preventing problems as they engage in the evaluation process.

CURRENT EFFORTS IN THE EVALUATION OF PRESERVICE TEACHERS

Both the competency-based movement and the humanistic movement in teacher education have received widespread attention in the last decade. The origins and essential features of these approaches were summarized in Chapter

2. This section considers the contribution of each approach in refining the process of evaluating preservice teachers.

Evaluation and Competency-Based Teacher Education Programs

Several writers (Kay 1978, McDonald 1978, Medley 1978) point out that one result of the emergence of CBTE programs has been the increased attention given to the evaluation component of teacher education. McDonald (1972) summarizes the reasons for this recent concern with evaluation: "Traditional teacher-education programs have not had to demonstrate the effectiveness of their graduates as teachers. However, in competency-based programs, the emphasis on accountability, on scientific inquiry, and on the use of evaluative feedback for program development all thrust evaluation into a prominent role" (p. 56).

Medley (1978) suggests, more specifically, that the development of competency-based teacher education has caused educators to view evaluation in a different light. Prior to CBTE, the first step in efforts to evaluate teacher competence was to define the term. That this attempt never resulted in consensus regarding the nature of teacher competence was a persistent problem for those concerned with evaluation. CBTE avoids the problem, according to Medley, by shifting attention from defining overall competence to defining a set of individual competencies. Medley explains the way in which this shift in focus affects evaluation:

> Assessing program outcomes becomes a matter of assessing a student's mastery of a set of competencies, one by one, rather than assessing some mysterious, global entity called teacher competence. Evaluating a prospective teacher becomes more a matter of taking an inventory of his/her repertoire of competencies than one of overall evaluation. (p. 38)

The CBTE program model calls for the identification of the means by which individual competencies will be assessed and the criteria that will be used to determine mastery. A wide range of assessment techniques is currently in use in CBTE programs. The following are three broad kinds of assessment frequently employed: (1) assessment of knowledge, (2) assessment of teaching performance, and (3) assessment of products (lesson plans, case studies, etc.). An example of a competency and assessment procedure in each of these categories is shown here. These examples are adapted from the examples provided by Arends, Masla, and Weber (1971) in *Handbook for the Development of Instructional Modules in Competency-Based Teacher Education Programs.*

KNOWLEDGE
> *Competency.* The student will be able to distinguish between behavioral and nonbehavioral objectives.
> *Assessment procedure.* The student is given a list of ten objectives and is

asked to indicate which are behavioral and which are nonbehavioral. Criterion level: 90% correct responses.

TEACHING PERFORMANCE

Competency. The student will be able to teach a lesson using indirect teaching behaviors.

Assessment procedure. The student prepares a fifteen-minute lesson in an area of his choice and teaches it using indirect teaching behaviors as defined in the Flanders interaction analysis system. Criterion level: 85% of the teaching behaviors are indirect.

PRODUCT

Competency. The student will be able to write three behavioral objectives for each of the taxonomic domains (cognitive, affective, psychomotor).

Assessment procedure. The student writes three behavioral objectives for each of the taxonomic domains. The instructor assesses the appropriateness of the objectives.

McDonald (1978) describes the evaluation component of competency-based teacher education as it was projected in the early stages of program development: "The competency-based movement called for a . . . detailed, fine-grained evaluation of and reporting on the specific skills, knowledge, and attitudes of each teacher trainee" (p. 9). He indicates that this plan has been implemented only in a few teacher education institutions because of the complexities and difficulties involved in developing such a comprehensive evaluation program. McDonald contends, however, that while the implementation of comprehensive evaluation programs has been limited, the CBTE concept of evaluation has significantly influenced the way in which teacher educators view the evaluation of preservice teachers: "But, although relatively little progress has been made in developing these programs of evaluation, the attitudes of teacher educators have shifted from relative satisfaction with the old system to a belief that a more comprehensive and detailed evaluation system is desirable" (p. 9).

Evaluation and Humanistic Teacher Education Programs

One of the most widely voiced criticisms of humanistic teacher education programs is that they fail to include specific procedures for assessing the achievement of objectives. Currently, many humanistic teacher educators are addressing this problem. One such effort is reflected in the monograph *Humanistic Education: Objectives and Assessment,* a report prepared by the Working Group on Humanistic Education of the Association for Supervision and Curriculum Development. The authors of this report make clear their view that if humanistic education is to become a reality, the goals must be stated and assessment must be possible.

Writing in this monograph, Arthur Combs (1978) describes the problems involved in humanistic assessment. Combs identifies three special problems of assessment in humanistic education:

1. Many humanistic objectives are general in nature and do not lend themselves to precise behavioral measurement. Objectives such as citizenship and creativity are expressed in so many ways that behavioral measurement becomes impractical.
2. Effective assessment of humanistic objectives may require searching for new means of evaluation. New assessment techniques may seem less precise when compared to behavioral measures. This is to be expected since these techniques are in the early stages of development.
3. Many humanistic objectives deal with such aspects of the inner life as attitudes, values, fears, and aspirations. Although these qualities are not open to measurement through traditional techniques, there are procedures by which they can be assessed in dependable fashion.

Combs suggests that many of the behavioral measurement techniques currently in use can be applied to the assessment of some humanistic objectives. Techniques such as tests of values and attitudes are a source of valuable information, for example. Another source is simple statistical data, such as a record of the frequency of interracial incidents. Combs points out that identifying the behaviors that would indicate the achievement of a particular humanistic objective often will suggest the assessment technique to be applied.

While behavioral measures can be useful in assessing some humanistic objectives, Combs stresses that additional techniques are needed. He contends, moreover, that the recent preoccupation with behavioral measurement has caused educators to overlook or mistrust potentially valuable techniques for assessing humanistic objectives. One such technique is that of gathering case history evidence. Combs points out that this technique is particularly well suited to the evaluation of humanistic objectives because many of these objectives are highly individualized. Another technique recommended by Combs is the use of self-reporting. He suggests that in situations in which expression is encouraged, self-reports can provide useful information on values, beliefs, and attitudes. Lastly, Combs proposes that professional judgment is a valid source of data. He asserts that when reasonable criteria for reliability are applied, conclusions based on professional experience can be very useful in assessing humanistic objectives.

In another chapter of the same monograph, Aspy and Hicks (1978) demonstrate the feasibility of designing specific procedures for the measurement of humanistic objectives. They present fourteen objectives, called "signs of creative teaching," and identify for each objective a specific assessment procedure. Three objectives, and the procedures for assessment, are shown here:

Sign II: Less teacher talk; more listening to children, allowing them to use the teacher and the group as a sounding board when ideas are explored.
Assessment Procedure
1. Describe the classroom interaction using Flanders' Interaction Analysis.
2. Tabulate the total behavior in categories 1 through 7 (teacher talk).
3. Tabulate the total behavior in categories 8 and 9 (student talk).
Sign III: Less questioning for the right answers; more open-ended questions with room for difference and the exploration of many answers.

Assessment Procedure
1. Tabulate the number of open-ended (divergent) questions asked by the teacher during a classroom interaction.

Sign IV: Less destructive criticism; more teacher help which directs the child's attention back to his or her own feelings for clarification and understanding.

Assessment Procedure
1. Tabulate the number of statements by the teacher which indicate to the student that he or she is deficient, for example, "You shouldn't feel that way" or "You should be able to do that."
2. Complete the ratio

$$\frac{\text{number of destructive criticisms}}{\text{time observed}} = ?$$

(Aspy and Hicks 1978, pp. 32–33)

Educators have long affirmed the value of humanistic objectives at every level of education. Humanists contend, however, that these objectives have typically received less attention than objectives dealing with cognitive areas. This criticism probably is as valid in teacher education as it is in any other segment of the educational scene. Undoubtedly, a major reason for this imbalance has been the lack of acceptable procedures for assessing humanistic objectives. Today, humanistic educators are making significant progress in their search for solutions to this problem. As they continue this search, they will make a valuable contribution to efforts directed toward refining the process of evaluating preservice teachers.

PROBLEMS IN IMPLEMENTING THE EVALUATION PROCESS IN CLINICAL EXPERIENCES

The overall problem of the evaluation of preservice teachers is an important concern for everyone involved in teacher education. In implementing the evaluation process in clinical experiences, cooperating teachers, teacher education students, and college supervisors frequently encounter additional problems. If these problems are not resolved, the evaluation aspect of the clinical experience will be viewed negatively by all participants, regardless of how satisfying other aspects of the experience have been.

Everyone who has worked with preservice teachers in clinical experiences can recall situations in which a student teacher or intern has felt that she was evaluated unfairly by cooperating teacher, college supervisor, or both. In discussing the evaluation of preservice teachers, McNeil (1972) describes the practices that can result in unfair evaluations:

Charges against college supervisors of student teachers and interns are similar to those leveled at supervisors in school systems. The college supervisor seldom has a preobservational conference with these novice teachers before a lesson is presented, and there is often a conflict between the expectations of the college supervisor and the master teacher in the classroom where the student teacher is doing his teaching. The training teacher or master teacher is not explicit in defining the competencies which the student teacher must acquire from his training: performance objectives which define these competencies have rarely been prepared; there is no sequencing of the order in which these competencies are to be won; and there seldom is a systematic ordering of experiences necessary for achieving desired changes in the student teacher.

Since rating scales used to assess student teachers lack objectivity, the use of the scales often reveals the characteristics and prejudices of the rater—the master teacher or college supervisor—rather than giving an accurate description of the student teacher's work with pupils. (pp. 8–9)

When the conditions described by McNeil exist in a clinical setting, it is highly improbable that a student will receive a fair evaluation. Because of the importance of the final evaluation to students, it is essential that cooperating teachers and college supervisors understand the problems that can prevent effective evaluation from taking place.

Two obstacles to effective evaluation can exist with regard to expectations for the student during the clinical experience. The first arises from the failure of cooperating teacher and college supervisor to identify clearly the expectations that are held for the student. The student can find, at the conclusion of the assignment, that she is being evaluated with regard to expectations of which she was totally unaware. The second difficulty arises when expectations for the student held by cooperating teacher and college supervisor are in conflict. The student may attempt to resolve the problem by shifting from one set of expectations to another as the situation demands, or by choosing one set of expectations in preference to the other. If she follows the latter course, the student risks being evaluated negatively by the person whose expectations she did not choose.

Subjective assessment of the student's performance by cooperating teacher and college supervisor represents another obstacle to effective evaluation. Not only is subjective assessment unfair, it is of no value to the student as a basis for improving her performance. To ensure that the evaluation is both fair and useful, it is essential to make every effort to document judgments with evidence that is as objective as possible.

Finally, effective evaluation will be hindered if cooperating teacher and college supervisor fail to discuss the student's progress in the areas included on the final evaluation form throughout the clinical experience. This lack of communication can create a particularly serious problem when a student's performance is rated as less than satisfactory in one or more areas. It is understandable that the student will feel that she has been treated unfairly if she has been given no prior indication that her performance in these areas was not satisfactory. Clearly, cooperating teachers and college supervisors have the responsibility to provide students with continuous feedback, both as a matter of fairness and as a means of helping students increase their competence.

A STRATEGY FOR IMPLEMENTING THE EVALUATION PROCESS IN CLINICAL EXPERIENCES

While they unfortunately occur with some frequency, problems in implementing the evaluation process are not unavoidable. When cooperating teachers, students, and college supervisors understand the essential features of effective evaluation, and work together in planning and implementing the process, they can significantly reduce the number of problems. In doing this, they will reduce the anxiety of everyone involved and create an atmosphere in which a positive view of evaluation can develop.

Essential Features of Effective Evaluation

Effective evaluation of learning is characterized by careful attention to specific elements of the process. Those features that are essential to effective evaluation, and their application in clinical experiences, are summarized here:

1. Evaluation involves a continuous process of collecting evidence of the learner's progress toward specified objectives. In clinical experiences, this means that data regarding the student's performance in those areas included in the final evaluation must be collected throughout the experience.
2. Evaluation requires adequate samples of the learner's behavior. It is essential, in clinical experiences, that students be given numerous opportunities, at different points throughout the experience, to demonstrate their ability in areas in which they are being evaluated.
3. The techniques used to evaluate the learner's behavior must yield information that is both objective and appropriate. The wide range of techniques available today makes the requirement of objectivity more achievable in clinical experiences now than in the past. In striving for objectivity, however, care must be exercised to avoid (a) ignoring humanistic competencies because techniques for their assessment are not yet as objective as techniques for assessing other objectives or (b) attempting to assess humanistic competencies by applying techniques that are objective but inappropriate.
4. The learner must participate in the evaluation process. A major goal of the clinical experience is to facilitate the student's growth in self-analysis, and so it is essential that the student be involved in collecting data and evaluating her progress throughout the experience.
5. The results of evaluation are most useful when they are shared, not only with the learner, but with others who are concerned with the learner's progress. In clinical experiences, cooperating teacher, student, and college supervisor must share their perceptions of the student's progress at frequent intervals throughout the experience.

Developing a Plan for Implementing the Evaluation Process

A major source of the misunderstandings that can develop in the evaluation process is the failure of the participants to plan ways in which they will work together in implementing evaluation. While responsibilities and procedures will be defined within the context of specific situations, several factors need to be considered regardless of the setting. Attention to these aspects of the evaluation process can help cooperating teacher, student, and college supervisor develop a plan that meets the needs and conditions of their unique setting.

It is essential, first, that the college supervisor provide cooperating teacher and student with copies of the final evaluation form the cooperating teacher will be asked to complete. Further, it may be necessary for the college supervisor to explain its use. Both cooperating teacher and student should be provided with answers to several relevant questions: Is this the form that the college supervisor will complete, or will she use a different form? Who will receive the various copies of the completed form? Will the cooperating teacher be asked to complete the form only at the conclusion of the student's assignment or at other times as well?

Typically, the evaluation form is a rating scale or checklist. Unfortunately, these scales and checklists often fail to provide a clear definition of the criteria to be applied by the rater in making a judgment. This results in a highly subjective assessment. An example of this lack of defined criteria is shown in Figure 8.1, which appears on the student teaching rating scale used at one university. The items on the scale are grouped in eight areas. The item shown in the figure is included in the area labeled *Preparation For Teaching: Resources*.

The following questions could occur to cooperating teachers who attempt to rate students' performance with regard to this item: What rating should be given to (1) the student who has prepared many teacher-made resources but has failed to evaluate their effectiveness? (2) the student who has prepared one or two resources and has evaluated their effectiveness? (3) the student who has prepared many resources and has found, in evaluating their use, that they were ineffective? In order to rate a student on this item, a cooperating teacher would

Figure 8.1 Preparation For Teaching: Resources

	Item Check					Comments
	1	2	3	4	5	
1. Prepares teacher-made resources and evaluates the effectiveness of their use.						

Rank Order: (1) Unsuccessful   (2) Poor   (3) Fair   (4) Good   (5) Excellent

SOURCE: This rating scale item and the items that appear on Analysis Guide 15 and Analysis Guide 16 were adapted from *Performance criteria for student teaching.* College of Education, Temple University, Philadelphia, PA, 1975.

have to develop his own criteria, which might not correspond to the criteria in the minds of the student and the college supervisor.

If the participants in a clinical experience are to avoid the misunderstandings that can arise from the application of different sets of evaluative criteria, they will need to establish criteria that will be accepted and applied in their particular setting. For example, a cooperating teacher, student, and college supervisor might agree that the following criteria will be applied in evaluating performance with regard to the item identified here, *Prepares teacher-made resources and evaluates the effectiveness of their use:* (1) number of resources prepared, (2) number of curricular areas involved, (3) variety of resources, (4) involvement of pupils in preparing resources where appropriate, (5) clear relationship shown between resource and lesson objectives, (6) pupils understand the purpose of each resource. They can then decide on the relationship of combinations of these criteria to the intervals of their evaluation form rating scale (i.e., which criteria must be met, and to what extent, to achieve a rating of *fair, good, excellent,* etc.). While the cooperating teacher, student, and college supervisor will recognize that the criteria they develop may differ from those developed by their counterparts in other settings, they will at least be assured that they are in agreement.

Once the student, cooperating teacher, and college supervisor have discussed the college's evaluation form, they can plan ways in which they will use the form. One way in which the evaluation form can be used is as a guide for planning the sequence of the student's experiences during the assignment. This will ensure that the student has opportunities to participate in each area in which she will be evaluated.

The form can also be used to select those aspects of the student's behavior that should be the focus of observations and conferences. This will direct attention to the continuous collection of data needed for accurate assessment of the student's performance.

A third use, of course, is as a means of evaluating the student's progress. To be effective, the evaluation process must involve the participants in sharing their perceptions of the student's progress at intervals throughout the experience. At evaluation conferences, cooperating teacher, student, and college supervisor can assess the student's growth in areas previously focused on, and select new areas as this is indicated by the student's progress.

It is important that the intervals at which evaluation conferences will be held are identified at the beginning of the clinical experience. If this step is not taken, these conferences can be overlooked as more immediate concerns occupy the attention of the participants. Some teacher education programs have developed procedures for assuring that planned, periodic assessment takes place. In the student teaching program at Tennessee Technological University, for example, assessment procedures are included in the guidebook used by students, supervising teachers, and university supervisors. Students work toward achievement of this program's objectives through three successive stages of activities. When a student has completed the activities within each stage, progress is recorded by student, supervising teacher, and university supervisor. On the basis of their analysis of the student's competence, they then identify those objectives achieved and those that require further attention. This assessment procedure assures that the student will receive feedback and engage in self-analysis at regular intervals throughout the student teaching experience.

The form used by the supervising teacher to record the student's progress in this program is shown in Figure 8.2 with four of the twenty-six program objectives. Parallel forms are provided for the student and university supervisor.

Figure 8.2   Student Teacher Rating Chart

Form for Supervising Teacher

Student Teacher _____   Supervising Teacher _____

Grade or Subject _____   School _____

Use the following continuum for rating the student teacher's performance on each of the objectives:

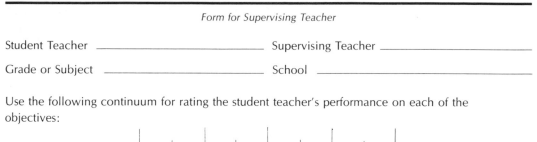

Poor   1   2   3   4   5   6   7   8   Excellent

Example: 1   2   3   4   5   6   7   8

Directions: After the student teacher has completed the activities suggested in a particular phase for each objective, rate him and record his progress on this chart. Use a numeral 1 to record each Phase 1 rating, a numeral 2 to record each Phase 2 rating, etc. When there is agreement between the student teacher, the supervising teacher, and the college supervisor that excellence for a particular objective has been achieved, the student teacher need not continue with subsequent activities in other phases designed to meet that objective. If the student teacher has made no progress in a particular phase, it may be necessary to write more than one numeral in the same space on the continuum. At the end of the student teacher's field assignment, multiply the final rating for each objective times the factor weight, and then total the far right-hand column to express the achievement numerically.

Instructional Aspects of Teaching	*Rating Continuum*	*Factor Weight*	*Total*
I-1 Achieves acceptance by students, accepts his students, and reacts successfully to all of the interplay between teacher and students.			
	1 2 3 4 5 6 7 8 ×	3	____
I-2 Demonstrates knowledge in the subject or grade he is assigned to teach.			
	1 2 3 4 5 6 7 8 ×	3	____

I-3 Demonstrates understanding of the processes involved in selection of course
content.

_____ |_|_|_|_|_|_|_|_| ×   1   ____
                                    1 2 3 4 5 6 7 8

I-4 Demonstrates skill in planning, in effi-
cient utilization of time, and in organization.

_____ |_|_|_|_|_|_|_|_| ×   3   ____
                                    1 2 3 4 5 6 7 8

SOURCE: Adapted from Robert E. DuBey, Virginia L. Endley, Betty D. Roe, and Daniel J. Tollett. *A performance-based guide to student teaching* (Rev. ed.). Danville, IL: The Interstate Printers and Publishers, 1975, pp. 143–44. Reprinted with permission.

Activity 15   In order to experience planning the evaluation component of a clinical experience, role-play a three-way conference with two other group members so that cooperating teacher, student, and college supervisor are included in the conference. Record the outcomes of the conference on Analysis Guide 15. Keep the information recorded on Analysis Guide 15 for use with Activity 16. Complete the following procedure for this conference:

1. Examine the two rating scale items, taken from a student teaching evaluation form, shown on the analysis guide. Develop criteria that could be applied in rating a student's performance with regard to these competencies using the following scale: (1) unsuccessful, (2) fair, (3) excellent.
2. The evaluation form from which the two items were taken includes items in the following areas: (1) Preparation for Teaching (a. resources, b. planning); (2) Teaching Behavior (a. presentation, b. socialization, c. control, d. evaluating pupil progress, e. professional identity and growth); (3) Home-School-Community Relations. Identify ways in which the evaluation form could be used during the student's assignment by (a) cooperating teacher and student, (b) college supervisor and student, and (c) cooperating teacher, student, and college supervisor.
3. Identify the intervals, during a seven-week full-time student teaching experience, at which assessment of the student's progress should be made by (a) cooperating teacher and student, (b) college supervisor and student, and (c) cooperating teacher, student, and college supervisor.

Sharing Evaluation Results

If cooperating teacher and student have worked together in assessing the student's progress throughout the assignment, they will be prepared to complete the final form cooperatively. Cooperating teacher and student can review the

Items for Evaluation

Teaching Behavior: Presentation

	1	2	3
1. Provides for individual differences in learning styles and capacities and for the personal contribution of each child, offering varied means for demonstrating achievement (Example: individual reports).			

Teaching Behavior: Socialization

2. Helps children to find acceptable ways of expressing emotions, both positive and negative.

Scale: 1 = Unsuccessful; 2 = Fair; 3 = Excellent

Assessment Criteria

1. _____   2. _____

_____   _____

_____   _____

Uses for the Evaluation Form

By Cooperating Teacher and Student _____

By College Supervisor and Student _____

By Cooperating Teacher, College Supervisor, and Student _____

Assessment Intervals

For Cooperating Teacher and Student _____

For College Supervisor and Student _____

For Cooperating Teacher, College Supervisor, and Student _____

student's overall progress and record her achievement on the evaluation form, which the cooperating teacher will submit to the college. Completing this final assessment jointly will reduce the anxiety often felt by cooperating teacher and student when this step is undertaken by the cooperating teacher independently. Of course, if the cooperating teacher records his assessment independently, he has the responsibility of discussing the completed evaluation form with the student before submitting it to the college.

The final assessment of the student's performance by the college supervisor will also be less anxiety-producing if college supervisor and student work together in completing the evaluation form that will become part of the student's permanent record at the college. Since it is the college supervisor who is responsible for indicating whether the student has completed the experience satisfactorily, it is essential that she help the student have a clear understanding of the basis for her assessment. By involving the student in completing the final evaluation, the college supervisor can not only share her perceptions of the student's progress but can also guide the student in identifying areas of strength that have emerged from the experience and areas on which she will want to focus attention in subsequent experiences.

An important step in sharing evaluation results, and one that is frequently overlooked, involves arranging a conference during which the cooperating teacher, and the student where possible, can provide the college supervisor with information beyond that recorded on the cooperating teacher's evaluation form. This additional input is especially necessary with regard to any areas of the student's performance for which the final rating indicates a need for further attention. In each of these areas, the cooperating teacher and student can share with the college supervisor their perceptions of the factors that prevented the student from achieving a higher level of competence. They can, in addition, suggest ways to help the student increase her competence in these areas. This information will be particularly useful if the college supervisor is responsible for planning subsequent clinical experiences for the student. Using the input offered by cooperating teacher and student, as well as her own assessment, the college supervisor will be able to provide the guidance needed to assure the student's continued professional growth.

One way in which cooperating teacher and student can share their analysis of evaluation results with the college supervisor is shown in Figure 8.3.

Figure 8.3   Sharing Evaluation Results

Item			
Preparation for Teaching: Resources	*1*	*2*	*3*
1. Prepares teacher-made resources and evaluates the effectiveness of their use.		√	
Scale: 1 = Unsuccessful; 2 = Fair; 3 = Excellent			

Information to Share with the College Supervisor	*College Supervisor's Follow-Up*
The student has had no background in preparing resources; therefore, she was not comfortable in developing materials and used only a few during her placement. Those resources were developed only in mathematics. The student felt that sometimes the learners did not see the purpose for the materials she developed. She would like more experience in integrating resources with activities.	• Acquaint the student with college's audio visual lab and the school district's Teacher Center for help in developing special resources. • Provide the student with references and sources for developing material in various curricular areas. • Place student with a cooperating teacher who consistently develops a variety of teacher-made resources in many curricular areas. • During the next assignment, review the student's plans in order to ensure that when resources are used the purposes will be clear to the learners.

Prior to a conference with the college supervisor, the cooperating teacher and student recorded information that they felt would help the college supervisor understand the student's inability to achieve a higher rating with regard to preparing and evaluating teacher-made resources. They then shared the information with the college supervisor in a three-way conference. Following this, college supervisor, student, and cooperating teacher participated in identifying ways in which the college supervisor could help the student make progress in this area in her next assignment.

Activity 16 In order to complete the evaluation process through sharing results, role-play the following conferences: (1) a two-way conference in which cooperating teacher and student identify information to provide for the college supervisor; (2) a three-way conference in which cooperating teacher, student,

---

Analysis Guide 16   Sharing Evaluation Results

Items for Evaluation

	1	2	3
Teaching Behavior: Presentation			
1. Provides for individual differences in learning styles and capacities and for the personal contributions of each child, offering varied means for demonstrating achievement (Example: individual reports).		√	
Teaching Behavior: Socialization			
2. Helps children to find acceptable ways of expressing emotions, both positive and negative.	√		

Scale: 1 = Unsuccessful; 2 = Fair; 3 = Excellent

Information to Share with the College Supervisor	*College Supervisor's Follow-Up*

---

and college supervisor plan for the college supervisor's continued guidance of the student. Role-play these conferences with the group members with whom you role-played the conference in Activity 15. Complete the following procedure for these conferences:

1. In the two-way conference, examine the two rating scale items, and the student's ratings for the items, shown on Analysis Guide 16. Next, identify factors that could have caused the student to have performed at the levels indicated by the ratings. You may find it helpful, in completing this step, to review the assessment criteria that you developed for these items and recorded on Analysis Guide 15. As the information that will be shared with the college supervisor is identified, record it in the appropriate column on Analysis Guide 16.
2. In the three-way conference, share the information recorded on Analysis Guide 16 with the member of the group who is assuming the role of the college supervisor. Identify ways in which the college supervisor can provide continued guidance for the student in the areas being discussed. Record this information in the appropriate column on Analysis Guide 16.

In concluding this discussion of evaluation in clinical experiences, it seems worthwhile to reemphasize a point discussed earlier in the chapter. Perhaps no dimension of the clinical experience has a greater potential for creating an atmosphere of anxiety than does the evaluation process. What has been suggested here is that the problems that produce the anxiety are not unavoidable. If cooperating teacher, student, and college supervisor are willing to cooperate in planning and implementing the evaluation process, they can reduce the number of problems they encounter, lessen the anxiety of everyone involved, and create an atmosphere in which a positive view of evaluation can develop.

REFERENCES

Arends, Robert L.; Masla, John A.; and Weber, Wilford A. *Handbook for the development of instructional modules in competency-based teacher education programs.* Buffalo, NY: The Center for the Study of Teaching, 1971.

Aspy, David N., and Hicks, Laurabeth H. Research on humanistic objectives. In *Humanistic education: Objectives and assessment.* Washington, DC: Association for Supervision and Curriculum Development, 1978.

Combs, Arthur W. Assessing humanistic objectives: Some general considerations. In *Humanistic education: Objectives and assessment.* Washington, DC: Association for Supervision and Curriculum Development, 1978.

Dussault, Gilles. *A theory of supervision in teacher education.* New York: Teachers College Press, 1970.

Kay, Patricia M. Assessing preservice teachers' competence. *Journal of Teacher Education,* March-April 1978, 29 (2), 7–8.

Lang, Duaine C.; Quick, Alan F.; and Johnson, James A. *A partnership for the supervision of student teachers.* Mt. Pleasant, MI: Great Lakes Publishing, 1975.

McDonald, Frederick J. Evaluating preservice teachers' competence. *Journal of Teacher Education,* March-April 1978, *29* (2), 9–13.

McDonald, Frederick J. Evaluation of teaching behavior. In W. Robert Houston and Robert B. Howsam (Eds.), *Competency-based teacher education: Progress, problems and prospects.* Chicago: Science Research Associates, 1972.

McNeil, John D. *Toward accountable teachers: Their appraisal and improvement.* New York: Holt, Rinehart and Winston, 1971.

Medley, Donald M. Alternative assessment strategies. *Journal of Teacher Education,* March-April 1978, *29* (2), 38–42.

PART 4

looking ahead

Today, perhaps more than at any time in the recent past, a discussion of the future of teacher education is not only relevant but essential. Indeed, in the light of the rapidly changing conditions that are having an impact on teacher education, it would seem a serious omission to fail to identify critical issues that must be addressed if new demands are to be met.

An extensive consideration of the many conditions, issues, and challenges being discussed in the literature of teacher education at the present time is clearly beyond the scope of this chapter. What can be attempted is an examination of the major forces that are creating demands for change and the implications of these demands for the future of teacher education.

CHAPTER **9** PERSPECTIVES ON THE fUTURE

TEACHER EDUCATION IN TRANSITION

Writing in a recent monograph, *Emerging Professional Roles for Teacher Educators*, Edward C. Pomeroy (1978), Executive Director of the American Association of Colleges for Teacher Education, describes his view of the status of teacher education:

> Teacher education today is in an unprecedented state of ferment. Barely two decades distant from the 21st century, the future direction of this important enterprise has been cast into confusion. Higher education institutions, teacher organizations, and state departments of education are engaged in efforts to reduce that confusion by seeking answers to basic problems, answers that will lead to more effective programs of education personnel development. The crucial issues at stake: Who shall control the preparation of education personnel for tomorrow's schools? And who shall determine the continuing staff development priorities— needs to be met, content of training programs, delivery systems, and quality control mechanisms? (p. v)

Pomeroy goes on to say that these crucial issues must be examined and addressed before the profession can begin to design new programs, reallocate financial and human resources, and prepare teacher educators who have the qualities necessary for implementing new programs.

Current Concerns in Teacher Education

Much of the confusion described by Pomeroy has its roots in the problems being faced by public school educators. Several of these problems, and their impact on teacher education, are considered here.

At all levels of government, education is competing with other segments of society for a limited number of dollars. As a result, as Mulhern (1978) phrases it, ". . . public education is into an era of accountability in which the central question is the 'learning effectiveness' of each expendable dollar" (p. 46). This concern for justifying expenditures in terms of pupil performance has led to efforts to define minimum levels of competence and to hold teachers accountable for pupil achievement of these outcomes.

The implications of the accountability movement are clear. Teachers who are being held accountable for pupil performance will, in turn, hold teacher preparation programs accountable for their ability to bring about desired levels of pupil achievement. It is appropriate that they do so. As Mulhern points out, teacher educators, like classroom teachers, must become accountable for their program graduates. He contends that teacher educators will have to reexamine their programs with regard to goals, content, and site location and make revisions, if necessary, in order to respond to this demand for accountability.

Howey, Yarger, and Joyce (1978) identify another pressure that has implications for teacher education: the call for increased attention to children with special needs. Passage of the Education of All Handicapped Children Act (PL 94–142) requires individual diagnosis and prescription for each handicapped child. In addition, there has been the development of bilingual and bicultural programs for pupils whose native language is not English. Finally, there is continuing pressure on the educational system to be more effective in responding to the needs of children in urban and rural areas.

Attempting to meet the special needs of pupils has created corresponding pressures for change in teacher education. Critics contend that teacher educators are not preparing teachers for meeting a wide range of pupil needs. Teacher educators must respond to this criticism through a careful evaluation of the correspondence between the objectives of their programs and the expectations that will be held for their graduates when they assume teaching positions.

A third force in public education that has been widely discussed is the shift in power in the politics of education (Haberman and Stinnett 1973, Massanari 1978, Mulhern 1978). The National Education Association and the American Federation of Teachers have gained considerable strength and support and now have influence on federal education policy. Another goal being pursued is self-determination with regard to teacher certification. Achieving this goal would mean that the professional organization, rather than the state, would determine who is to be certified to teach.

Mulhern points out that the issue of control over teacher certification has significant implications for teacher education programs. The current pattern of university control over programs and recommendations for certification would change considerably if the profession were self-determining. Mulhern argues that this shift would make it necessary for college-based teacher educators to form partnerships, characterized by equality of decision making, with school personnel in order to retain their influence in the profession at large.

Teacher Effectiveness Research and Teacher Education

The importance of the issues facing educators today points to the critical need for increased efforts to relate research on teaching to teacher education. Without the knowledge base this relationship would provide, it cannot be expected that educators will develop viable, long-range solutions to current problems. While this need has not gone unrecognized in the past, attempts to establish a strong connection between teacher effectiveness research and teacher education have been blocked by several obstacles. There are encouraging indications, however, that movement toward overcoming these obstacles has begun.

Medley (1977) identifies three problems that have thwarted efforts to strengthen the connections between research on teaching and teacher education. First, because of the difficulties inherent in conducting research on teacher effectiveness, many of the earlier findings were inaccurate and, as a result, inconsistent with each other. Medley indicates that recent research has been better designed, and that it is now possible to report more findings that are consistent. His report of the strongest and most dependable findings of process-product research reflects this promising development.

As the number of studies of teacher effectiveness increased, a second obstacle to the establishment of a link between this research and teacher education emerged: the inaccessibility of the growing body of literature in which findings were reported. Medley contends that in addition to being vast and inaccessible, much of the literature was difficult to comprehend and evaluate. He suggests that teacher educators can hardly be blamed if they abandon the difficult and time-consuming task of attempting to sift these findings. It is encouraging to find steps being taken to overcome this obstacle. In the introductory section of his own report, for example, Medley makes this statement of purpose: "It is the primary purpose of this report to provide the teacher educator with access to the meaningful findings of research in teacher effectiveness" (p. 1). Another recent work in which the findings of research on teaching are reported in a straightforward, readable manner is *Research on Teaching*, edited by Penelope L. Peterson and Herbert J. Walberg (1979). Both the Medley report and the Peterson and Walberg text were used as sources for the summaries of teacher effectiveness research presented in Chapter 1.

A third obstacle that has blocked efforts to link research on teaching and teacher education is the lack of close collaboration between reseachers and practitioners. Medley points to a serious consequence of this lack of collaboration: Researchers do not seem to be studying the teacher behaviors that teacher educators consider important. He notes that when a list of behaviors studied by researchers is compared with the list of competencies that define the objectives of a competency-based teacher education program, it is evident that the lists are far from congruent. Medley says: "The way out of this situation is for future process-product research to use as process variables the same competencies that the teacher education programs are trying to help teachers acquire. Researchers and teacher educators should get together to investigate the validity of the latter's program goals" (p. 67).

Several statements support Medley's position and indicate a developing awareness of the need for the participation of all educators in the effort to establish a strong connection between teacher effectiveness research and teacher education. In his discussion of the forces impinging on the future of teacher education, Karl Massanari (1978) writes: "Meanwhile, there has been a growing realization of the inadequacy of the knowledge base which supports the education of teachers, as well as an increased awareness that education research should focus on current problems faced by classroom teachers and that teachers themselves should be involved in such research activity" (p. 4).

Nathaniel Gage (1978) examines the prospects that lie ahead in research on teaching and predicts the involvement of teachers in the development of the scientific basis for teacher education programs:

> Within the field of teacher education, the knowledge of better ways to teach will be applied more effectively. The applications will be more warmly welcomed because teachers will have much greater say in determining the substance, method, and organization of the education. The voice of teachers on these matters will be more enlightened because they will have understood and shared in developing, through collaboration with research workers, the scientific basis for the objectives and methods of teacher education programs. (p. 94)

Thus, a clear call for collaboration in strengthening the knowledge base of teaching and teacher education is being sounded. It is essential that all participants in programs of teacher education respond to this challenge.

EMERGING ROLES AND PRIORITIES IN CLINICAL EXPERIENCES

In the initial section of this chapter, several of the forces and conditions that are creating demands for change in teacher education were explored. The call for cooperative efforts in responding to these and other pressures is being voiced as strongly today as is the call for collaboration in meeting research needs. There is a growing awareness that effective responses to current conditions cannot be developed through the efforts of single educational agencies working independently of each other. The development of responses that are comprehensive enough to be effective will require the cooperation of various sectors of the profession: schools, colleges, state departments of education, and professional organizations. If it is to be productive, this cooperation will necessarily involve the participants in a process of mutual decision making in defining emerging roles and in establishing the priorities toward which their efforts will be directed.

Emerging Roles in Clinical Experiences

In no aspect of teacher education is the need for cooperation, particularly between college and school personnel, more apparent than it is in the clinical component. While the long-standing relationships that exist between many colleges and school districts would seem to support this view, Howey, Yarger, and Joyce (1978) contend that although school-college relationships are extensive, they are relatively superficial. They report that only rarely are teachers and other school personnel involved in designing preservice programs, developing admission procedures, or conducting research activities. Moreover, they note that little support and training are provided for cooperating teachers. If their survey accurately reflects school-college relationships, it is clear that these relationships will need to be restructured if teacher educators are seriously interested in developing cooperative approaches to addressing the issues they face today.

One dimension of this restructuring will involve the redefinition of the roles of college-based teacher educator and school-based teacher educator.[1] What expectations for the occupants of these roles can be anticipated as a result of this effort? In his contribution to *Emerging Professional Roles for Teacher Educators*, William H. Drummond (1978) responds to this question by (1) analyzing the context of teacher education and (2) identifying roles that seem to emerge from this analysis. Several aspects of his role descriptions have particular relevance for the clinical component of teacher education programs. The following discussion of selected aspects of the roles of school-based teacher educator and college-based teacher educator is based on Drummond's projection of how these roles will be defined "in the not too distant future" (p. 23).

[1] Drummond (1978), in *Emerging professional roles for teacher educators*, uses the term "college-based teacher educators" to refer to personnel who work in schools, colleges, or departments of education. Houston (1978), in the same monograph, uses the term "school-based teacher educators" to refer to personnel who are responsible for preservice, inservice, or continuing education and whose primary base of operations is in an elementary or secondary school.

Drummond bases his projections for the future, in part, on a very significant assumption concerning funding for teacher education programs. This assumption is that preservice programs that are entirely campus-based, and lack the approval of school district personnel and teacher organizations, will no longer receive public funding. As this situation occurs, according to Drummond, college-based teacher educators will direct increased attention to preservice programs that are field-oriented and developed in cooperation with school-based teacher educators and members of professional organizations.

The preservice programs Drummond forecasts will be "competency based and site specific" (p. 21). Emphasis will be on students' acquisition of those competencies that will enable them to work successfully with children and youth of different socioeconomic and cultural backgrounds. The assessment of these and other competencies that students will be expected to develop will take place throughout their professional sequence. The development and implementation of assessment techniques and procedures will be the responsibility of both school and college personnel.

Drummond projects several dimensions for the roles of college-based teacher educator and school-based teacher educator. As is the case now, however, some school-based and college-based teacher educators will direct their energies primarily toward working with preservice students in the capacities of cooperating teacher and college supervisor. Drummond identifies the competencies that will be expected of teacher educators who assume these particular responsibilities. He predicts that eventually every certified teacher will be expected to demonstate the skills associated with the role of cooperating teacher. Central to this role is the ability to implement the process of clinical supervision (discussed in Chapters 3 and 7). College supervisors will be expected to work closely with teachers, through staff development programs, to help them develop the clinical supervisory skills they need in order to assume the role of cooperating teacher.

In summary, if Drummond's predictions are accurate, the roles of teacher educators participating in clinical experiences will acquire new dimensions in response to the following developments:

1. School-based teacher educators and college-based teacher educators will collaborate in the development of preservice teacher education programs.
2. Preservice teacher education programs will be field-oriented.
3. School-based teacher educators and college-based teacher educators will share responsibility for the assessment and retention of prospective teachers.
4. College supervisors will provide instructional programs to help classroom teachers develop the skills associated with the role of cooperating teacher.

Emerging Priorities in Clinical Experiences

Perhaps the most significant recent development in programs of teacher education is the national trend toward providing earlier and increased clinical experiences. College and school personnel applaud this trend, but they are also aware of the needs that arise from efforts to expand the clinical component of teacher education. Those needs that should be given priority in a given setting will be based, of course, on the participants' analysis of their particular situation. There seem to be several areas of concern, however, that must be addressed by teacher educators regardless of their specific college/school context. In concluding this chapter, then, we examine these emerging priorities.

Clearly, one of the first tasks to be undertaken in designing a preservice program that provides a variety of clinical experiences is that of differentiating the experiences to be included. Competencies need to be identified for each experience in which students will participate. A clear sequence for acquiring these competencies must also be established so that students are provided with a gradual induction into the teaching role. The failure of program planners to address the need to differentiate and articulate clinical experiences will imply that students benefit from increased experiences "out in the schools" regardless of what they do while they are there. Certainly, this represents an inadequate and unjustifiable approach to teacher education.

The preparation of personnel who have the ability to work with preservice students in a variety of clinical experiences is another task to which attention must be given. An emerging priority is that of providing training opportunities for the increasing numbers of cooperating teachers who will be working with students as the clinical component of teacher education programs expands. Because of the greater demand, many cooperating teachers undoubtedly will occupy this role for the first time. They cannot be expected to provide effective guidance for students unless they are given planned, systematic opportunities to develop the skills associated with the role of cooperating teacher.

It is encouraging that teacher education institutions, state departments of education, and school districts are evidencing an increased awareness of the importance of helping cooperating teachers acquire needed competencies. Since the fall of 1979, for example, Northern Illinois University has required its cooperating teachers to take a course designed to help them develop the skills they need to supervise a variety of clinical experiences. Dr. Charles Moore (1978), Director of Early Clinical Experiences at the university, explains that this requirement was initiated in response to the recently mandated Illinois guidelines which recommend special training for cooperating teachers.

In Texas, recognition of the need to provide training opportunities for cooperating teachers has resulted in a state mandate that all teachers who work with student teachers participate in a program of inservice education. The formation of the Austin Cooperative Teacher Education Center was the response of one school district to this mandate. This consortium regularly offers a wide range of workshops from which cooperating teachers select those that they wish to attend.[2] As the trend toward increasing clinical experiences continues, it can be expected that other states will follow the lead of Illinois and Texas.

Concern for the effectiveness of college supervisors does not seem to parallel the concern for the competence of cooperating teachers that is currently in evidence. On the basis of responses from 94 teacher preparation

[2]Austin Cooperative Teacher Education Center, Office of Staff Development and Student Teaching. *Supervising teacher staff development.* Austin, Texas, 1979.

institutions, Bowman (1978) reports that the methods used by these colleges and universities to ensure the competency of supervisors are (1) cooperating teacher and student teacher evaluation, (2) faculty and departmental evaluation, and (3) evaluation on the basis of teaching experience rather than through formal efforts. Bowman concludes that his findings give "little assurance that the supervision of student teachers holds a great priority among teacher preparation institutions" (p. 64). While Bowman's sample is not large, his findings make it clear that there is an urgent need, in some institutions at least, to define the competencies required by college supervisors and to develop systematic, reliable techniques for their assessment. This need becomes particularly critical as clinical experiences increase and additional personnel, many of whom may lack formal preparation for the role, assume the responsibilities of college supervisor.

The final concern to be discussed here involves research efforts in clinical experiences. Zeichner (1978) reports that most studies of student teaching have collected data by administering questionnaires before and after the student teaching experience. Few studies have examined the process itself as it evolves over time. He then notes the increasing tendency in the literature of teacher education to call for research that focuses on the student teaching process and that includes observations of students throughout the experience. Zeichner finds it disappointing, however, that as yet only a few researchers have responded to this call.

As the clinical component of teacher education expands, it can be hoped that other researchers will join with the participants in clinical experiences in examining what occurs not only during the traditional student teaching experience but also during different kinds of pre-student teaching and internship experiences. It is essential to have this knowledge in order to assess the effects of expanding clinical experiences and make sound judgments with regard to their design.

The foregoing discussion of concerns, predictions, and priorities is by no means exhaustive. Many other issues in teacher education are being discussed and debated. Is it possible to identify a recurring theme that gives direction to the search for solutions to current problems? It seems that it is, and this theme is twofold: (1) that major changes in teacher education need to be brought about; and (2) that a unified effort by the entire profession will be required to effect these changes.

Many teacher educators are optimistic about the possibility of achieving a unified effort that will result in significant changes. Others, pointing to present educational and societal conditions, are far more pessimistic. More important than the question of which of these positions is the more valid is this question: Where does the ultimate responsibility for determining the future of teacher education lie? Howey, Yarger, and Joyce (1978) leave no doubt as to who is responsible for the future of teacher education. Because this response is one which every teacher educator must confront, it seems appropriate to end this discussion of the future with their statement:

> In the final analysis, after the dust has settled and the rhetoric has diminished, the
> onus for creating major improvement in the profession will be with the profession

itself. In simplistic terms, it will require the collegial efforts of many individuals who believe that children can be better educated if their teachers are better prepared. Although boosts may come from external sources such as the public media and various federal, state, and local government agencies (including the courts), real improvement will occur only as a result of the efforts of the people within our profession. (p. 50)

REFERENCES

Bowman, Novy. Student teacher supervision practices and policies. *Action in Teacher Education,* Summer 1978, *1* (1) 62–65.

Drummond, William H. Emerging roles of the college-based teacher educator. In *Emerging professional roles for teacher educators.* Washington, DC: American Association of Colleges for Teacher Education and the ERIC Clearinghouse on Teacher Education, 1978.

Gage, N. L. *The scientific basis of the art of teaching.* New York: Teachers College Press, 1978.

Haberman, Martin, and Stinnett, T. M. *Teacher education and the new profession of teaching.* Berkeley, CA: McCutchan, 1973.

Houston, W. Robert. Emerging roles of the school-based teacher educator. In *Emerging professional roles for teacher educators.* Washington, DC: American Association of Colleges for Teacher Education and the ERIC Clearinghouse on Teacher Education, 1978.

Howey, Kenneth; Yarger, Sam J.; and Joyce, Bruce R. *Improving teacher education.* Palo Alto, CA: Association of Teacher Educators, 1978.

Massanari, Karl. Changing conditions and perspectives about them. In *Emerging professional roles for teacher educators.* Washington, DC: American Association of Colleges for Teacher Education and the ERIC Clearinghouse on Teacher Education, 1978.

Medley, Donald M. *Teacher competence and teacher effectiveness: A review of process-product research.* Washington, DC: American Association of Colleges for Teacher Education, 1977.

Moore, Charles. Required training for cooperating teachers. *ATE News Letter,* November-December 1978, *12* (2), 6.

Mulhern, John. Charting new directions in teacher education. *Journal of Teacher Education,* July–August 1978, *29* (4), 46–51.

Peterson, Penelope L., and Walberg, Herbert J. (Eds.). *Research on teaching: Concepts, findings and implications.* Berkeley, CA: McCutchan, 1979.

Pomeroy, Edward C. Foreword. In *Emerging professional roles for teacher educators.* Washington, DC: American Association of Colleges for Teacher Education and the ERIC Clearinghouse on Teacher Education, 1978.

Ziechner, Kenneth M. The student teaching experience. *Action in Teacher Education,* Summer 1978, *1* (1), 58–61.

appendixes

appendix A EXPECTATIONS for THE ROLE of STUDENT TEACHER[1]

Instructions: On the line to the left of each of the items (1–76), please indicate your opinion regarding what should be expected of a student teacher by writing the letter corresponding to one of the following statements:

A. Absolutely must
B. Preferably should
C. Preferably should not
D. Absolutely must not

Example: If you feel that a particular item represents a function that a student teacher *absolutely must* be expected to perform, you would write *A* on the line preceding the item. If you feel that the item represents a function that a student teacher *absolutely must not* be expected to perform, you would write *D* on the line preceding the item. Please respond to all items.

Planning

_____ 1. study the cooperating teacher's unit and daily plans
_____ 2. work with the cooperating teacher in planning a unit
_____ 3. plan a unit independently
_____ 4. develop written lesson plans for his teaching activities
_____ 5. prepare daily plans a week in advance
_____ 6. use a consistent format for writing lesson plans
_____ 7. submit lesson plans to cooperating teacher prior to teaching
_____ 8. revise lesson plans in accordance with cooperating teacher's suggestions
_____ 9. use the same format as that used by the cooperating teacher for planning
_____ 10. rely on the recommendations provided by the teacher's manual for a lesson in an area such as reading
_____ 11. conduct cooperative planning sessions with children

Observation

_____ 12. study the cooperating teacher's plan before observing a lesson
_____ 13. take notes while the cooperating teacher is teaching
_____ 14. if notes are taken, make these notes available to the cooperating teacher

---

[1]Colden B. Garland. An exploration of role expectations for student teachers: Views of prospective student teachers, cooperating teachers, and college supervisors. (Doctoral dissertation, The University of Rochester, 1964). *Dissertation Abstracts,* 1965, 165–68. (University Microfilms No. 65-8557). Reprinted with permission.

A. Absolutely must
B. Preferably should
C. Preferably should not
D. Absolutely must not

_____ 15. observe in the classroom for a week before beginning to teach
_____ 16. settle a disturbance while the cooperating teacher is teaching
_____ 17. contribute to class discussions while the cooperating teacher is teaching
_____ 18. observe in the classrooms of other teachers
_____ 19. observe the teaching of another student teacher

Studying Children

_____ 20. seek to acquire an understanding of the characteristics of the community in which the school is located
_____ 21. observe children at age levels above and below that to which the student teacher is assigned
_____ 22. maintain an anecdotal record of the behavior of one child during student teaching
_____ 23. observe children in school situations outside of the classroom
_____ 24. use a specific form for recording observations of individual and group behavior
_____ 25. study the abilities of mentally retarded children
_____ 26. prepare an individual case study
_____ 27. participate in one related community agency
_____ 28. administer a sociogram

Guiding Learning Activities

_____ 29. begin teaching by working with a small group
_____ 30. create his own instructional materials in the absence of suitable materials
_____ 31. teach at some time when the cooperating teacher is not in the room
_____ 32. work with one child who needs special assistance (diagnosing deficiencies, applying remedial procedures)
_____ 33. assume responsibility for guiding the activities of temporary and/or permanent groups
_____ 34. express his own imagination and creativity in his teaching
_____ 35. do substitute teaching in other classrooms
_____ 36. teach groups of different abilities
_____ 37. assume responsibility for grouping for an activity
_____ 38. do substitute teaching in assigned classroom
_____ 39. organize and conduct a field trip
_____ 40. follow the same instructional program as that of the cooperating teacher
_____ 41. assume total responsibility for the teaching program before the conclusion of the student teaching experience
_____ 42. use community resources in teaching
_____ 43. teach at more than one grade level during the student teaching semester or period

A. Absolutely must
B. Preferably should
C. Preferably should not
D. Absolutely must not

Evaluating Learners

_____ 44. construct, give, and interpret tests
_____ 45. develop and maintain pupil progress charts
_____ 46. contribute information to cumulative records
_____ 47. participate with the cooperating teacher in pupil conferences
_____ 48. guide children in developing group standards
_____ 49. conduct group evaluation sessions
_____ 50. conduct individual conferences with pupils to discuss their growth
_____ 51. administer an interest inventory
_____ 52. use non-test methods of evaluation

Range of Teacher Activities

_____ 53. requisition supplies and instructional materials
_____ 54. work at some time with consultants or special teachers
_____ 55. assume major responsibility for lunchroom supervision at some time
_____ 56. participate in changing school policies
_____ 57. spend two or three days working with the building principal
_____ 58. participate in parent-teacher conferences
_____ 59. attend faculty meetings
_____ 60. become a member of a faculty committee or group in an area in which he has special competence
_____ 61. attend PTA meetings
_____ 62. accompany the cooperating teacher on home visits
_____ 63. conduct a parent-teacher conference alone
_____ 64. keep attendance records
_____ 65. attend a conference of the principal and cooperating teacher when the cooperating teacher is discussing some aspect of his work
_____ 66. collect money for such purposes as milk, lunch, Community Chest, etc.
_____ 67. correct papers/tests administered by the cooperating teacher
_____ 68. evaluate reference books

Additional Activities

_____ 69. keep a daily log of experiences
_____ 70. visit the classroom before student teaching begins
_____ 71. contact the cooperating teacher prior to student teaching
_____ 72. maintain anecdotal records for children in the classroom
_____ 73. be available either before or after school for conferences with the cooperating teacher
_____ 74. accept social invitations from parents

A. Absolutely must
B. Preferably should
C. Preferably should not
D. Absolutely must not

_____ 75. discuss activities of student teaching seminars with the cooperating teacher
_____ 76. organize a professional file of teaching material of both pictures and subject matter

appendix B expectations for the role of college supervisor[1]

Instructions: On the line to the left of each of the items, please indicate your opinion regarding what should be expected of a college supervisor by writing the letter corresponding to one of the following statements:

> A. Absolutely must
> B. Preferably should
> C. Preferably should not
> D. Absolutely must not

Example: If you feel that a particular item represents a function that a college supervisor *absolutely must* be expected to perform, you would write *A* on the line preceding the item. If you feel that the item represents a function that a college supervisor *absolutely must not* be expected to perform, you would write *D* on the line preceding the item. Please respond to all items.

Planning

_____ 1. study the supervising teacher's unit and daily plans
_____ 2. work with the supervising teacher in planning a unit
_____ 3. study the student teacher's unit and daily plans
_____ 4. work with the student teacher in planning a unit
_____ 5. work with the student teacher in developing lesson plans
_____ 6. conduct cooperative planning sessions with supervising teacher and student teacher
_____ 7. conduct in-service planning sessions with cooperating school faculty

Observation

_____ 8. observe children in the classroom assigned to the student teacher
_____ 9. observe supervising teacher prior to placement of student teacher
_____ 10. observe supervising teacher during period of student teaching
_____ 11. take notes while supervising teacher is teaching
_____ 12. if notes are taken, make these notes available to the supervising teacher

---

[1]Leonard Kaplan. An investigation of the role expectations for college supervisors of student teaching as viewed by student teachers, supervising teachers, and college supervisors. (Doctoral dissertation, The University of Rochester, 1967). *Dissertation Abstracts,* 1967, 103–5. (University Microfilms No. 67-8985). Reprinted with permission.

A. Absolutely must
B. Preferably should
C. Preferably should not
D. Absolutely must not

_____ 13. if notes are taken, make these notes available to the building principal
_____ 14. take notes while the student teacher is teaching
_____ 15. if notes are taken, make these notes available to the supervising teacher
_____ 16. if notes are taken, make these notes available to the student teacher
_____ 17. if notes are taken, make these notes available to the building principal
_____ 18. observe in the classrooms of other teachers for purposes of selecting supervising teachers

Evaluation

_____ 19. assume total responsibility for evaluating student teacher
_____ 20. share responsibility of evaluation with the student teacher
_____ 21. share responsibility of evaluation with student teacher and supervising teacher
_____ 22. designate total responsibility of evaluation to the supervising teacher
_____ 23. use evaluation procedures designed by the college
_____ 24. use evaluation procedures designed by the school or school district
_____ 25. evaluate effectiveness of the supervising teacher in this capacity
_____ 26. make this evaluation available to the supervising teacher
_____ 27. make this evaluation available to the building principal
_____ 28. guide student teacher toward the goal of self-evaluation

Additional Activities

_____ 29. assist supervising teacher in fulfilling her role
_____ 30. act as liaison between student teacher and supervising teacher
_____ 31. assist student teacher's adjustment to public school and college policies
_____ 32. serve as resource consultant for student teacher
_____ 33. serve as resource consultant for supervising teacher
_____ 34. serve as consultant with local P.T.A. groups
_____ 35. serve as resource consultant for all teachers in the building
_____ 36. conduct student teaching in-service programs
_____ 37. clarify the obligation of the school to the college and the college to the school
_____ 38. work with the college staff in developing the total teacher training program
_____ 39. attend faculty meetings in cooperating schools
_____ 40. work toward the improvement of the total school program

appendix C expectations for the role of cooperating teacher[1]

Instructions: On the line at the left of each of the items, please indicate your opinion regarding *what should be expected of cooperating teachers* by writing the letter corresponding to one of the statements below:

A. Absolutely must
B. Preferably should
C. Preferably should not
D. Absolutely must not

Example: If you feel that a particular item represents a function that cooperating teachers *absolutely must* be expected to perform, write *A* on the line preceding the item. Use only one letter for each item. Please respond to all the items.

_____ 1. Work with the college supervisor in planning the student teaching program.

_____ 2. Participate actively in seminars and in-service training for cooperating teachers.

_____ 3. Develop a well-balanced program of student teaching activities for the student teacher.

_____ 4. Explain to the pupils the responsibility of the student teacher.

_____ 5. Arrange for contact between parents of the pupils and the student teacher.

_____ 6. Provide the student teacher with a place for his personal materials.

_____ 7. Assist the student teacher in finding accommodations in the community.

_____ 8. Take the student teacher for a tour of the community.

_____ 9. Introduce the student teacher to members of the administrative staff, co-teachers, and other school employees.

_____ 10. Invite the student teacher to participate in faculty meetings.

_____ 11. Explain all school routines, rules, and policies.

_____ 12. Show the student teacher the physical set-up of the classroom, the school building, and the school grounds.

_____ 13. Inform the student teacher of the aims and objectives of teaching in the school district.

---

[1]Jovito B. Castillo. The role expectations of cooperating teachers as viewed by student teachers, college supervisors, and cooperating teachers. (Doctoral dissertation, The University of Rochester, 1971). *Dissertation Abstracts*, 1971, 94–97. (University Microfilms No. 71–22, 329). Reprinted with permission.

A. Absolutely must
B. Preferably should
C. Preferably should not
D. Absolutely must not

_____ 14. Explain the over-all plan of the course of study for each subject.
_____ 15. Plan for the student teacher the different phases of his training.
_____ 16. Explain the principles related to certain teaching techniques.
_____ 17. Prepare a set of observation guidelines for the student teacher.
_____ 18. Show the student teacher how daily or unit plans are prepared.
_____ 19. Demonstrate for the student teacher the different methods or procedures of teaching.
_____ 20. Share with the student teacher information about the interest and abilities of the pupils.
_____ 21. Tell the student teacher proven techniques of classroom management.
_____ 22. Involve the student teacher intimately in planning and directing the learning activities of the children.
_____ 23. Instruct the student teacher how to establish "close" rapport with the pupils.
_____ 24. Give precise guidance on how different types of teacher-made tests are prepared.
_____ 25. Give the student teacher detailed information as to how report cards, attendance forms, and permanent records are prepared, used, and kept.
_____ 26. Demonstrate operation and use of the different audio-visual equipment and office machines.
_____ 27. Supply reference books, professional magazines to be used by the student teacher.
_____ 28. Supply the student teacher with copies of the teacher's guide, teacher's manual, textbooks, and other types of teaching aids.
_____ 29. Allow maximum freedom for the student teacher as he assumes more teaching responsibility.
_____ 30. Share with the student teacher the ideas, discoveries, and innovations in education.
_____ 31. Help the student teacher to develop interest and skill in doing simple educational research.
_____ 32. Assist the student teacher to search for valid principles that would support his activities or teaching methods.
_____ 33. Counsel the student teacher about "proper" grooming and decorum in the classroom.
_____ 34. Make the student teacher aware of his voice, pronunciation, and level of vocabulary.
_____ 35. Evaluate the progress of the student teacher.
_____ 36. Develop the basic criteria for judging success of the student teacher.
_____ 37. Act with vigilance in protecting the educational welfare of the pupils from the inefficiency of the student teacher.

A. Absolutely must
B. Preferably should
C. Preferably should not
D. Absolutely must not

_____ 38. Assume the sole authority in deciding the student teacher's readiness to assume full responsibility in teaching.

_____ 39. Check the unit or daily plans of the student teacher.

_____ 40. Hold scheduled conference periods with the student teacher.

_____ 41. Review the written report of the student teacher about his student teaching experiences.

_____ 42. Arrange for the student teacher to observe other classrooms in the school building or district.

_____ 43. Help the student teacher interpret his observation notes of other classrooms.

_____ 44. Keep a comprehensive record of the activities and progress of the student teacher.

_____ 45. Shield the shortcomings of the student teacher from the critical view of the college supervisor.

_____ 46. Evaluate the activities and progress of the student teacher with the college supervisor at regular intervals.

_____ 47. Involve the student teacher in extra-curricular activities that are sponsored jointly by the school and the community.

_____ 48. Explain to the student teacher the merits and demerits of the unsolved issues of the profession: e.g., salary scale, certification requirements, desegregation, or grouping of pupils.

_____ 49. Clarify for the student teacher the provisions of the teachers' "code of ethics."

_____ 50. Take the student teacher to teachers' conventions and other organizational meetings.

appendix D RESULTS of STUdiES of EXPECTATIONS fOR THE ROLES of STUdENT TEACHER, COLLEGE SUPERVISOR, ANd COOPERATING TEACHER

Table A   Expectations for the Role of Student Teacher on Which There Was Disagreement Among Prospective Student Teachers, Cooperating Teachers, and College Supervisors

Item	Differences in Direction**	Differences in Intensity**
5. prepare daily plans a week in advance	PST*: − CT*: +	
10. rely on the recommendations provided by the teacher's manual for a lesson in an area such as reading	PST : − CT : +	
15. observe in the classroom for a week before beginning to teach	PST : + CS*: − CT : + CS : −	
28. administer a sociogram	PST : − CT : +	CS : AM CT : PS
46. contribute information to cumulative records	CT : − CS : +	
57. spend two or three days working with the building principal		PST : PSN CS : AMN
67. correct papers/tests administered by the cooperating teacher	PST : + CS : −	PST : AM CT : PS

```
 *  PST = Prospective student teachers
    CT  = Cooperating teachers
    CS  = College supervisors
 **   + = Should ─────────────── Reflects disagreement on
      − = Should not ─────────┘  direction of expectation
     AM = Absolutely must ─┐
     PS = Preferably should ─── Reflects disagreement on
    PSN = Preferably should not ─ intensity of expectation
    AMN = Absolutely must not ─┘
```

194

Table B **Expectations for the Role of College Supervisor on Which There Was Disagreement Among Student Teachers, Supervising Teachers, and College Supervisors**

Item	Differences in Direction**	Differences in Intensity**
1. study the supervising teacher's unit and daily plans	CS*: − ST : +	
	ST*: + Sup. T*: −	
6. conduct cooperative planning sessions with supervising teacher and student teacher	ST : + Sup. T : −	
8. observe children in the classroom assigned to the student teacher	CS : + Sup. T : −	
	ST : + Sup. T : −	
9. observe supervising teacher prior to placement of student teacher	CS : − ST : +	ST : AM Sup. T : PS
10. observe supervising teacher during period of student teaching	CS : + Sup. T : −	
	ST : + Sup. T : −	
12. if notes are taken, make these notes available to the supervising teacher		ST : PS Sup. T : AM
13. if notes are taken, make these notes available to the building principal		CS : AMN ST : PSN
		ST : AMN Sup. T : PSN
18. observe in the classroom of other teachers for purposes of selecting supervising teachers	CS : − ST : +	ST : AM Sup. T : PS
19. assume total responsibility for evaluating student teacher		CS : PSN Sup. T : AMN
21. share responsibility of evaluation with student teacher and supervising teacher	CS : − ST : +	
23. use evaluation procedures designed by the college	ST : − Sup. T : +	
25. evaluate effectiveness of the supervising teacher in this capacity		ST : AM Sup. T : PS
26. make this evaluation available to the supervising teacher	CS : − Sup. T : +	CS : AMN ST : PSN
	ST : − Sup. T : +	

Item	Differences in Direction**	Differences in Intensity**
27. make this evaluation available to the building principal	CS : − Sup. T : +	CS : AMN ST : PSN
35. serve as resource consultant for all teachers in the building	CS : + ST : −	

```
 *      ST = Student teachers
 Sup. T = Supervising teachers
     CS = College supervisors
**      + = Should ──────────── Reflects disagreement on
        − = Should not ──────── direction of expectation
      AM = Absolutely must ─┐
      PS = Preferably should ─┤── Reflects disagreement on
     PSN = Preferably should not ┘  intensity of expectation
     AMN = Absolutely must not
```

Table C Expectations for the Role of Cooperating Teacher on Which There Was Disagreement Among Student Teachers, Cooperating Teachers, and College Supervisors

Item	Differences in Direction**	Differences in Intensity**
4. explain to the pupils the responsibility of the student teacher	ST*: − CS*: +	
10. invite the student teacher to participate in faculty meetings		ST : PS CT : AM
11. explain all school routines, rules, and policies		ST : AM CS : PS CS : PS CT : AM
12. show the student teacher the physical set-up of the classroom, the school building, and the school grounds		ST : AM CS : PS CS : PS CT : AM
13. inform the student teacher of the aims and objectives of teaching in the school district	CS : − CT*: +	
14. explain the over-all plan of the course of study for each subject		ST : AM CS : PS
15. plan for the student teacher the different phases of his training	ST : − CT : +	

Item	Differences in Direction**	Differences in Intensity**
	CS : − CT : +	
16. explain the principles related to certain teaching techniques	ST : + CS : −	
19. demonstrate for the student teacher the different methods or procedures of teaching	ST : + CS : −	
	CS : − CT : +	
21. tell the student teacher proven techniques of classroom management	ST : + CS : −	
	CS : − CT : +	
23. instruct the student teacher how to establish "close" rapport with the pupils	CS : − CT : +	
25. give the student teacher detailed information as to how report cards, attendance forms, and permanent records are prepared, used, and kept		ST : AM CS : PS
		CS : PS CT : AM
27. supply reference books, professional magazines to be used by the student teacher	CS : − CT : +	
28. supply the student teacher with copies of the teacher's guide, teacher's manual, textbooks, and other types of teaching aids		ST : AM CS : PS
		ST : AM CT : PS
29. allow maximum freedom for the student teacher as he assumes more teaching responsibility		ST : AM CT : PS
		CS : AM CT : PS
31. help the student teacher to develop interest and skill in doing simple educational research	ST : + CT : −	
	CS : + CT : −	
36. develop the basic criteria for judging the success of the student teacher	ST : − CT : +	
	CS : − CT : +	
38. assume the sole authority in deciding the student teacher's readiness to assume full responsibility in teaching	CS : − CT : +	

Item	Differences in Direction**	Differences in Intensity**
39. check the unit or daily plans of the student teacher	ST : − CS : +	
	ST : − CT : +	
45. shield the shortcomings of the student teacher from the critical view of the college supervisor		ST : PSN CS : AMN
		CS : AMN CT : PSN
47. involve the student teacher in extra-curricular activities that are sponsored jointly by the school and the community	ST : − CT : +	
48. explain to the student teacher the merits and de-merits of the unsolved issues of the profession: e.g., salary scale, certification requirements, de-segregation, or grouping of pupils	ST : + CT : −	
50. take the student teacher to teacher's conven-tions and other organizational meetings	ST : − CS : +	

*   ST = Student teachers
     CT = Cooperating teachers
     CS = College supervisors
**   + = Should ⟶ Reflects disagreement on
     − = Should not ⟶ direction of expectation
   AM = Absolutely must
   PS = Preferably should ⟶ Reflects disagreement on
  PSN = Preferably should not ⟶ intensity of expectation
  AMN = Absolutely must not

Table D   Expectations for the Role of Student Teacher, Cooperating Teacher, and College Supervisor on Which There Was High Consensus* Among Student Teachers, Cooperating Teachers, and College Supervisors

Student Teacher	Cooperating Teacher	College Supervisor
2. work with the cooperat-ing teacher in planning a unit (+)**	1. work with the college supervisor in planning the student teaching program (+)	3. study the student teach-er's unit and daily plans (+)
4. develop written lesson plans for his teaching ac-tivities (+)	2. participate actively in seminars and in-service training for cooperating teachers (+)	22. designate total responsi-bility of evaluation to the teacher (−)***

Student Teacher	*Cooperating Teacher*	*College Supervisor*
6. use a consistent format for writing lesson plans (+)	6. provide the student teacher with a place for his personal materials (+)	28. guide student teacher toward the goal of self-evaluation (+)
7. submit lesson plans to cooperating teacher prior to teaching (+)	9. introduce the student teacher to members of the administrative staff, co-teachers, and other school employees (+)	31. assist student teacher's adjustment to public school and college policies (+)
8. revise lesson plans in accordance with cooperating teacher's suggestions (+)	22. involve the student teacher intimately in planning and directing the learning activities of the children (+)	32. serve as resource consultant for student teacher (+)
20. seek to acquire an understanding of the characteristics of the community in which the school is located (+)	40. hold scheduled conference periods with the student teacher (+)	37. clarify the obligations of the school to the college and the college to the school (+)
21. observe children at age levels above and below that to which the student teacher is assigned (+)	46. evaluate the activities and progress of the student teacher with the college supervisor at regular intervals (+)	38. work with the college staff in developing the total teacher training program (+)
23. observe children in school situations outside of the classroom (+)		
30. create his own instructional materials in the absence of suitable materials (+)		
31. teach at some time when the cooperating teacher is not in the room (+)		
32. work with one child who needs special assistance (diagnosing deficiencies, applying remedial procedures) (+)		
33. assume responsibility for guiding the activities		

Student Teacher	Cooperating Teacher	College Supervisor
of temporary and/or per- manent groups (+)		
34. express his own imagin- ation and creativity in his teaching (+)		
36. teach groups of differ- ent abilities (+)		
42. use community re- sources in teaching (+)		
44. construct, give, and in- terpret tests (+)		
45. develop and maintain pupil progress charts (+)		
48. guide children in devel- oping group standards (+)		
54. work at some time with consultants or special teachers (+)		
59. attend faculty meetings (+)		
61. attend PTA meetings (+)		
64. keep attendance records (+)		
73. be available either be- fore or after school for conferences with the co- operating teacher (+)		
76. organize a professional file of teaching material of both pictures and subject matter (+)		

*An item was considered to reflect high consensus when 86–100% of the respondents of the three groups indicated that the behavior should or should not be performed.

** + = Should

*** − = Should not

index